UTOPIAS

Architectural Utopias in Search of the Ideal City

Ece Ceylan Baba

TABLE OF CONTENTS

Happiness, Falling

Preface by David Turnbull,
Los Angeles, USA – Professor of Architecture,
Critic and Writer

Ece Ceylan Baba concludes her extensive but inevitably inconclusive search for the Ideal City, with an exclamation, of misery or joy?

I do not know, but suspect both.

With the desire called 'Utopia', unfulfilled, held in abeyance, like unrequited love, despair would be appropriate, exasperation, perhaps, frustration, certainly. If 'the secret will to arrive at the brink of destruction is implicit in the utopian hypothesis' as Manfredo Tafuri suggests in 'Architecture and Utopia' (1973), and if, as Fredric Jameson, 'who is unwilling to recognise anti-utopian prejudice as a positive force' claims, utopia is, and is not, 'the evocation of a perfect society, or a 'blueprint' for a better one', the 'constitutive undecideability of a representation which affirms and foregrounds Utopia in the very same act by which it calls it fundamentally into question' must be offered, as it is, by Ursula K. Le Guin in 'The Lathe of Heaven' (1971), and, in this volume, by Ece Ceylan Baba — a profound ambivalence:

> Utopias are speculative,
> Utopias are fantastic,
> Utopias afford consolation,
> Utopias permit fables and discourse, indeed, they are...
inscribed in the fabula,
> > (Foucault)
> Utopias are elusive,
> ... the Utopian city — even if we never catch sight of it,
we will not stop looking
> > (Calvino)
> Utopias keep a promise.
> Utopias can be found 'in limine' — in the correspondence
> of architecture and literature.
> Utopias keep a secret.
> Utopias are found on the other side of the looking-glass.
> Utopia is no place, it is also a good place — Eutopia.
> The architecture of Utopia, is always 'une architecture de
la jouissance'...
> > Bliss.
> Utopia is a dream, of happiness, rising.

Dystopia is not.

Not a mirror image or inversion of Utopia, not a counter-utopia or anti-utopia, dystopia is, for Ece Ceylan Baba, the ultimate disappointment.

Symptomatic of the abuse of power, 'surrender to the politics of things brought about by the laws of profit', or both, dystopias, governed by an administrative elite or benevolent dictatorship, maintain the contradictions of capital — good for some, bad for many. In a tangled relationship of politics and planning, pleasure and pain, in dreams and nightmares, the utopian impulse is condemned, and every planned community, indeed any emergent 'society of jouissance', is doomed. Dystopia is an embodiment of the seventh circle of Hell, in Dante's 'Inferno' (c. 1320) — Violence.

The ideal city and the infernal city share a common root — the city, governed well or badly. In the past, the present or the future, allegorical frescos painted in 1338, by Ambrogio Lorenzetti (1290 - 1348), in the 'Sala dei Nove' in the 'Palazzo Pubblico' in Siena, confronting each other across the room, persist as exemplary representations. Good government stimulates the economy, maintains a diverse ecology, on the land and in the water, abundant agriculture, happiness and health... bad government thrives on the exploitation of people and resources, leading to pollution, the destruction of terrestrial and aquatic ecosystems, widespread dissatisfaction, famine, drought, disease and death.

I remember reading the recently published 'Collage City' in 1978. Opening the book at Chapter One, 'Utopia — Decline and Fall', I hear Colin Rowe's voice. I did not know him then, but years later I would hear him speaking, in Fred Koetter's house in New Haven, Connecticut, on the 'phone with Susie Kim, after dinner — distant, but close, intimate but unreachable, like Utopia. While not exactly an embodiment of St. Augustine's 'City of God' or Plato's 'Republic', Thomas More's Utopia, for Rowe and Koetter, is a 'city of the mind', 'an object of contemplation', 'the terrestrial shadow of an idea...' an 'icon of the good society'. As 'a reference and no more than this', they write, 'both utopia and the ideal city, the combination—however belated—of Filarete and Castiglione, of More and Machiavelli, of manners and morals, produced results. It was a combination which sponsored a convention; and then a convention which, while it did not seriously alleviate the social order, became responsible for the form of cities which are still today admired'. While their reference to sixteenth century 'manners and morals', elaborated in Baldessare Castiglione's 'The Book of the Courtier' (1528), and Niccolò Machiavelli's 'The Prince' (1532), may seem unreasonably remote, the conventions — typological and morphological prescriptions, governing the architecture of the 'Ideal City' have been remarkably persistent.

In the nineteenth century 'realist utopias' are imagined with streets and squares, narrow alleys, broad avenues, tree-lined boulevards and beautifully planted parks. It is no accident that the author of 'Le Droit à la ville The Right to the City' (1968), Henri Lefebvre (1901 - 91), walked through the galleries and arcades of the Palais-Royal, in Paris, discussing the possibility of 'une architecture de la jouissance', on French television, in 1972, with the 'phalanstery' (1842) a 'palace for the people' proposed by Charles Fourier (1772 - 1837), in mind. It is also no accident that the Palais-Royal is included as a 'plaque-tournante' in Guy Debord and Asger Jorn's 'Naked City' (1958), or, I would wager, that Machiavelli's 'The Prince' (1513), Sir Thomas More's 'Utopia' (1516), and Martin Luther's 'Ninety-Five Theses' (1517) are included in one volume, No. 36, of the Harvard Classics series, edited by Charles W. Eliot (1834 - 1926), president of Harvard University from 1869 to 1909, published by P. F. Collier & Sons, in 1910.

In the twentieth century, notably the mid 1970s, the publication of Manfredo Tafuri's 'Progetto e utopia' (1973), Francoise Choay's 'La règle et le modèle' (1974), anticipated by 'L'urbanisme, utopies et réalitès' (1965), and Colin Rowe and Fred Koetter's 'Collage City' (1978), tracing continuities of thought, from the sixteenth century to the present, was accompanied by a period of reflection and critique, with seminal publications and exhibitions, among them — 'Rational Architecture' (1978), assembled Leon Krier (b. 1946), with Anthony Vidler (1941 - 2023), and Maurice Culot (b.1939), published by AAM, focussed on the 'Reconstruction of the European City'. Reconstruction, not reinvention, but notably reviving the spatial hierarchies and typological conventions that informed the speculative construction of the Ideal City, from Sforzinda (c.1464) to Chaux, Arc-et-Senans (1773-5), Antonio di Pietro Averlino, Filarete (c.1400 - 69) to Claude-Nicolas Ledoux (1736–1806). Utopia lingered, engaged in a covert operation negotiating with everyday life — under-cover. In the United States, visionary architects drew fantastic architectural accumulations addressing the corrosive impact of 'sprawl', and the critical intersection of architecture and ecology. Radical projects for biomorphic, biospheric architecture, alternative lifestyles and technologies, experimental communities, proliferated around the world. Some vivid, some less so, all addressing a difficult but possible future, learning from Lewis Mumford's writing, notably 'The Myth of the Machine' (1967 - 70), Buckminster Fuller's 'Synergetics' and 'Whole Systems' approach, Yona Friedman, building more with less, Paolo Soleri's ecstatic frugality — the technics of survival.

I am perplexed by the hiatus that followed this period of exuberant experimentation, the acceleration of environmental degradation, poverty, migration, and destructive conflict, the repetition of broken promises, and shattered dreams. And, while it is clear that the pursuit of the ideal, of the city as built Utopia is inevitably fraught, as Paolo Soleri declared in his 'Sixty-Three Topics', topic 46: 'The City as Symbol', in 'Arcosanti — an Urban Laboratory?' (1983), 'whenever utopia is afloat, failure is paradigmatic', I believe that failure is never absolute. For Colin Rowe and Fred Koetter, utopia's decline and fall, anticipates utopias restored, by way of a digression, actually a few — imagining Filarete's 'Sforzinda' as a garden, contrasting Louis XIV's Versailles with Hadrian's Villa, the Acropolis with the Forum, Hedgehogs and Foxes, the bricoleur — in one of two 'reservoirs of ethical content', utopia and tradition, and an 'open city', that is 'hostile to neither', predicated on the possibility that the pleasures of a utopian poetics can be be disentangled from utopian politics.

Italo Calvino draws 'Invisible Cities' to a close with a provocation that resonates with Ece Ceylan Baba's entanglement of Utopia and Dystopia, of the just with the unjust city — 'in the seed of the city of the just, a malignant seed is hidden'... qualified by 'an intrinsic quality of this unjust city germinating secretly inside the just city: and this is a possible awakening... of a later love of justice, not yet subject to rules, capable of reassembling a city more just than it was before it became a vessel of injustice.' Perhaps here there is a clue, and a possible explanation for my fascination with her conclusive exclamation, and conclusions in general — one, in particular, the last four lines of 'The Tenth Elegy', that close 'the whole cycle of Rainer Maria Rilke's 'Duino Elegies', transcribed by Cy Twombly onto a 'cartouche' on the 'pedestal' of the sculpture 'Untitled' (1984), discussed in Giorgio Agamben's short essay, 'Beauty That Falls' — four lines that end, 'when happiness falls'.

Ece and Utopias

Preface by Emre Arolat,
Istanbul, Turkey – Architect Hon. FAIA, RIBA

It is fair to say that in the geographical area in which we live most of the major problems in the architectural world result from a kind of disconnect, deepening by the day, between academia and the active fields of architecture. With a few notable exceptions, it can be asserted that in recent years Turkish academic institutions have almost completely closed their eyes to what is happening "out there" in the wider world. So much so that the groups engaged in swiftly expanding their dominance of these institutions have been focusing their attention and activities either on infighting or on attempts to curry favour with the centralized administration. As a result, and in much the same way village inbreeding leads to genetic disorders, academic institutions are steadily degenerating into increasingly incompetent structures overrun by pseudo-intellectuals whose world view extends only as far as their own somewhat limited spheres of knowledge. On the other hand—or on the opposing side, let's say, once again bearing in mind that there are undoubtedly exceptions—there has emerged a strikingly self-entitled, self-indulgent field of architectural practice that is bereft of scientific data and tends to emphasize the speed and quantity of production at the expense of quality. A group of architects completely ignorant of global developments and the current professional trends of their international colleagues in advanced societies are presenting work that is uniformly sloppy and of inferior quality. And, unfortunately, the actors in these two arenas no longer produce together, form interdisciplinary teams, or even engage in dialogue with one another...

It must have been about twelve years ago that I first became aware of the name Ece Ceylan Baba through the publication of her book *Istanbul and the Democracy of Design*. I later learned that she had attended my father's course on projects at Mimar Sinan University, of which I, too, am an alumnus. I remember noticing her book on the office shelf of a close friend as we were chatting, and then studying it with some curiosity. The intellectual framework was interactive design processes and the democratic platforms that can emerge when designer and city dweller cooperate. At first glance, it could be argued that the text addressed the buzzy questions of that time in the context of the then-current new world environment of smoothed sharp edges and the evaporation of concrete particulars. What really struck me about the book, though, was the unaffected and intriguing intellectual depth, as well as the posing of certain questions some would consider downright mischievous. The book was further enhanced by the inclusion of a dialectical flavour rarely encountered in the academic writings of that period.

From that day onward I began observing Ece Ceylan Baba, albeit from a distance, as she gradually became a more prominent actor in the architectural world. It was remarkable that despite her relative youth she participated in so many different professional activities. She appeared to be a serious and engaging woman who was becoming increasingly visible due to both her productivity and to her refreshing originality when contrasted to our neighbourhood academics.

Ece Ceylan Baba's second book, *The Loft: The Transition from Modernism to Post-Modernism and Loft Architecture's Repercussions in Istanbul,* was published in April of 2015. This time, the work focused on the very specific subject of loft architecture in an intellectual trek stretching from New York to Istanbul, simultaneously examining the then-current trend in both socio-cultural and economic terms as it succeeded in expanding the boundaries of comprehension and interpretation for the reader. The most significant link to her first book was a starring role for Istanbul and the dizzying transformation specific to Istanbul.

On January 24, 2020, an earthquake struck Türkiye's Elâzığ province. The earthquake killed 41 people and impacted the entire Eastern Anatolia Region, but mostly Elâzığ and Malatya. Nearly 1500 people were injured. A few months later, at the instigation of a friend, I found myself on a plane headed for Elâzığ with a civilian volunteer group that included Ece Ceylan Baba. We aimed to examine the city on the ground post-earthquake and meet with local actors, including municipal authorities, to determine how we could contribute to rehabilitation efforts in the area. With that trip, I began getting closer to Ece. After spending a few intense days with her, I realized that some of the preconceptions I had formed from afar were well off the mark. I was surprised and relieved in equal measure to find that behind that strong, even steely, exterior was a personality soft as silk. Yes, she was clearly uncompromising on many subjects. After all, she had managed to launch an academic career without allowing herself to become entangled in or ground down by the vicious cogs of the system, and had done so without becoming indebted to authority. But what I found most astonishing about her was a diversity and depth of market experience, as well as an ability to conduct business, that one would not expect from a typical academic.

Umut-Elâzığ is the first project that Ece Ceylan Baba and I completed together. This post-earthquake effort executed on a completely voluntary basis was of great personal importance to me as well. With the participation of students from the Yeditepe University Department of Architecture, where she is both the Department Head and Dean, we worked at a furious pace, night and day, for approximately a year. Located on roughly sixty hectares, the Umut-Elâzığ project was completed and turned over to the Umut-Elâzığ Municipality as a sustainable, environmentally friendly, and multi-layered settlement. During this process, I saw up close what a multi-faceted academic dedicated to her profession Ece Ceylan Baba is.

At the beginning of 2020, Ece signed a copy of her newly published book *Architectural Utopias in the Search for the Ideal City*. After returning to Istanbul from our trip to Elâzığ I read it in one sitting. The first section delves into the concept of utopia, and, after coming to terms with that idea, then deals with Utopia and the Ideal City, from antiquity and Atlantis up to the present day, supported by examples and in an impartial manner that is easy to grasp and mostly presented chronologically, thus allowing readers to form their own opinions virtually free of authorial prodding. The author's own views are found between the lines as commentary on the optimistic naiveté that colours most of the examples cited in the book.

In the pre-dawn of February 6, 2023, another earthquake struck eastern Türkiye, with Kahramanmaraş the epicentre this time. This one was far more devastating. Eleven provinces in the Southern and Eastern Anatolian regions suffered first degree damage. Worst of all was the destruction in Antakya, ancient site of Antioch and home to numerous civilizations and cultures over millennia. It was nearly wiped off the map. My path crossed with Ece's immediately after this earthquake, most likely due to our experience together in Elâzığ. We both became part of a core group of four that, by the end of the month, launched an independent civilian platform called Collective Mindset-Antioch. This multi-layered initiative with a transparent volunteer recruitment process was designed with the objective of setting up a qualified study and planning group, and it continues to operate today with the participation of hundreds of people from a diverse range of disciplines. Together, we have embarked on a process that considers Antakya's physical and cultural values to be our guiding data as we heed the failed centralized urban planning lessons of the past by ensuring that the process is fully open to the participation of real stakeholders.

A step has been taken away from a single mind seated at a desk designing an entire city to the designing of the micro areas, buildings and formations that comprise a city's micro elements. The indexing of cities to the common consciousness and to the evolving needs of city dwellers is now replacing the concept of utopias that seek absolute order, by employing a 'floating' approach that manages chaos. History has shown us that an insistence on utopic visions always produces the same result: Dystopia!

The italicized lines above are from the 'Conclusion' of Ece's latest book: *Architectural Utopias in the Search for the Ideal City*. Upon revisiting those lines, I was struck once again by what a profound privilege it has been to collaborate both on the Collective Mindset-Antioch platform and in all other areas with a professional who does not fit the typical profile of an academician in this part of the world, someone who ponders, reads, wonders and at the same time 'does'. I fully expect that anyone who reads this book, which will also be available internationally, will enjoy similar feelings.

Utopian Cities, Environmental Determinism, and the Urban Context

Preface by Davide Ponzini,
Milan, Italy – Professor of Architecture

The reference to an ideal and absolute order of the urban environment and of society is indeed a very powerful rhetorical tool, a sort of central trope in architectural and planning disciplines. It became, at times, a prominent literary genre on its own. Over the past centuries this tool served planners and designers as well as social reformists and more-or-less visionary politicians and rulers. This book provides an informative overview of the origins and evolutions of utopian thinking with specific reference to urban and architectural design. The book searches the roots of utopia in Western culture, from antiquity to the Renaissance, from the Enlightenment to modern times, by arguing that the West provided certain conditions for it to emerge and then spread worldwide.

Although the author never uses the term "environmental determinism", she explains very well that the utopian design of cities and communities often implies the expectation that a good city will generate a good society. Citizens are seen as part of these urban and social projects where rationality forges space and society at once. The mastermind that stands behind the understanding of urban and societal problems and that single-handedly crafts a comprehensive and consistent solution derived legitimacy from utopian exercises. Le Corbusier is often used as the epitome of this kind of figure. This "great man paradigm" still affects the layman's understanding of what urban planning, design, and architecture are about: the realization of a dream-like vision – somewhat like a machine – that is laid out in detail by an expert or a visionary, rather than derived from a collective enterprise. Also, a certain level of de-politicization gained ground from ideal designs – despite the fact that early utopian communities had a strong political, even anarchic, stance as in the case of Owen and others. I see environmental determinism as problematic and especially underestimated. It is still present in the public debate and even in many schools of architecture.

In the history outlined in the book, the utopian plans and designs translated into reality have been understood as techniques more than political acts. Social engineering and the limitations in individual freedom that these plans implied are justified by the promise of maximizing collective wellbeing as if this did not imply distribution of benefits to given groups and not others (that is politics). By definition, utopian models and their universal validity defy context. Especially modernist models adopt a tabula rasa approach. On the contrary, the actual city as the West and most part of the contemporary world know it derives from endless transformations and adjustments, even when a scheme for it is heavily planned to start with or at given moments in history.

As Peter Hall (2013) masterfully explained, the urban planning discipline owes much to this translation of ideal models into urban realities, often leading to bad results, both for the local communities and the discipline's reputation. Baba's book warns against the side effects of unwittingly translating utopias into reality: dystopia. The latter is analyzed as an almost natural – and very present in history – counterpart that opposes the urban realm to its society, in terms of dysfunctional settings, political control, loss of local identity, and individual oppression. In this sense, both utopia and dystopia tend not to value what makes and remakes real cities, that is social interaction and political actions. The growing social complexity and cultural diversity of our cities, in my view, call for more politics, and not less, as well as for more contextualized policies, plans, and projects, and not less. In this framework, the reflection on utopian city design provides an important ground for technical innovation that in my view should be tested, adapted or rejected depending on the context it is going to be applied to.

As a conclusion of this short preface – or as a start of the book – it is worth considering the geographic and historical context of the book. The Middle East today is an important testing ground in attempting to turn ideal designs into real cities whereas the power of national and local authority is expected to do it all. Among other radical projects, Turkey witnesses today the Canal Istanbul plan and the redesign of a large quadrant of the city of Istanbul. This project will generate massive new infrastructure and significant discontinuity in the urban form, changing the coastal ecosystem and the social structure of local communities. It is an instrument for the political elite that comes from the very top (i.e. the President of the country) down without considering the reasons of growing oppositions. Another project of perhaps greater size and ambition is Neom's Line in Saudi Arabia. It is a project for a linear urban environment of 170 kilometers, from the Red Sea coast to the northwest inland of Saudi Arabia – again a strong vision by the de-facto ruler of the country.

One can easily find antecedent ideas for these and many other current projects in the book. Whether these designs are utopian or dystopian is a matter of discussion and I believe that this book provides solid historic background and intellectual means for the readers to build their own opinion. Similarly, after two decades of celebration of smart city planning and at the dawn of AI-powered planning and design, this book raises awareness about the flawed expectations of defining urban order based on technology rather than by the political process of adaptation of the city to ever-evolving human and societal life.

Utopian Visions in City Planning

Preface by Tim Cutts,
London, England - City Planner

For any city planner and urbanist it can be all too easy to bury your head in a world of policy, regulation and standards and lose sight of the wider ambition and vision for our cities. This book serves as a reminder of some of the great utopian ideals that have influenced the history of our cities and which can be traced through the streets and townscapes of our cities today.

Some of our most familiar townscapes, such as Haussmann's grand boulevards in Paris and Trafalgar Square in London, did not come about accidently but through the destruction of swathes of the city to make way for grand avenues and squares, befitting the capitals of emerging empires (Utopias of the Nineteenth Century). New townscapes often sought inspiration from antiquity in laying out streets, squares and parks, bringing order and atheistic beauty founded on neo-classical design. More cynically we are also reminded that new designs made it harder to foment worker revolt and helped consolidate the rule of governments at the time.

Enduring poverty and insanitary conditions in the nineteenth century later influenced Ebenezer Howard's garden city movement (Modernism and Twentieth Century Utopias). Howard and others sought to create calmer environments, less overcrowded and away from the bustle of the city. Residents could be more closely connected with nature, with access to cleaner air and healthier lifestyles. As well as influencing the design of new towns, these ideas can be seen in the leafy suburban environments which grew up across Europe and the US in the 1920s and 30s.

Following the Second World War cities around the world looked towards the ideas of Corbusier and his radiant city. The allure of addressing housing needs by building high rise blocks often set within parks and landscaped spaces proved attractive to a generation of city leaders looking to clear slums and build quickly. The model was allied to the growth of the motor car and a perceived need to separate vehicles from pedestrians. The better examples of this approach, such as the Alton Estate in Roehampton now have statutory protection. The less successful examples, such as the Aylesbury Estate in Southwark, are gradually being demolished.

What these utopias have in common is that they sought to address issues facing civic leaders and thinkers at the time. How do we respond to the challenges of today and are there lessons we can draw from these examples?

Many of the models referred to are founded upon the idea of starting afresh and building from a clean slate. However, the climate emergency facing the planet and the overriding need to reduce carbon emissions today push us increasingly towards retention and reuse of buildings rather than demolition and rebuild. The concepts of densification around transport hubs, encouraging travel by sustainable modes of transport and reducing car use are also prevalent.

More recent concepts such as the 15 minute city, where jobs, shops, schools and parks are within easy reach of homes have echoes of Howard's garden city. They also hint towards other key issues which city planners and designers are seeking to address around healthy environments, cleaner air, active lifestyles and strong local communities.

The utopian ideals reviewed in this book emphasise the fact that cities are not just about buildings and spaces, but people and the way societies organise themselves. For all the benefits and progress which utopian ideas have brought, deprivation and poverty endure in urban environments, along with a sense of alienation from the benefits which city living can bring. The charge of gentrification has often accompanied large scale regeneration projects and the emphasis today is much more upon generating value for existing as well as future communities.

The final chapter reminds us that utopian ideals are often the ideas of a single person, often motivated by a paternalistic instinct and sometimes also for other reasons, such as a desire to improve worker productivity (Utopias in Post Industrial Society). The execution has often been misguided. The current focus is much more on pluralistic ways of working, involving local communities with approaches such as co-design, planning-for-real and urban rooms becoming more embedded.

While utopias might be out of fashion, the ideas explored in this book are important in helping understand our cities and their development and can provide inspiration for the way in which our cities can evolve to address the needs of tomorrow.

The Concept
of Utopia

Utopia is an imagined but as yet unimplemented, unrealized place (Noble 2009:12). Being a modeled design of perfection, it aspires to overthrow and replace the current imperfect system. By transcending beyond being an abstract design, its goal is to become concrete by preserving all the features of its design. The most salient features of utopia include the claim of a perfect design, a rational order, an absolutism adorned with an authoritarian and totalitarian attitude (Mumford 1962: 362-63). Utopias strive to build, with the help of modern technology, an ideal universe where all conflicts of conscience and self-interest in society are eliminated, where all obstacles to a dignified life are eradicated, and to create an environment where peace, prosperity and virtue will be eternal and universal (Kateb 1975:17). Such characteristics lead utopia to close itself to all possible proposals and options.

Utopia originated as a literary genre from the theory of the state. In later years, even though the types of utopias have diversified and turned into architectural utopias, they have been always hand in hand with the theory of the state. Thus, even in its most architecturally oriented version, utopias are situated within the tradition of political philosophy and seek the ideal order (J.C. Davis 1983:27). Utopias are often produced during periods when societies are struggling with crises and decay (Usta 2015:18). Utopias aim to produce a city-state within the framework of state theory, and even though they seem to produce a single product, by claiming that these city-states should dominate the whole world, they declare their candidacy to transform the whole world (Usta 2015:18-19). In utopia, the already existing world is abolished, transcended (Havemann 2005: 20), and final as well as eternal perfection is achieved.

Utopias represent ideals, and therefore, even the slightest departure from the ideal will disrupt its status as an ideal and destroy the utopia. This explains why, although many utopian ideals have been sought to be put into practice in history, these ideals have never been realized without loss due to many different factors that have not been taken into account on paper or in theory. Nevertheless, just because they could not be realized in their ideal form, utopias cannot be seen as ineffective constructs. On the contrary, their greatest impact in history has been their ability to transform history and society. While utopian ideals have not succeeded in the literal realization of utopias, they have always succeeded in radically changing the world. Utopias have been the most crucial levers of motion as they have interrupted history with the pure ideas developed by the human mind against the existing conditions, allowing for leaps and bounds.

UTOPIA'S EVASION FROM DEFINITION

Utopia, by virtue of its references scattered across a vast territory, winks at many definitions under the same concept. This leads to the emergence of numerous definitions of utopia. There is a vast literature on what the concept is, offering a wide range of different answers. Every researcher emphasizes a different characteristic of utopia and builds their definition around this attribute. Since each of these definitions focus on a different aspect of utopia, they may examine utopia in depth in a particular field while overlooking its features in others. For a comprehensive understanding of what utopia is, it would be useful to examine its most emphasized features one by one.

DESIRE

Since utopia is always a thought or a design that is thrown into the future, it is a structure that one wants and desires to establish in the future in place of the existing order. Fundamentally, utopia is the expression of a desire; to transform the city, whose current structure is unsatisfactory, into a structure that would be satisfactory. It is the desire for a better existence and a better life (Levitas 1990: 119). Through its design, utopia attempts to visualize and make visible the city that is still in the minds and hearts as a desire, by projecting it to the world. In Moylan's words, it is "the images of desire" (Moylan 1986:1). In this view, the motivation that brings utopia into being is desire. Utopia pursues a perfect order that is designed in pursuit of an optimistic desire.

HOPE

When the desire for a better world to be built in place of the present one is supported by a belief that this desire is realizable, then hope arises. Hope is holding on to the possibility of something that has yet to be realized. It arises from the "inadequacy of the present" and yet it affirms the future (Moylan 1986:22). In Bloch's words, it is the expression of the human longing for a future in which he will feel at home (Çörekçioğlu 2015:55). It is the optimism that an urban design organized with reason can yield much better results than one that has developed on its own over the years. This is why, according to some researchers, hope, whether big or small, is always a utopia at its core (Havemann 2005: 20). Hope, like desire, is a fundamental element of utopianism concerning the possibility of a better world for humanity (Kateb 1966:257). That is, the hope that comes from the belief that a future which can be taken under control will be much better than the present.

The horizon of utopias is, without exception, a society of harmony. The universe it reflects does not yet exist, but it has taken it upon itself to spread the message that the society of harmony on the horizon is attainable, that it is a realizable design. Utopia, the critique of the existing order, offers a comprehensive description and prescription for the attainment of the harmony on the horizon, gives hope to society for the realization of this world of harmony. Utopia urges the society strive for the utopic future. Every utopian text conveys a social craving and sows deep the seeds of a deep hope. Utopias trigger social unification and create a common purpose for a common future. They build and guide hopes.

UTOPIA IS REBELLION AGAINST THE STATUS QUO

Utopian consciousness is the refusal of assimilation with the situation surrounding existence. In this sense, utopias are designs that declare a will to transcend reality and, not satisfied with this, put forward actions that aim to dismantle the existing order partially or completely (Mannheim 1979:173). Utopian thought seeks to shatter the closure of the ideological stasis that legitimizes the *status quo*. It is a radical attitude towards the operating system of minds. It is the search for an alternative and perfect world that it deems possible. Every utopia is a radical criticism and rebellion against the injustices, unfairness, discrimination, inefficient use of resources and especially irrationality created by the political, economic, cultural and social conditions experienced by the mind that produces it. It is the dream of a better world (Eurich 1967:vii). Often with the emergence of a new means of production, it emerges from the conflict between the world as it should be and the world as it is. It not only aims to transform society, but also to eliminate and transform the inadequacies of the social order of production

(Abensour 2009:66). Severing all ties with the past is one of the fundamental characteristics of utopia (Coşkun 2004:74). Utopian criticism breaks all ties with the current situation and reveals that it is in favor of a total rejection of the past. Its criticisms are not directed against certain individuals or some aspects of the system, but against the system as a whole. It is a manifesto of rebellion against the current system, rejecting it in its entirety.

PURE RATIONALITY

Formation of cities in the historical process involves many components such as geography, trade, politics, climate, culture, beliefs, etc. Without a specific plan, these elements materialize certain patterns through overlapping randomness. These cities, which emerge as a result of the contention of many different constituents and conflicting social interests, sometimes with partial compromise, or by getting used to some conflicts and inefficiencies, are structured not in forms required by rationality, but in an evolutionary line, with the accumulation of buildings, roads, habits and tendencies. In utopias, on the other hand, cities that emerge through evolutionary accumulation, through patterns formed by the overlapping of randomness, are completely rejected and crossed out in one fell swoop. As the reason for this rejection, the fact that cities evolve without observing rational criteria is indicated. Whereas in utopia, reason is positioned as the sole criterion of everything (J.C. Davis 1983:14). Everything that is thought to be incompatible with rationality is dismantled by utopians. Instead of evolutionary development, a revolutionary *coup d'état* guided by pure reason is proposed. With a single blow, all that belongs to the past must be erased, razed to the ground, and the rational alternative must be built in its place, from scratch, from the very beginning. Traditions, tendencies, customs, buildings, roads, designs that have been incorporated into the city in different ways at different periods are to be abolished on the grounds that they do not serve a single rational mind. This is one of the most criticized aspects of utopians. These criticisms suggest that the issues that utopians claim to have solved with ease on paper, by the purely rational mind, do not take into account the complexity of the human psyche and psychological needs, and that while they glorify the most efficient use of resources and standardization for the sake of rationality, they undermine human aesthetics, the practices of everyday life, and the sense of being in a safe and familiar space. In Cioran's words, "what is most striking in utopian narratives is the lack of psychological olfaction and intuition" (Cioran 1999: 85). This is because everything is tied to pure rationality. Its value is reason, its symbol is the plan (Kumar 1991:35). However, life goes beyond the plan at every step, and drifts into terrains that rationality cannot explain. According to this idea, which asserts that cities cannot be produced with purely rational designs, the destruction of buildings and city plans that have proven to be functional in the historical process, with a single stroke of a pen, puts the existence of society at risk with a single move. Setting out for utopia leads to dystopias.

UTOPIA IS A MODELING

Utopia is the modeling of a social ideal from a point of view that has its own history and character (Kumar 1991:13). Rather than the transformation of the pre-existing, it anticipates the production of something entirely and almost completely new from the beginning. In this sense, it is based on a fundamental rejection of the old. In line with the nature of modernism, utopia is based on first designing and then realizing. Everything is a subset of reason. The pure reason will design and humans will build. What has not yet been realized, what does not exist but seems realizable will be created in the human mind (Usta 2014:32). And then, an implementation that corresponds exactly to this creation will be pursued. Moreover, this modeling will be valid not only for one place, but for everywhere in accordance with the logic of modeling. In other words, once the model is produced, it will be standardized and universalized. Modeling is necessarily a mental leap and is theoretical, not practical. In utopia modeling, the opinions, feelings or desires of the people who live and are likely to live in the city are considered irrelevant. The underlying idea behind this attitude is the conviction that the inhabitants of the city cannot know which urban design would make them happier (on the grounds that they are uninformed about urban design and are not rational enough in their general outlook on life). According to utopian thinkers, in such a social environment, social consensus or democratic collective decision-making to design a better city will not yield good results. For utopians, it is much more appropriate for a single enlightened mind, who has studied urban design and can think rationally, to design the entire city on its own, even if it is contrary to the daily desires of all its inhabitants. This leads to the assumption that "the modeling generated by a single mind should be valid for all the cities of the world". This attitude of utopians has also been heavily criticized. The design of cities by the modeling of a single mind, rather than by the inhabitants of that city, is not only anti-democratic, but is also accused of leading to dystopia on the grounds that it will disrupt the functional mechanisms of the city, as it will allegedly fail to find answers to many practical problems.

UTOPIA IS UNIVERSAL

Utopia, constituted as a new structure built on an empty space after a comprehensive rejection of the existing one, is completely divorced from locality as it destroys all organic ties with the old. In essence, utopia is not a structure designed for a single place. As a modeling, it aspires to all kinds of urbanization. Therefore, in line with the definition of modeling, it claims to be universal, not unique. Utopian modeling is done once and then the whole world is expected to be renewed in accordance with this model. Utopias deny that they are historical and claim universal general validity. They are not for one place, but for everywhere. In this sense, utopias distinguish between "place" and "space" and refer to a defined space rather than a defined place. Thomas More, the inventor of the word 'utopia', derived this word –the title of his book– by combining *ou-* which means "non-existent" in Ancient Greek with *topos* which means "place". This derivative word, which literally means "non-place", semantically supports that the utopian space does not belong to a specific place (Köksal 2014: II-III). Although utopia can only coexist with a space, it cannot be produced specifically for a single space. Although it is built in space, it does not vary in each space in the logic of a tailor-made piece. Rather, it is an abstraction that spreads across all spaces. Utopias are independent of a particular place. They are proper for everywhere.

UTOPIA IS THE PROPOSAL FOR AN ALTERNATIVE ORDER

Utopia aims at the construction of a certain way of life, free from the imperfections of the existing order. It is an alternative paradigm born out of the critique of the status quo (Goodwin 1980:384-85). Utopians think that in a perfect society, all kinds of antagonism would cease (Cioran 1999:87). The alternative order offered by utopias is, without exception, a conflict-free society. Here, conflicts of interest are overcome, all classes and members of society are identified and positioned in such a way that they act as cogs in a whole for the common good of society. The "I" is replaced by the "we" (Ağaoğulları 1986:34). The utopian starts from the idea that the order they live in is problematic and creates a positive vision for the future (Erdem 2005:78). Problems such as class struggles, inequality, injustice, unfairness, war and misery that exist in the current world are transcended in this vision. Utopians are of the opinion that the alternative but perfect order is directly supported by the redesign of the physical design of the city. They think that the physical infrastructure affects the sociocultural superstructure. By rebuilding the physical layout in a completely rational way, after all remnants of the old have been cleared away and completely destroyed, it is assumed that many aspects of the alternative layout will become more efficient than ever before — from the way people use the city to the opportunities the city will offer them, from the way the new urban design organizes the way minds work to the most efficient use of commerce and leisure time.

UTOPIA IS A PERFECT IDEAL

Utopia is Platonic, i.e., it is a perfect ideal. In the Platonic sense, the "reality" consisting of fallen and distorted representations that fell from the "ideal" to the material universe, is sought to be restored to the ideal world. In utopia, an ideal life gets established in which everything goes well, every detail is worked out, all human actions are calculated, determined, designed, in other words, a life in which almost all problems are solved (Alver 2009:141). The fall from perfection will be reversed in utopia. At least this is the utopian's belief. Thus, people will build their paradise on earth. Since utopia claims to be perfect, it lacks a dynamism that will allow for a continuity of change within itself. Any possible change that may occur in this perfect structure can only be in the direction of deterioration. For utopia is so perfect that further progress in a positive direction is no longer possible. For this reason, utopian designs are completely closed to any kind of change and development. Not even a single stone of the design should change. Utopias are characterized by "the monotony of perfection" (Reader 2007:163). The aim of utopia is to build social integrity, order and perfection, and it is willing to realize this at any cost (J.C. Davis 1983:8). This value is usually determined by the pruning of many of man's spiritual fulfillments. This sharp stasis arising from the perfection of utopia —its claim to be perfect— condemns the individual in the name of "happiness" (Ağaoğulları 1986:33). The first place where this perfection, which is thought to be detected by pure rationality, seems to block is the spiritual, intellectual and actional freedoms of human beings. Utopias created in the name of offering a better life seem to produce areas of tension instead of happiness, authoritarian structures and more flawed environments than before, as they often contradict the desires of urban dwellers. Utopias that set out for perfection seem to result in dystopias by generating unprecedentedly flawed cities.

ONE-MAN REGIME

Utopias are not built on social consensus or compromise. They are produced in the pure rational mind of a single person. Therefore, utopia is closed to social consensus. The entire society is expected to obey this utopian modeling that claims a modernist "reality" and "truth". Those who oppose utopia are simply incompetent people who cannot see where their own interests lie. For these masses who do not know where their own interests lie, utopians impose an order on their behalf, in spite of them. The "knowing" person is superior to all "unknowing" interest groups in order to ensure the general welfare of society. The utopian acts as a philosopher, an architect, a planner, an engineer, a sociologist, a jurist and a monarch. Although they do not say it, they aspire to be a god. By standing up against the whole society, utopians declare that everything that has been done so far has been wrong, that these wrongs stem from ignorance, yet from then on, they are the subject who knows, and that they will use their knowledge for society and, if necessary, in spite of society. From now on, this single supermind determines everything from social rules to the design of the economic order, from the control of production forms to the organization of entertainment areas, from how housing and domestic life should be to working hours, from the architecture of the city to how many people should live in the houses. The utopian sees this power in themselves and always draws that power from rationality – at least they say and believe that they do. Having such faith in their own project, utopians expect absolute obedience. Thier design is as precise as a Swiss watch, and each part supports the other. Like a watch that becomes inoperable in the absence of any one part, they think that if any part of their design is not realized, their utopia cannot be realized either. Utopias are therefore non-negotiable: It is either what the one man has designed, or it does not exist.

SOCIAL ENGINEERING

Utopias do not agree with the idea that human beings have a nature and that all life should be built in harmony with and around this nature. On the contrary, they believe that people and society can be changed by changing environmental conditions (Kurt 2007: 160). These beliefs have a methodical content. In other words, they think that they can predict in advance what kind of changes in environmental conditions will bring about certain social changes. Therefore, they have unlimited confidence that they can build the physical conditions of the city in a way that will create the society they want to attain. They assume that the ideal form of the city will also idealize the society and social structure (Yüksel 2012:11). Therefore, every utopia is an architectural utopia. Transforming the physical conditions of the city will shape society in the desired direction. Utopians see the architecture of the city as the key to the perfect ideal society. And they fully believe that they can redesign society from top to bottom.

UTOPIA IS ILLIBERAL

Utopia is a structure that relegates freedoms to a secondary place in the name of order. The order of social functioning does not care what the individual will feel under this order. It is an order where free will is shelved and no irrational step is accepted. Utopia is only interested in increasing the quality of measurable results. In the name of the maximum rational functioning of society, it eliminates free will, excludes and prohibits everything that is not rational for society, without exception. In this sense it is oppressive and illiberal. It does not trust the individual and therefore does not give them the right to choose. The utopia designer, alone, has defined what is "best" for everyone, and the freedom to go beyond this definition is taken away from the individual from the very beginning. The individual's personality is dissolved in the society and the individual is reduced to a facsimile of any other individual in the society. In utopias, private life is frequently interfered with, and in many utopian designs, private property is taken away from the individual, even the right to own a house is abolished, and the individual is forced to live a public life in the name of efficient use of resources (it is highly doubtful that these designs can provide such efficiency). Individual freedoms and the right to choose are sacrificed for the sake of the ideal design of society. The individual is turned into a fiction, a symbol. Here people do not live, they merely fulfill the functions assigned to them. The human being no longer has a personality (Izetbegović 1987:244-46). The duty of the person has taken precedence over the rights granted to them. In utopias, for the sake of maximizing social interest, the individual is dissolved and reduced to an organic limb of society. The service of the individual to the city has become more important than the service of the city to the individual. It is predicted that the order achieved in total will create a better life for all people. In utopias, the duties and statuses of all citizens are determined, and these qualities designated from the center cannot be changed (Kurt 2007: 160). There is no social transitivity. In the name of absolute equality, the freedom of individuals to be different is destroyed. The equality in utopias is the most restrictive equality that social consensus can realize. Equality is achieved not in the sense of freedoms, but in an illiberal way. In utopias, there is material prosperity for all citizens. There is no room for poverty in these ideal designs (Meyerson 1996:119). However, just as in the case of equality, the price imposed on citizens in the name of material security is the transfer of their freedom to the centralized system. In utopias, individual freedom is sacrificed to secure material assurances. Utopia takes away the individual's right to choose and behavior for the sake of creating a perfect society, while relying on bureaucracy and technology. It invests in bureaucracy to keep people under constant control and oppression, and in technology to produce the methods and tools necessary for the bureaucracy to fulfill this function properly. Utopian dreams tend to result in totalitarian nightmares (Kołakowski 1982:247). The authoritarian veins of utopias are always on standby as a threat for ideological abuse.

UTOPIA IS MAINLY A CITY

Utopia is primarily a design for a location, a space and essentially a city (Alver 2009:140). It has an urban form (Harvey 2005:192). In fact, according to Mumford, the first utopia is the city itself (Kumar 1991:25). Utopia is the form of space that has been liberated from its existing state and structured in an imaginary way from the very beginning. For this reason, utopias determine and describe almost all spatial organizations. From houses to buildings, from workplaces to fields, from streets to alleys, from the center of the city to its borders, utopias directly construct how the entire architecture of the city will be built within its framework. Thus, cities become projections that create the ideal society. Every city is essentially a utopia and every utopia is mostly a city (Yüksel 2012:11). Starting from the idea that form determines content as much as content determines form, utopian thought finds the architecture of the utopia it determines on a city scale vital. Architectural form, in utopia genre, determines the material and spiritual content and fate of the city and everyone living in it. According to this idea, the good society should be built by reasoning systematically, i.e., in the light of the principles of mathematics, geometry, in short, rationality (Kumar 1991:35). The ideal city wants to contain and control all kinds of possibilities within its walls. Utopians do not find it right to create a compatible architecture by thinking of human beings first. They first design the proper architecture following rational principles, and then advocate that society should be determined and created by this rational architecture. In this sense, every utopian architecture is a social engineering (Alver 2009:143). Utopia is a proposal for an ideally designed urban order.

UTOPIA IS STATIC

Utopians desire to change the existing structure in its entirety. Therefore, they are radical and revolutionary. However, if they succeed in achieving the new urban architecture and social structure they aim for, they no longer accept any change (Kurt 2007:160). This is because every change that will take place after that means a deviation from the ideal society that was reached or created, and a corruption from the perfect structure. For this reason, utopias aim for unlimited conservatism from the moment they realize themselves. However, since no utopia in history has ever built itself in such a way as to perfectly realize the design on paper, it has not been tested whether this unlimited conservatism is actually possible. However, the theoretically revolutionary utopia, as soon as it constructs itself, is thrown into theoretical conservatism and places itself in this stasis for eternity.

UTOPIA IS PROGRESSIVE

The equality, prosperity and order envisioned in utopias have never achieved the perfect structure that utopias aim for. Moreover, even though utopias have made progress in many areas compared to their predecessors, once they are built from scratch, they are criticized for not being open to innovation and taking on an authoritarian form. These criticisms are not without merit. However, although they have been criticized for various reasons, utopian initiatives have always offered new, progressive solutions for the city and urban space and have succeeded in implementing some of them (Kahya 2007:21-22). Today, the point reached by urban planning, its enhanced design power and the ability of technology to continuously articulate new designs have all taken their origins and power from utopias. Therefore, even though utopias have failed to produce perfect societies, orders or cities, they have sometimes provided significant improvements compared to their predecessors and have brought about irrefutable advances in the *status quo*.

UTOPIA IS EGALITARIAN

Utopias are always egalitarian, pro-sharing, and usually envision a society based on common property (Gürsel 2005:69). Utopia defends all these to the end, even at the cost of abolishing the free will of the individual. However, since this egalitarianism suspends the freedoms of individuals and imposes them to adhere to a certain modeling, it actually overlooks what it essentially aims for: the design of a city consisting of happy people. The egalitarianism of utopias is often accused for being an equality achieved at a lower level of prosperity, rather than an equality achieved at a higher level of prosperity as it was conceived in their modeling stages.

IS UTOPIA A GENRE PECULIAR TO THE WEST?

There are contradictory views on this issue. Against the view that utopia is a genre unique to the West, it has been argued that in various periods, similar texts were created in different parts of the world. Yet, at times, this second claim seems to be attempting to reach this conclusion by pushing the definition of the utopia genre and over-expanding its framework.

For example, according to the Turkish thinker Sadık Usta, who argues that utopia is not a genre peculiar to the West, the utopian tradition in Muslim cultural realm began with Mazdak in Iran, and was followed by the Karmatis and the Black Iraqis in the Arabian Peninsula, the Khurremids in Azerbaijan, the Alevis and Babai rebels in Anatolia, Rumi (who was influenced by the Kalenderis), the Bedreddinists and others (Usta 2015:22). Again, alongside the transfer of knowledge from Egypt to Ancient Greece, it is argued that various texts on the design of the ideal city were also transmitted.

The counter thesis, on the other hand, argues that utopia is a genre that can only emerge after certain historical conditions are met, pointing to the European Renaissance as the period when these conditions were fulfilled. Accordingly, there is no real utopian tradition and utopian thought outside the Western world. Various types of ideal societies such as "golden ages" and "paradises" abound in non-Western societies, but they are not utopias (Kumar 2007:26). Utopian desire can be found in all world cultures. In this sense, utopian thinking is a universal phenomenon. Nevertheless, no matter how universal it is to accept that there is a possibility that the future can be perfectly constructed, it is unique to the West that this possibility is arranged in a certain way and textualized in a written form (Moylan 1986:2). Outside the Western world, the infrastructure necessary for writing utopias failed to materialize.

In my opinion, the full realization of the utopian ideal city design is only possible with the existence of a purely rational thought (*reinen Vernunft*). And such pure rational thought can only be related to modernism, which came into being in a certain geography at a certain time. This corresponds to the European region of the fifteenth century. As such, the crystallization of utopia as a concept is only possible from this time onwards and in this region.

Designs with utopian characteristics before this date can only be called proto-utopias. As pure rationality is a prerequisite for the transition from proto-utopias to utopias, histories and regions without pure rationality cannot successfully produce utopias. The main difference between the West and the East is that modernism — which was realized in the West on the back of pure rationality — was not possible through an internal transformation in Eastern societies, but only through an external imposition, and therefore it does not seem possible for the proto-utopias in the East to turn into real utopias. Moreover, just as modernism can be exported to other societies, albeit in a top-down manner, it is also possible for utopias to be exported to other societies. In other words, while the spontaneous emergence of utopia as an idea is unique to the West and it is a reality that the West has provided more favorable conditions for the production of utopias, there is always the possibility that the utopias produced can later be brought to the East. Utopias, which are products of a certain historical period in the West in terms of production and discovery, can be adapted to any part of the world by virtue of their claim to universality. The only problem is whether the utopias on paper will turn into utopias or dystopias in practice as a result of these adaptations.

The Search for the Ideal City

All utopian authors shared the values of a perfectly organized, rational environment of happiness, free from all randomness and away from anything accidental. Utopia, which envisions an ideal living space, always needs a habitat to create this space.

As all the desires of utopia can be realized only in one place, the determination, design and construction of this place is of vital importance for utopia. The space takes shape according to the dream map of utopia. In the design, the Utopist includes everything from where the utopia will be located to spatial organizations, such as houses, neighborhoods, buildings, streets, avenues, and what will be located where. The author thinks, determines and standardizes the size, parts, regions and geographical location of utopia down to every detail. Acting like an engineer and planner, the author of utopia speaks on behalf of society and people —despite them— regarding the distribution of utopian space, makes suggestions and adapts the space to the map of society in his mind (Alver 2009:141). Indeed, utopia can only realize itself through the utopian design of the space in which it is constructed.

Utopias, simply "having an urban form", are intertwined with the image of the city and "always constructed in urban settings" (Harvey 2005:192). The fact that the social model in utopian proposals is limited to the city arises from the concern to create a social model that can be called micro, which is realizable, capable of maintaining a balance within itself, and controllable (Coşkun 2004:186). Utopia is both a proposal for an urban order and the delineation of its ideal dimensions (Alver 2009:142-43). While they were criticized for producing standard, homogeneous and uniform urban environments, utopian pursuits offered new and progressive solutions for the city and urban space.

Underpinning the design of the ideal city is the idea that the good society should be built through systematic reflection. Reason is its value, and the plan is its symbol. In the ideal city tradition, man as philosopher-architect-craftsman is a co-creator with God. Like God, humans, with the intellect gifted by Him, should live for the purpose they are conscious of. And as much as possible, nothing should be left to chance. The ideal city wants to contain and control all kinds of possibilities within its walls.

Utopian urban approaches and their critics always start with the following question: "What is the ideal city?" Utopists argue that the ideal city is founded on rational principles (Cunningham 2007:3). Yet, utopian visions that design the city like a machine are seen by many as a nightmarish dystopia.

Since the Utopia designer recognizes the untransformed state of the space as raw and sees this raw state as imperfect, s/he starts by creating the image of the environment in which the society will live in order to eliminate these imperfections.

Without this image, concretization cannot be achieved. Thus, during the design process of utopias, the artificial organization of the environment is a priority (Aktan 2012:69). In the creation of the environment, the construction of what should be as it should be will lay the foundations of the "ideal". Without exception, this makes every utopia a function of space.

It is only natural that modern utopias envisioning harmonic, congruent, measured, rational societies would be interested in the arts, especially architecture, as an expression of proportion, symmetry, arithmetic and geometry. When they set out to spatially design the ideal societies they envision, the forms they usually use derive from many different geometric forms, starting with the sphere and the circle, which are considered to be the most perfect forms in the cosmos.

For Plato and Aristotle, the city is perceived as the most optimal form of social organization and the most favorable environment where the ideal society can be created (Baczko 1989; Ertan 2003:146). In their search for the ideal society, which began in antiquity and has continued to the present day, utopias have found the most suitable place for themselves in the city (Binboğa 2012:138; Bumin 1986). Utopists, believing that humans are shaped by their physical environment, have begun by establishing an "ideal city" for the "ideal society" they envision. In Ancient Greece, the search for an ideal order, such as Plato's *Republic*, was founded in the *polis* (πόλις, city). In his work titled *Republic*, Plato designed his ideal government of philosophers in the *polis*. Thomas More grounded his ideal order on urban organization; in the same period, Tommasso Campanella grounded the administrative and religious oppression based on gender discrimination in *La città del Sole* (*The City of the Sun*) upon the city. In *New Atlantis*, Francis Bacon laid the foundations of a social order based on the principles of empirical science in the city. The nineteenth-century utopias such as Étienne Cabet's *Voyage en Icarie* (*The Voyage to Icaria*), Edward Bellamy's *Looking Backward: 2000–1887*, H.G. Wells's *A Modern Utopia*, Charlotte Perkins Gilman's *Herland*, in which he fictionalizes a society of women, and the work entitled *The Island*, in which Aldous Huxley describes his utopian society, are examples of classical utopias based on orderly and planned cities.

Reflecting the social and spatial projection of a civilization, the city is a settlement where non-agricultural production is generally carried out, where control functions are gathered, and which has reached certain levels of size, heterogeneity and integration (Aslanoğlu 1998:13). City is a structure formed by the close proximity of many people for the purposes of residence and production (K. Davis 1973:1; Saunders 1986:7). It is above a certain quantitative size and is complex (Elliot & Macrone 1982:5). From the *polis* of Ancient Greece to the organization of the nation-state, the city has maintained its role at the center of social designs (Ertan 2012:39). People of thought and action alike have sought a utopian design in which the urban space of the future can be rationally organized, thereby fulfilling the requirements of transparency set by the impersonal reason (Bauman 2005:50).

The cities in utopias and the theme of an ideal city are very much related. The endless interplay between utopia and the search for the ideal city takes place under the auspices of a dual need (Sacrey, Bouchet & Picon 2003: 117). While the utopian city bears the legal, administrative, social, economic and environmental traces of the period in which it emerged, it also depicts the space shaped by the utopian/ideal society in accordance with the vision/ imaginative horizon of its designer (Yüksel 2012:11). Ideal city adds the element of design to utopia. The urban space that adorned the dreams of Utopists would be a place that would never be polluted by history (Bauman 2005:50). As the product of a pure rationality that could be perpetuated forever, this city would not feel the need to change. Much like Habermas' notion of an objective legitimacy of propositions and norms that can only be universal and therefore demand the "erasure of space and time" (Habermas 1987:323), the vision of the perfect city implied a total rejection of history and the destruction of all its concrete traces. The city in the utopian approach is a dream that attempts to challenge the authority of both time and space by eliminating the qualitative differentiation of space.

In a sense, in terms of spatial management, modernization necessarily results in utopianism. However, it does not seem possible to establish a monopoly in a city that was founded by the successive coincidences of history, that built itself by evolving under different social impulses, and that moves through time by changing constantly in the practices of these different groups. Establishing a monopoly is easier if the city is built from scratch. In other words, if the city becomes a realization of a utopian mind's spatial dreams on paper and if urban realities are implemented without any deviation from that model throughout its entire history, it would be easier to establish a monopoly. Only then can meanings and functions be truly precise and clear. For these reasons, Utopists emphasized the need to tear down and rebuild to implement their paper model in a space. The architects and urban planners of utopia clearly wanted to build their ideal city from scratch in order to realize their utopia. In this sense, social history can be seen as a history of cities that were desired to be built from scratch.

The concept of "utopia" entered into circulation in 1516 with Thomas More's famous book about the imaginary space he designed as part of his criticism of contemporary British politics (More, 2003). Utopia conclusively established its existence as a genre after this book. However, there were also designs before *Utopia*, which, although they did not completely bear all the characteristics of utopia, contained various important utopian features.

Pre-utopian utopian-like designs were not only political and cultural, but they also put forward ideas on urban planning and followed a rational trajectory. Besides, although utopia today stands out as a Western idea, it also has non-Western sources. The earliest utopian designs can be traced back to the invention of writing.

IDEAL CITY DESIGNS IN ANTIQUITY

The first utopia-like works of history that have survived to the present day are found in the Mediterranean basin, the Indian Vedas and Chinese classics (Usta 2015:20-21). These utopia-like works date back 5,000 years. Setting off from Sumer, Egypt and Greece, utopia stops by Rome, China and India, and after pausing for a while, it spreads again to the Middle East and Europe. These works share the common characteristic of referring to a "golden age" thought to have existed in the past, and comparing the past with the present, while criticizing the moral decay and deterioration that has taken place over time. These texts, written as a nostalgia for the egalitarian social structure of the golden age, underline the fact that human beings lived a free and happy life before the emergence of classes, exploitation and social hierarchy, and investigate what needs to be done in order to return to that golden age.

Ancient utopias are the first embryos of the ideal city/state theory. These texts in search of the ideal city are the transcribed forms of ideas designed to overcome the problems, crises and impasses experienced by the societies and cities in which their authors lived. They are efforts to determine *what should be* in the face of discomfort with *what is*. Ancient utopias are rational designs that make little reference to religious references. At the same time, they are ideas that aim for universality and in this sense render themselves the common heritage of humanity. Ancient utopias are mostly found in literary works mixed with legends and myths. While these narratives speak of an equal society where all people live in prosperity, prosperity and abundance, they are actually a reaction to the negativities/problems of the period in which they emerged (Yüksel 2012:14). Although there are debates about how far utopia-like texts from this period can be considered real utopias in this regard, it should not be ignored that they had a significant impact on the utopias that would emerge in the Middle Ages and that they had thoughts/dreams far beyond their time.

The first known utopian text in history was inscribed on clay tablets by the Sumerians exactly 5,000 years ago. The Sumerians described a "golden age" to refer to a "very ancient era" when humanity was not yet sinful and knew abundance and peace (Usta 2005:14). "Dilmun Island", depicted as a paradise in Sumerian legends, is an inaccessible place. There is no room for war or any conflict on this island (Usta 2015:20-21). As the example of the Sumerians shows, utopian initiatives and ideal city designs seem to have begun to manifest themselves with the birth of civilization. This proves that the history of abstract reason's attempt to determine the concrete space and the form of the state is quite ancient.

Interestingly, the centuries in which island narratives on state and society were most frequently published were the third and first centuries BCE (Usta 2015:27). Similar currents would only appear in the Middle East in the tenth century and then in Europe in the sixteenth century during the Renaissance.

Atlantis, the world's oldest known and most famous utopian city/country, reaches the present day through Plato's texts. In *Timaeus* and *Critias*, Plato narrates the conflict between the civilization of Atlantis and Athens (Plato 1977). In these narratives, Atlantis is an island that gives its name to the ocean in which it is located. A powerful civilization with a very advanced technology lives there. According to Plato, who describes the plan of the capital of Atlantis in detail, in the center of the city, there is an inner fortress that also houses the royal palace and a huge temple of Poseidon separated from it by a wall made of gold. The whole city consists of circles around this temple. In order to reach the center from the sea and to connect the center with other ports, a canal 90 meters wide, 30 meters deep and 10 kilometers long was opened (Usta 2005:56). Bridges and aqueducts were built to connect the land circles surrounding the sea and to connect the capital with the other islands of the Atlantean Empire. There is an intertwined canal system that connects the entire network for communication and irrigation (Yüksel 2012:13-14). The social hierarchical order in Plato's narrative shapes the spatial organization of the cities of Atlantis.

Atlantis, which is described as an ideal society in Plato's narrative, when it attempts to conquer its neighbors to the east, comes into conflict with the Greek cities led by the state of Athens. During this struggle, even though the Greek cities abandon Athens over time, Athens continues its struggle alone and eventually triumphs over Atlantis. After this victory, extraordinarily violent earthquakes and floods occur at sea and the island of Atlan-

tis disappears overnight, sinking to the bottom of the sea (Plato 1977:38).
While describing the struggle of Atlantis and Athens, Plato tries to depict
the ideal society (Kumar 1991:37-40). The myth of Atlantis, as articulated
by Plato, had a great influence on the later utopian tradition. Even Francis
Bacon named his utopia *New Atlantis*, in reference to Atlantis (Bacon 2010).
Plato's Atlantis and ancient Athens are a conscious fiction. Both societies
are embellished and worked out for didactic purposes.

Plato's contribution to utopian literature is not limited to *Timaeus* and
Critias. In his book *The Republic*, written in response to the corruption in
the Athenian administration in Ancient Greece, the philosopher designs
a new ideal state order. He designs the city and urban structure from its
foundation to its functioning, from architecture to traffic, from production
to waste management. Such a detailed description of design is a turning
point in the history of utopianism. In Plato's *Republic*, society will be guided
by wise and educated intellectuals, i.e., philosophers. In the social hierarchical order of the *Republic*, the philosopher-kings constitute the top tier of
the ruling class, the auxiliaries and the protectors form the military class,
and the farmers, artisans and merchants form the lower ranks. However,
among Plato's utopias, *The Republic* is the one in which urban planning is
least mentioned (Ertan 2012:42). Plato's suggestions about the image of the
city in this book are only small details. For example, by design, city should
be surrounded by walls consisting of the houses of the guardian class as
a means of screening against attacks from the outside, and these houses
should have simple designs.

Plato discussed in much more detail in *The Laws* how the urban planning in his ideal city should be. According to Plato, the ideal city should be
neither on the seashore nor far from the sea. According to him, being on
the seashore would stimulate trade and business life, but it would also lead
to an increase in the power of the masses as a result of intensive foreign
trade overseas, and the administration would shift to democracy, causing
unqualified minds to have a say in the administration. Establishing the city
far from the sea, on the other hand, protects the city by making it difficult
for foreigners who may cause disorderly developments to come to the city,
but at the same time, it reduces the volume of business and the wealth of the
city. For these reasons, Plato's ideal city is located about 15 kilometers inland
from the sea. In order to be self-sufficient, the city relies on agriculture for
its economy. Plato also advises that there should be no other city-state near
the city. He limited the city's population to 5,040 citizens so that the people
could get to know each other directly. Thus, he predicts that there will be
no alienation among the people, but rather a close friendship will develop.
Plato envisions one house for each citizen in the city; in other words, he
proposes 5,040 houses for 5,040 citizens. Population cannot be increased or

decreased. The land is equally distributed among the citizens, and the size of existing houses and land cannot be increased or decreased. Plato's circular city is located on a hill for security and hygiene reasons (Plato 1998:189-90). Plato's design can be considered as the first ideal state that includes detailed city plans. However, Plato created an anti-utopia instead of a utopia, as he predicated the "ideal city" model that he tried to realize on the oppressive and antidemocratic form of government of Sparta, and projected this model on the Athenian city plan (Danışman 2005:66). In the ideal state designed by Plato, just like in More's *Utopia*, freedom is given up in order to ensure social justice and equality, and the whole society is forced to live under strict rules determined by the state. Plato not only sought solutions to the problems of the old world, but also raised urban issues such as optimal city size, transportation and population, all of which are still debated today. As a utopian, he wants to change the *status quo* completely and create a city as per his desire, and then he aspires for a static structure that suspends all possible changes, for a land based on uniformity and excluding diversity (Kurt 2007:161-62). Plato, just like other utopians, wants to create a perfect and unbreakable/unchanging site that is a copy of the city in the realm of ideals. Plato's ideal will directly affect future urban utopias.

With Plato, the urban planning of ideal state designs devised by a single mind in a utopian manner begins to gain importance. Hippodamus will expand this tradition initiated by Plato and realize the first principles and designs for an ideal city design. Hippodamus, who is considered to be the first urban planner in history, proposes a rational planning emanating from a single mind, as in urban utopias, and writes a book on urban planning and management. Hippodamus' book on urban planning has not survived to the present day. We learn his name and the existence of his book through Aristotle's *Poetics* (Aristotle 2009:54). Hippodamus argues that the city population should be 10,000 people in utopian ideal city planning. The inhabitants of this city of 10,000 people are divided into three classes: craftsmen, farmers and soldiers. The city lands are divided into three parts: religious, public (or state-owned) and private (Alsaç 2007:110-11). These distinctions, made with a highly abstract rationale, also manifest themselves in urban planning. Hippodamus, who organized the city with roads cutting each other perpendicularly and square or rectangular building islands between them, creates the first grid-shaped city plan in history. He then applies his theory in Miletus and Thurii, a Greek colony in Italy. After his death, his plan becomes even more widespread. Hippodamus' urban planning comes to life in Priene and Cnidos in Anatolia, Olynthos in Macedonia, Alexandria in Egypt and Rhodes. As can be understood from the example of Hippodamus, ideas about urban organization began with utopias; ideal urban design has close ties with utopias.

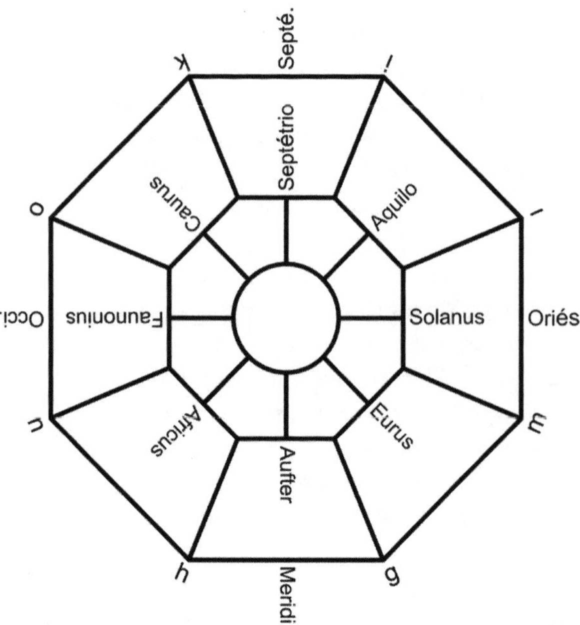

Ideal city
plan,
Vitruvius

Vitruvius was one of the leading designers in producing an ideal city design in Antiquity. This Roman engineer wrote his theoretical ideas in *De architectura libri decem*, i.e., "Ten Books on Architecture" (Vitruvius, 1999). This work is recognized as the first work on architectural theory. In addition to vast amounts of information on architecture, it covers in detail what kind of structure the ideal city should have and the issues that should be considered when building a new city. Vitruvius' ideal city design and his thoughts on the subject will be reread during the Renaissance, translated into many languages, and will directly affect the approaches to architecture and urban planning, especially in Europe (Alsaç 2007:111-12).

In Antiquity, the utopian city aims to perfectly reflect the social hierarchical order in space. The planning of the city should fulfill all kinds of social, economic and political functions. The utopian tradition in Antiquity takes a long break with Europe's entry into the Middle Ages. Since abstract reason and rational thought, which constitute the basis of utopias, were de-emphasized during the Middle Ages, the necessary infrastructure for the formation of utopias also disappeared. The phenomenon that gave the period its dominant character in the Middle Ages was dogmatic thinking shaped within the framework of church influence. Rather than criticizing the status quo and attempting new breakthroughs, it was more important to preserve the status quo and to do so based not on abstract reason but on superstition. The ideas of the island of happiness conceived within the Christian tradition have been no more than a shadow of the concept of paradise. In the imaginative realms of the Middle Ages, it is seen that the imaginative designs of the Antiquity or the Renaissance period were not based on the work that was celebrated in utopias, but on the paradises on earth where everything was readily available. For example, "Cognagne", the utopia of French writers in the twelfth century, is a paradise for those who have good taste and those who enjoy debauchery. There is neither work nor toil in Cognagne. Idlers are rewarded. There are tables for the hungry on the roads and in public places. The rational utopian design is thus put on hold until the Renaissance, until rationality reasserts and proves itself as an important component in the construction of society.

IDEAL CITY DESIGNS IN RENAISSANCE

Throughout history, ideas about the organization of the environment in which we live have primarily targeted the social structure and then the physical environment in which this structure will take place, indicating that periods concentrated on the field of literature. Only at one point in the historical process these ideas were elevated to the level of design: Renaissance. In other words, thoughts and ideas about changing the environment were first put forward in the form of designs during the Renaissance. In this period, Italy was the epicenter of an act of intellectual architectural production.

The Italian Renaissance coincides with the beginning of secularization in society. While the power of the merchants was growing stronger, the desire to control human destiny and the living environment accompanied the emerging movement of humanism. The Renaissance is a period of leap forward in which reason is once again transformed into an important tool for understanding the world. The prioritization of reason allowed for the intrusion of radical and rational intellectual designs that threatened the ideologically conservative closure of the traditional world. This innovative paradigm demonstrated itself in many examples in Europe during this period showing that existing urban designs were not the only option and that better cities could be designed in accordance with changing conditions and developing technology. In parallel with the Renaissance, these ideal urban designs started in Italy and influenced the continent. These designs are known as the "ideal city designs of the Renaissance period" in the history of architecture and urbanism (Alsaç 1978:31).

The plan to build ideal cities was not just an architectural project. It was believed that through this ideal urban architecture, a peaceful and harmonious society could be built with a rational government that respected the freedom of its citizens. It was thought that there was a linear relationship between urban architecture and social order (Russano 2012:23). The structure of the city also determined the structure of society.

From the birth of Renaissance architecture in Italy, architectural design increasingly aligned with Vitruvius' idealization of architectural proportions and order. This development led, in the architectural culture of Western

Europe, to the emergence of the "competent architect" who investigated and measured the remains of the past and revitalized correct and beautiful architecture through the interpretation of texts and the power of his understanding, hence the formation of "Academies" (Tuztaşı & Civelek 2012:12). Thus, texts and drawings become intertwined in architectural thought and architectural theory is structured by the network of interrelations between these two.

Perspective, which seems to have been discovered by Brunelleschi, the architect of the dome of the Duomo in Florence, and later theorized by the humanist Leon Battista Alberti, offers architects the possibility of a universe that can be geometrized and measured. Thus, with the Renaissance, the city began to be seen as an object that could be projected in perspective or design, just like a building. It is thought that the city can be designed as an order emerging from the pure mind. This leads to the understanding that a perfect city can be produced by utilizing the fact that the city is something that can be built mentally (Sacrey, Bouchet & Picon 2003:22). As a result of the reflection of artistic ideas and ideals on the urban plan, geometric, precise urban schemes are projected. Thus, different ideal city designs developed throughout the fifteenth century, with references to antiquity, manifest themselves as plans managed from a single center, perfectly organized, and often with geometric features.

Idealist Renaissance urban planners aim to reproduce the hierarchical and aristocratic order of Plato's *Republic* in the centralized and circular cities they designed. With its centralized and circular structure, the utopian city of the Renaissance period seems to be a microcosm not only of the society it is a candidate to host but also of the entire universal order (Eaton 2002:98). Since aesthetic perfection was seen as a function of mathematical perfection in this period, Renaissance urban planners strictly adhered to ideal measurements and applied mathematical principles to cities. Comprehending the city with an absolute utopian approach, they combined the writings of the Roman architect Vitruvius with Platonic idealist concepts in their urban plans and attempted to produce physical copies of them (Kumar 1987:19).

The city, which was designed at the highest possible level and in an orderly manner, strives to present a rational, hierarchical and humanist approach to the disorder and chaos of the existing cities in the nature dominated by human beings (Yüksel 2012:16-9). In this period, the path to the ideal city passed through the ideal world of mathematical reason. What emerged were utopian cities.

Leon Battista Alberti (Morris 1994:170), known as the first urban planning theorist of the Renaissance period, gained this reputation in 1452 when he wrote a 12-volume architectural work entitled *De Re Aedificatoria* (On the Art of Building) and delivered it as a manuscript to his patron Pope Nicholas V (Grafton 2002:266). This book presents the first known ideal city designs of the Renaissance. With the printing of the manuscripts in 1485, *De Re Aedificatoria* is considered the first modern attempt to systematize architecture (Roccasecca 2009). The book becomes a milestone in the attempts to organize cities in an ideal and systematic way through architectural theories.

Alberti was directly influenced by Vitruvius in his designs. According to him, only Vitruvius is everlasting among the ancient authors who wrote about architecture (Eck 1998:280). Following Vitruvius, Alberti first starts by discussing the most suitable locations for the construction of ideal a city before its construction. For Alberti, there is no city design that can be deemed appropriate for every region without exception. It is necessary to design an ideal city in accordance with the characteristics of each geographical region. Since he was able to propose different solutions to different situations, his book does not contain a single ideal city model, but many ideal city designs. Among these ideal city designs, there are plans that can be built on plains, slopes, riverbanks and hills. For Alberti, the roads of cities are particularly important. He differentiates the roads of the cities according to their locations and arranges them in accordance with the topographical conditions. While the roads he designed for large and important cities were wide and straight, he proposed curved roads for smaller cities whose defense was secondary. He argues that curved roads will make these small cities look more beautiful and larger (Alsaç 1978:32). The wide and linear street form he envisioned for large cities clearly differs from early Renaissance urban planning principles (Morris 1994:170). This approach manifests itself as an innovation unique to Alberti.

Alberti, who put forward various ideas about the forms of cities, the nature of their defenses, how water resources should be used, and how sewage networks should be realized in his ideal city designs, mostly designed his city plans in the form of stars. The roads of his cities open radially from the center to the edges. In the city center where all roads intersect, there is a church, a palace or a castle according to different ideal city designs realized by Alberti.

Alberti divides his ideal cities into various regions. He allocates areas and resting places for each region. He expels factories and other production units from the city on the grounds that they emit outputs such as noise, pollution and odor that reduce the quality of life in the city. He creates special places outside the city for workshops; clusters similar business lines and groups them according to their relations with each other (Alsaç 1978:33). He tries to provide forms of insulation that will increase the total happiness of the city dwellers. Although Alberti's designs are considered to be the first ideal city designs of the Renaissance, according to some views, Alberti was not interested in designing an ideal city, but in setting general rules to create a productive sphere of influence (Pearson 2011:21) and in realizing the functional adaptations the city needed for the development of trade (Rosenau 2007:44).

Antonio di Pietro Averlino, known as "Filarete" (means lover of virtue in Greek), was the second architect following Alberti among the ideal city designers produced during the Renaissance period (J.R. Spencer 1958:10). The ideal city plan he designed was published in his 25-volume *Trattato di Architettura* (Treatise on Architecture), written between 1461-64 (Lang 1972:391). He dedicated a copy of the book to Francesco de Medici, the father of Lorenzo de Medici, the famous ruler of Florence, and another copy to Duke Sforza of Milan, his protégé between 1451-65 (Moffett, Fazio & Wodehouse 2004:308). These names indicate that he was a highly popular urban planner and had good relations with influential city rulers.

Filarete named his ideal city, which he designed in the shape of an eight-pointed star through its outer walls, "Sforzinda", referring to the name of his patron Francesco Sforza (Alsaç 2007:112-13). The angles on the walls were designed to provide an advantage during the defense of the city. Sforzinda is an ideal city project that Filarete presented to Duke Sforza of Milan as a model of how Milan could be structured if he were made chief architect.

Filarete constructs the social structure of Sforzinda based on the model described by Plato in the *Laws*. From the property rights of citizens to the institutions of the city, there is a direct influence from the *Laws*. However, while Plato does not mention any architectural features of the institutions, Filarete both describes and draws them in detail. However, from time to time, various inconsistencies between the text and the drawings have been noted (Lang 1972:391).

Filarete placed the House of Vice, where sexual needs were satisfied, and the adjacent House of Virtue at the very center of Sforzinda. While the ground floor of the House of Vice is a brothel, the upper floor is an astronomical observatory (Thomson 1993:64). The city expands by centering on this building. The interior of the city is relatively empty. Next to the cathedral and the castle, there is a labyrinth garden consisting of seven parts. All

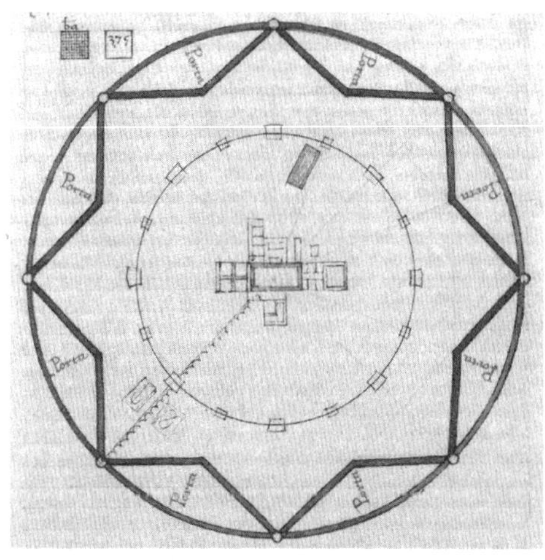

Sforzinda city plan, Filarete

the paths in the garden lead to a circular area at the center of the garden. From the center of the city, 16 axial avenues lead to the city's peripheries (Morris 1994:170).

Filarete designed the city down to the details of the clothing of its citizens. Accordingly, each social class in the city would be recognized by their attire. There is order, pleasure and abundance in Sforzinda; Filarete writes that the architecture of the buildings in the city reflects this harmony (Thomson 1993:64). Thus, while Filarete, like his predecessors, relies on architecture in designing the ideal city, he goes beyond architecture in his design and attempts to identify other visual aspects directly related to social life. Going beyond the guidance of the city's architecture, he also directly intervenes in people's dress. Thus, half a century before the publication of Thomas More's *Utopia* in 1516, two Italian architects, Alberti and Filarete, created the first spark of a utopian tradition in designing the ideal city. Alberti's proposals and Filarete's Sforzinda, like More's *Utopia* paved the way towards a desirable order for future life – but without specifying how to achieve it (Meyerson 1996:113). They opened up new horizons and mobilized new approaches for the urban planners that followed them.

Francesco di Giorgio Martini (1439-1502) was another author of a multi-volume book on ideal urban design during the Renaissance. Due to the increasing influence of firearms at the time, Martini gave priority to the security and defense of the city in the design of the ideal city. In this sense, he is one of the earliest theorists of ideal military city designs. One volume of his seven-volume *Trattato dell'architettura civile e militare* (Treatise on Civil and Military Architecture) deals entirely with urban planning.

In the *Trattato*, which took 20 years to write (between 1475-95), he defines architecture as a scientific discipline based on arithmetic and geometry and realized through drawing, creativity and invention (Merrill 2013:1). In line with this definition, he designs different ideal cities. These consist of designs that are located on a plain, slope or riverbank or have a harbor, rectangular, in various polygonal shapes, with roads either in a network perpendicular to each other or in a concentric-radial pattern (Alsaç 1978:33-4). In Martini's ideal city designs, there are areas in the center of the city where all roads converge and on which major important buildings are located.

Another important designer in the Renaissance search for the ideal city was the renowned Leonardo da Vinci. Da Vinci (1452-1519), better known for his work on the defense of cities, also produced numerous studies on

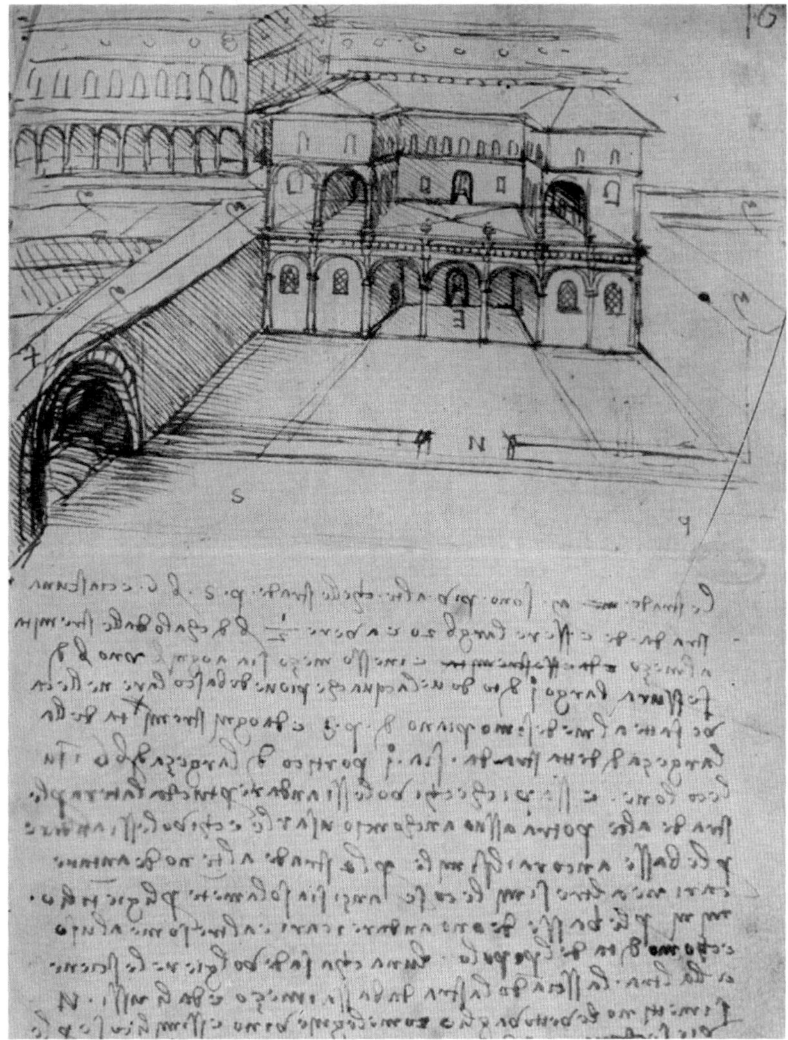

Sketch of one
of Leonardo
Da Vinci's
ideal city
designs

urbanism, but his main contribution to the field was his thoughts on the theory of urban planning. Da Vinci's ideas can be found *Codex Atlanticus*, the posthumous collection of his drawings. His proposed city is located on a river. The river was divided into branches by canals and these branches were passed through the city. Each branch of the river, which will be divided into six or eight branches before reaching the city, will flow through the city in parallel to each other and the flow direction of the river, and will be reunited after leaving the city (Alsaç 1978:34). The aim is to meet the water needs of the city and its sanitation.

The first proposal for the separation of pedestrian and vehicular traffic at different levels emerges in Da Vinci's urban design. According to Da

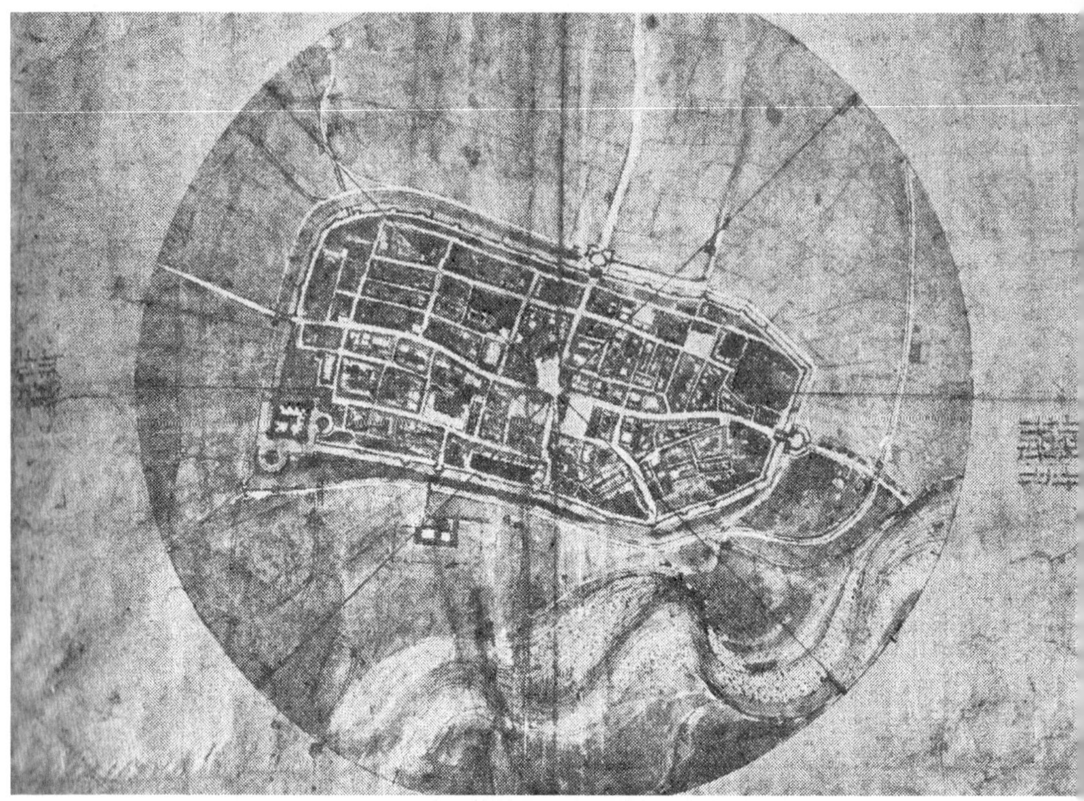

Vinci's suggestion that urban transportation should be solved at different levels, the lowest level would include loading, stables, water transportation and sewage functions. Above this would be the level where car and horse traffic would take place. The third level, where the city's elite would live, would be devoted entirely to pedestrian transportation.

Thinking well ahead of his time, Da Vinci designed portable dwellings for those working in the fields. He thought that these could be moved from one place to another in rural areas at harvest time, which would be beneficial for the health of those living in them as well as being functional. From this comes the idea of creating a green belt around cities.

Another suggestion of Da Vinci was to build satellites around the city for the workers in Milan. By doing so, he aims to relieve the ever-growing city of Milan and ensure the orderly growth of the city. With these ideas, it is almost as if he found the principles of modern urban planning on his own (Alsaç 2007:114). For the Renaissance period, however, these principles were literally utopias.

Instead of ideal urban designs, Da Vinci seems to have produced functional ideas that would practically meet the requirements of the time. Some

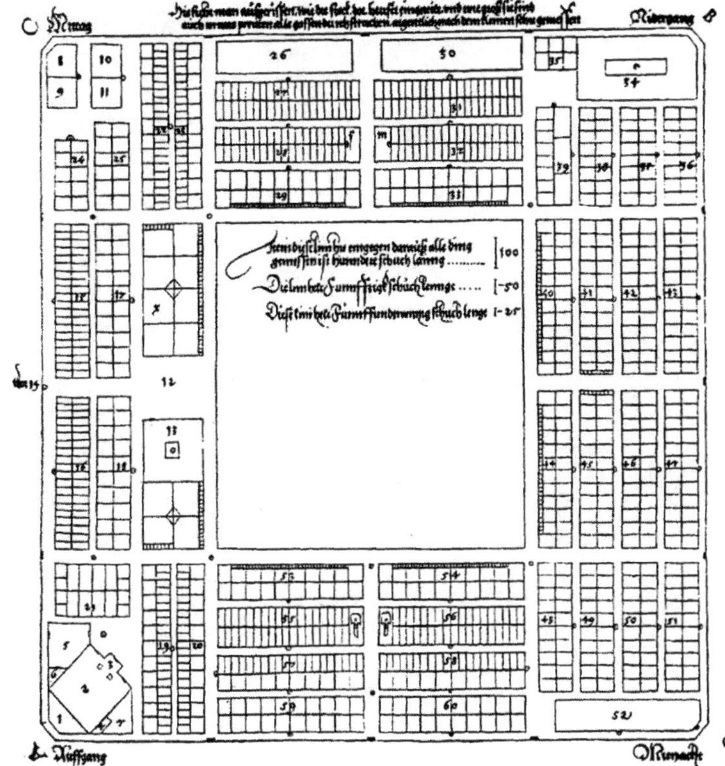

A plan of Albrecht Dürer's ideal city design

of these ideas, such as those related to urban defense, were implemented immediately, whereas his ideas suggesting that enlarging cities or making functional improvements in the city were taken to be pointless, and thus they never materialized. Ideas such as the need to separate different types of traffic, and the necessity of determining road dimensions as a function of the height of the buildings above them, could only be addressed later, in contemporary urban planning practices.

Francesco de Marchi (1504-77), another important urban planner who worked on and produced ideal city designs during the Renaissance, proposed a large number of rectangular, square, circle, various polygons, star and cross-shaped city plan schemes. The roads are concentric rings and radial networks, all meeting in a central area. He also emphasized the problems of ideal cities on plains, slopes, riverbanks and port cities. For example, there is an ideal design of a port city around a circular area. In another design, in which a river is assumed to flow through, the road network is arranged parallel to the river, that is, in the form of curves, indicating that terrain data were also taken into consideration in the shaping of the plan (Alsaç 1978:35). De Marchi not only made ideal city plans, but also produced ideas on how old cities could be reorganized according to these ideal plans.

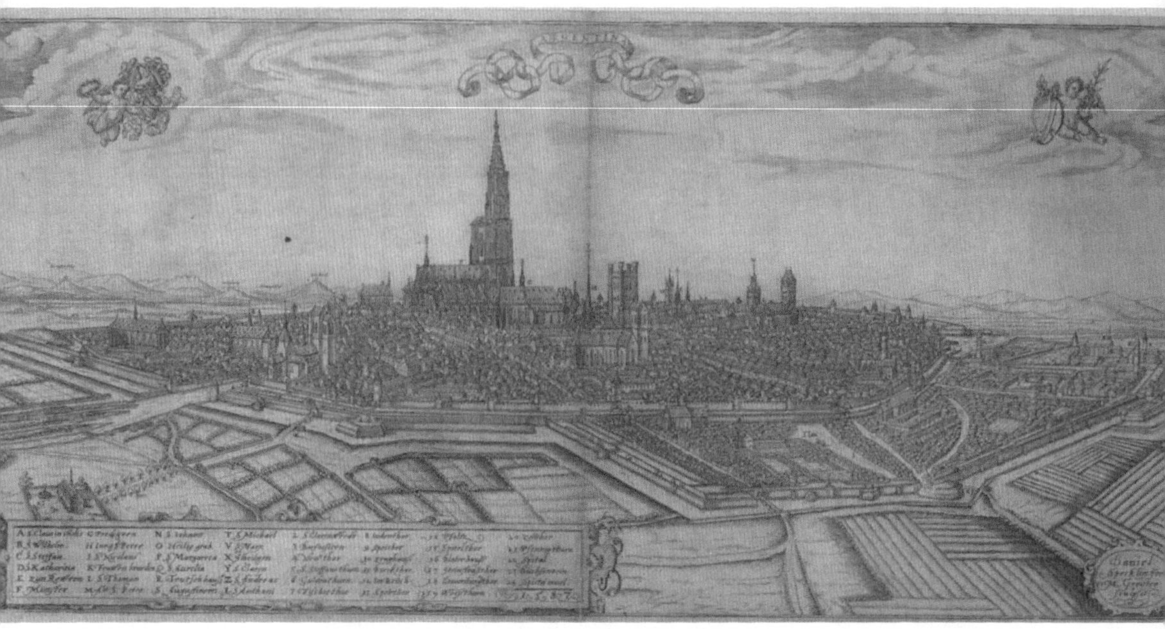

In the Renaissance period, Italy produced the most ideal city designs, to be followed by Germany. Albrecht Dürer is one of the most important urban designers in terms of ideal city designs made by Germans. Dürer's (1471-1528) designs are included in his work *Etliche Unterricht zu Befestigung der Stett, Schloss und Flecken* (Several Instructions for the Fortification of Towns, Palaces and Localities) published in 1527. The first German translations of Vitruvius also coincide with these years. It is known that German theoreticians and designers had already read Vitruvius' texts in Latin or Italian and were aware of the theoretical work done in Italy during the Renaissance. For this reason, some of the German ideal city designs are clearly influenced by Italian models.

From the title of Dürer's book, it is clear that he focused his work on the defense of cities. In this work, Dürer developed two ideal cities. The first plan is an octagon; a concentric-radial road network provides transportation. There is an octagonal area in the center of the city. Dürer's second design is based on a square plan. The city is placed so that the four corners of the square point in four directions. The various functions were examined in detail and environmental conditions such as the predominant wind direction were taken into account in order to prevent the disturbing fumes and odors of the foundries from entering the city. In his design, Dürer proposed separate building blocks for various functions or social groups, and designed places where everyone could store a year's worth of food. Since the dimensions envisaged for various functions are given in detail in the work, it is possible to calculate that one side of the square-planned city will be 734 meters long. In both designs, there is an area in the center of the city. This is an octagon in the first example and a square in the second. Unlike the Italian designs, these are left empty and the church is located on another building island adjacent to this area. In Italian designs, on the other hand, the church is usually conceived to be located in the geometric center of the city.

One of the most important urban planning theorists of Germany in this period is Hans van Schille. Van Schille's work, published in 1580, contains various ideal city designs. However, it is understood that these are copies of designs made by the Italian Francesco di Marchi. In this work, ideal cities with square, pentagonal, hexagonal, octagonal plans are discussed together with their walls and their views. In addition to these, there are also plan drafts in which the central area is a square or a circle. In Van Schille's designs, defense problems rather than the functional problems of the city predominate.

Another German urban planning theorist from this period is Daniel Speckle. Speckle became famous with his work *Architectura von Vestungen* (Architecture of Fortifications) published in 1589. In his ideal city designs, he starts from a basic module in which the distance between the wall towers is taken as approximately 305 meters. Ideal city plans are usually star-plans derived from octagons. Speckle became famous especially in Northern Europe with these designs and was appointed as a consultant by the princes there.

Another theoretical work or utopia in Germany was the *Reipublicae Christianopolis descripto* (Description of a Christian Republic) by Johannes Valentin Andreae (1587-1654), a theologian, published in 1619. Andreae's work is the most detailed of the utopias created in the sixteenth and seventeenth centuries.

Another example of ideal city designs in Germany is found in Joseph Furttenbach's (1591-1667) *Gewerb und Stadtgebaeu*, published in 1650. In this example, starting from a rectangular plan scheme, Furttenbach achieves an oval form by covering the short sides of the rectangle with a wall system consisting of half-octagons. The long axis of this oval form is oriented east-west. He also places the entrance gates of the city on this axis.

Furttenbach organizes the rectangular area that forms the interior of the city by dividing it into certain functional zones, thus creating a design that emphasizes functional requirements rather than feudal requirements. He discusses in detail the church, municipality, school, hospital and housing structures that must be present in the city.

Leonhard Christoph Sturm (1669-1719) was another German architect interested in theoretical urban planning problems. In his *Prodomus Architecturae Goldmannianae* (Reference to Goldmann's Architecture), published in 1714, and *Der Auserlesenste Verneuerte Goldmann Oder Die Ganze Civil-Baukunst* (Goldmann revised, or Civil Architecture in its entirety), published posthumously in 1721, Sturm proposed very simple forms, usually square and rectangular, as ideal urban designs. Another German ideal city designer, Wilhelm Dilich (1571-1650), in his work *Peribologia seu muniendorum locorum ratio oder Bericht*, which was written in 1640 but published only in 1689, proposed ideal city designs and designed different ideal cities for different land geographies.

During this period, it is also seen that new cities were established in Germany where the ideas developed through ideal city designs were implemented. Cities such as Hanau on the banks of the Main River, the construction of which began in 1597; Freudenstadt, the construction of which began in 1599 on the order of Prince Friedrich I of Württemberg; and Friedrichstadt on the Eider River, the construction of which began in 1619, can be shown as attempts to realize ideal city designs in Renaissance Germany (Alsaç 1978:36-39). Freudenstadt is very reminiscent of Dürer's ideal city designs with its square plan, square-shaped area in the center and the church located in one corner of it.

In addition to Italy and Germany, ideal city designs can also be found in European countries such as France, Switzerland, the Netherlands, Denmark and Sweden during the Renaissance period. In France, the first examples that come to mind are the ideal city designs of Antonio Cordiani, Jacques I Androuet du Cerceau and especially Jacques Perret, the author of *Des Fortifications et Artifices, Architecture et Perspective* published in 1601.

In France, just like in Germany, there were attempts to put these ideal urban designs into practice. One of the typical examples of these implementations is Vitry-le-François commune, designed by Girolamo Marini and the construction begun in 1545. This city was formed from a square plan with each side measuring 612 meters. The city walls are shaped like a star with pointed projections at the corners and the center of the square. In the center of the city, which is divided into four parts by two main roads, is a square plaza.

In Switzerland, Prince Henri II of Neuenburg attempted to establish an ideal city named Henriopolis after himself. Prince Henri II, who dreamed of an ideal city on the shores of Lake Neuenburg where both Catholics and Protestants could live together, was not successful despite many incentives to realize this city and bring the necessary population here.

Henriopolis was planned on paper as a semicircle. The center of the city is the marketplace, located right next to the harbor on the shore of the lake. The roads were designed perpendicular to the diameter of the circle parallel to the lake and perpendicular to each other. In the center of the semicircle, there is a square surrounded by churches and the municipality building. Fountains, which were planned to be placed in various parts of the city, were hoped to provide an aesthetic appearance as well as a functional one.

In the Renaissance period, ideal city studies in the Netherlands also manifested themselves in both design and implementation. Simon Stevin (1548-1620), one of the most important Dutch ideal city designers of this period, published a book called *Het burgherlick leven* in 1590, which was also a kind of sociological study. This book was followed by *Sterctenbovwing*, a work on the construction of city walls, published in 1594. Stevin's book, which collectively expressed his ideas on ideal city planning, was published only after his death in 1660. In his works, it is seen that instead of polygonal or star plans, Stevin proposes regular, symmetrical, rectangular plans consisting of repeating squares (Weebers, Ahmad & Zuraini, 2011:179). In his ideal urban designs, he also envisions roads reserved only for pedestrians, and explains that he thinks this is so that everyone, rich or poor, can walk without being disturbed by horse and car traffic. Stevin also designed and worked on topics such as the "ideal house" and the "ideal building block".

One of the ideal city designs created for implementation in the Netherlands was Willemstad, the construction of which began in 1583. Its designer was Frans de Traytorrens, most probably a Scot. Willemstad's plan consists of an equilateral heptagon, with the main axis of the city oriented north-south and perpendicular to the harbor in front of it.

Another attempt to build an ideal city in the Netherlands is Scherpenheuvel. The plan of this city, which was designed in 1606, is also a heptagon. The reason why the ideal city designs in the Netherlands are usually a heptagon is that it carries a symbolic meaning representing the seven regions of the Netherlands. In Scherpenheuvel, a Catholic city, in addition to this reference, there is also a reference to the seven sorrows and seven joys of Mary. The road network and building islands of this ideal urban practice follow a radial-concentric scheme. In the city center is a seven-armed star square with a church in the center.

The influence of Italian and German ideal city designs is evident in the ideal city designs of Renaissance Denmark. Especially the colonial cities established by the Danes in the Scandinavian countries show serious similarities with the Italian and German ideal city designs. Two Danish cities, Kristiansand and Christianshavn, whose plans were drawn up in 1665 and 1617, resemble ideal city designs in terms of their plan schemes.

Kristiansand has a square plan, its roads are perpendicular to each other, and there is a square plaza in the center of the city. Christianshavn, on the other hand, has an octagonal plan with the corners of the city walls protruding like stars. The road network and building islands are made up of concentric squares. In addition, the diagonals of these squares radiate radially from the square area in the center to the edges of the decagon, that is, it connects it to the city walls.

An example of ideal city designs in Sweden is Erik Dahlberg's project for Landskrona in 1680. Landskrona, which has a circular plan with roads cutting each other perpendicularly, was planned as a city of 1,500 people.

During the Renaissance period, England differs from continental European countries in terms of ideal urban design and implementation in terms of intellectual and architectural framework. Ideal urban designs were not realized in England during this period. Some researchers attribute this to the fact that Vitruvius' English translations appeared very belatedly. According to this thesis, without the influence of Vitruvius, theoretical studies in terms of ideal urban design were not realized. However, England would become pioneer country for a much more important step forward. Indeed, utopia as a genre would emerge right in England.

What is interesting is that despite the lack of ideal city designs, the field of thought has focused on this subject, and one of them has even gained such fame that the title of one of its works is used as a general name for such works and designs. The work in question is Thomas More's *Utopia*, published in 1516.

In this work, an island with 54 imaginary cities is described. It is observed that the writers who produced works in the field of thought in England emphasized the social structures of cities rather than their physical appearance. As a matter of fact, *The New Atlantis*, the most famous work in this field after Thomas More's *Utopia*, deals with the subject from this angle. Written by Francis Bacon (1561-1626) and published posthumously in 1627, *The New Atlanits* deals with the society of a port city surrounded by walls.

Another example of intellectual architecture from England is *Eximenic*, a fifteenth-century walled, square-planned city with a large central square in the center and small squares in every quarter of the square. Again, in *Oceana*, published in 1656 by James Harrington (1611-77), the physical appearance of the city is not mentioned, but the structure of an ideal society governed by a republic is discussed. In another example, John Evelyn (1620-1706), in his work *Fumifugium*, published in 1661, talks about air pollution and suggests the creation of a green belt surrounding London in order to prevent this.

However, Thomas More's *Utopia*, which is considered to be the text that established utopia as a genre, is of particular importance and requires a detailed analysis.

THE EMERGENCE OF UTOPIA AS A GENRE

It was only with Thomas More's *Utopia* that utopia emerged as a distinct genre with a narrow definition of its own. Thomas More's *Utopia* represents a breakthrough that gives this genre its name. It bears all the qualities that make utopia a utopia and defines the characteristics of the genre. The work is a special literary innovation that effectively drew the boundaries of the utopian field for the next five centuries (Kumar 1991:45-6). In the utopia he created, Thomas More went much further than Plato and planned everything about the utopian country down to the finest detail.

With a humanist and modernist approach, Thomas More is convinced that the source of eternal peace and happiness can be found in the pursuit of rationality. More complains about the injustice of the world and the existing system. He chooses to respond to the world he complains about by designing a world in which no one will complain.

The world Thomas More envisions is a perfect world, free from the evils of his time, well-governed, with just laws, where wealth and ignorance, which he sees as the source of injustice, are eliminated, and where, once established, people will live happily ever after.

While writing Utopia, *More* had in mind Plato's *Republic* and new information coming to Europe from the New World. The New World civilizations that emerged with the discoveries showed European civilization that their model was not the only possible alternative, and that other models were also possible. Far, far away from Europe, on the other side of the dividing ocean, there are people who, without knowing Plato, Aristotle or Aquinas, are forming societies, building cities, developing a different economic and administrative system, and applying laws. When the Spaniards set foot in America, they encountered the Inca Empire, which had a rational, geometric urban planning; it was seen that a world that had not experienced the adventure that Europe had gone through could also exist.

For a European, The Inca Empire in South America at the beginning of the fifteenth century resembled a kind of "utopia". The country was divided into regions where a certain number of people lived, uniformity in clothing and housing was adopted, and state warehouses and stores were established.

In this country, where everyone had to work except the sick and those over the age of sixty, everything was so well planned that even the visually impaired were made to sort corn kernels to avoid unemployment, and marriages were supervised by officials. Although everything that adorned the great temple and sacred garden in the capital Cuzco was made of gold, the Incas lived a simple life without luxury and ostentation. This was the way this society, which fascinated Europeans, was governed (Bumin, 1986:23-24). It was as if another version of the fictional city that Plato created in his dreams and thoughts was being practiced in South America.

Thomas More, who encountered examples of a utopian city or country both in literature and in practice, thus found the courage to design an alternative grand order for England, which he was dissatisfied with its current situation. In this way, the famous humanist Thomas More, who also served as prime minister to King Henry VIII of England, was the first to introduce the concept of "utopia" into the field of literature with exactly this name and in its current scope. In his work *Utopia*, More describes an imaginary island whose founder is "Utopos", hence its name.

This concept, *U-topia*, derived from ancient Greek with a simple word play, means "no country", "dream country" and "imaginary country". *Topos* (τόπος) means place and space in Greek, and the prefix "u" (οὐ) gives the word a negative connotation. Utopos takes the suffix "ia" (-ῐᾱ) in Greek and Latin because it must ultimately be a land and a country. Thus, a meaning such as no country, unknown country, imaginary land emerges. However, in More's work, the word "utopia" also has a connotation of "good place" and "happy place". As More's contemporaries and close successors would discover, the author also puns on the homonymy between the word "ou" and the Greek word "eu" (εὐ-), which means "good", "ideal", "perfect" and "prosperity". In this way, the word "eutopia" (εὐτοπία) is obtained, which has meanings such as "good place", "perfect place", "ideal place". Thus, "utopia" means "a place that is perfect but does not exist", "a place of prosperity but cannot be found", "an ideal but nowhere" (Çörekçioğlu 2015: 23-24).

Utopia was written in the midst of a great crisis in Europe's order of values and the world of meaning. This crisis is the crisis of the transition from the Middle Ages to the Modern Age; it expresses the collapse of all cultural elements and institutions of the Middle Ages, economic, moral and political, in the face of the new values and institutions of the emerging modernity. In this respect, More's text emerges in a contingent world between two different paradigms, that is, between the closed cultural structure of feudalism and the open cultural structure of nascent modernity.

More's *Utopia* consists of two separate parts written at different times. Contrary to expectations, the first part was written after the second part and was not included in the first edition of the work. The first part was included in *Utopia* only in later editions. There was a reason why he wrote the second and then the first part: After describing the perfect order he envisioned, More wanted to emphasize how terrible the situation in his own country and in the whole of Europe was compared to the order of Utopia. For this purpose, he wrote the second part later and put it at the beginning of his book (Urgan 1984:47). He wanted his readers to see for themselves the difference between Utopia and the order they were already living in and to be disturbed by this dichotomy.

The first part of *Utopia* is more of a satire in terms of genre, whereas the second part is a story of a journey that would later turn into a literary genre called utopia. While the first part is about the current situation in the England of the period, the second part is a description of the socio-political structure of Utopia, a country where a perfect society lives in an unknown place.

More's Utopia is a metafiction. The narrator in this metafiction is a Portuguese traveler named Raphael Hythlodaeus. In More's fiction, Hythlodaeus is a sailor who accompanies Amerigo Vespucci on his journey to the continent just after Columbus' discovery of the New World. After Vespucci's fourth voyage to the Americas, Hythlodaeus remains in the New World and continues his voyages alone, eventually coming across the island of Utopia on one of these voyages.

In the first part of *Utopia*, Raphael Hythlodaeus begins his story when Thomas More, both as an official of the British government and as a humanist, asks Raphael for information about his travels to the New World and the new countries he has discovered. Another person listening to Raphael is Peter Giles. The narrative is constructed as a conversation between this trio. In this conversation, Raphael attempts to convey to More and Giles what he had previously discussed during a conversation between Cardinal Morton, an English lawyer, a jester and a mendicant monk at a table in the cardinal's house. The subject of the narrative is directly related to the social, economic and political problems of England in More's time. Raphael's surname Hythlodeaus, which More derives from two Greek words (ὔθλος + δαιζω), means "teller of tales", "expert in idle talk" and "peddler of sophistry".

The second part of the work is the story of Raphael's journey to the island of Utopia. In this part, Raphael assumes the role of a storyteller and describes in detail the founding of Utopia, its customs, traditions, economic and political structure, religious rituals, relations with neighboring countries and many similar issues. This travel experience resulted in Raphael's admiration for the country of Utopia. At the end of the work, More, who is presented as one of the characters of the book, finds most of Raphael's descriptions strange and concludes that they are unlikely to be practiced.

More seems to have constructed the two parts in contradiction to one another. The first part deals with the realpolitik troubles of England and Europe. In this part of the book, More makes heavy accusations against the England under the Tudor dynasty. In the second part, he includes descriptions of the customs and institutions in Utopia. In both sections there are subtle allusions to the works of the Renaissance humanists. *Utopia* is clearly constructed to hold up a mirror to the England of More's time. On the other hand, the second part gives news from a completely different world and talks about a new socio-political and economic order (Çörekçioğlu 2015:95). Thus, the new world of Utopia is proposed as an alternative to the miserable old world.

The fact that the space of Utopia is imagined geographically as an island is meant to underline its independence from the outside world. More thought that an imaginary and ideal settlement and life could be more easily established in a place unaffected by the outside world. Utopia would be an earthly paradise cut off from the world.

More, dissatisfied with the inequalities in England, envisions an egalitarian society and reflects his dream on the imaginary island of Utopia. Utopia is separated from the mainland after King Utopos had a canal dug. With this detail, More refers to the fact that in order to reach the paradise on earth, people must transform the existing natural givens with their own power, as opposed to accepting the existing natural conditions. The ideal society is not found in nature, but can only be built by pure reason. More will emphasize this point again and again throughout *Utopia*.

Utopia in More's narrative is named after the first founder and King Utopus. Utopia is entirely the design, a plan and implementation of King Utopus. It even owes its being an island to Utopus. For Utopia is not a region with a natural geographical form of an island. It became an island when King Utopus cut through the isthmus of about 24 kilometers connecting these captured lands to the land and turned Utopia into an island. Therefore, even the geography of Utopia has undergone a direct architectural intervention. This situation is important in terms of seeing the intense relations between utopia and architecture as well as urban planning.

City image,
Thomas
More's *Utopia*

On this island, which is approximately 805 kilometers long and 320 kilometers wide at its widest point, there are 54 rectangular cities designed by King Utopus, all of which are built on the same plan, although there are minor detail differences in their formation according to the geographical characteristics of the region. The number of these cities cannot be increased or decreased. Amaurote, the capital city in the center of the island, was also planned by Utopus, but was not finished during his lifetime, but was later completed exactly according to his plan. The city was preserved unchanged afterwards. Amaurote (meaning "not clearly visible") was made the capital, because it was in the center of the island and everyone could easily reach it. Neither larger nor more beautiful than the other cities of Utopia, Amaurote, with its walls, stone bridges, wide and mud-free streets, comfortable houses, cleanliness and freshness, is nothing like the chaotic, dirty and restless London of the sixteenth century. On the contrary, it is the very antithesis of London.

Amaurote is surrounded by a thick and high wall with towers and bastions. Outside these walls are natural barriers such as wide and deep ditches, hedges, thorn bushes and rivers. The walls surrounding the capital, which is shaped like a quadrangle in the center of a circle, mark the boundary between the urban space and the natural space of the countryside.

On the island of Utopia, which shows a uniform structure in every sense, all of the cities are located at an equal distance of approximately 38.5 kilometers from each other. It is possible to go from one city to another in a day. However, since work is highly valued in Utopia and many measures are taken to ensure that no citizen falls into idleness or laziness, people's traveling from city to city is also subject to various conditions. Citizens can go sightseeing in different cities of Utopia, but this is subject to permission; if they stay in a city for more than a day, they must continue their daily work in that city. The daily working time is six hours. Utopians also have the right to rest, but for them rest means changing their occupation.

Whereas in sixteenth-century England the wealthy classes, nobility, landowners, clergy, clergymen, most women, in other words more than half

of the total population, were completely idle, in Utopia every adult, male or female, has to work, unless health prevents it. In Utopia, which is a classless society, every man and woman is engaged in agriculture, works in a craft, becomes a soldier when necessary, and spends a lot of time reading and writing.

Since Utopia is an agricultural country, agricultural work is the main occupation of Utopians. Even children are trained in these jobs, which helps them develop physically. Near every city there are large areas of land devoted to agriculture. Every Utopian, male and female, must settle in groups on farms on this land and work in shifts for two years. Thus, since there is no peasant class settled in the countryside and everyone takes turns working as peasants, the deep distinction and inequality between peasants and urbanites in the England of the period is eliminated (Urgan 1984:62). When the Utopians complete their two-year agricultural service, they return to their professions in the city in order not to be worn out for a long time in jobs that require hard muscle power. However, those who also enjoy agricultural work can ask for permission and work on farms for as long as they wish.

In Utopia, everyone has to work, but working or being worked to death, as seen in other countries, is considered harmful for both the soul and the body by Utopians. Utopians work only six hours a day, three hours in the morning and three hours in the afternoon. They rest for two hours at noon. One of the main tasks of managers is to check that everyone is working. Idleness is not tolerated, even when traveling. In countries outside Utopia, the vast majority of the population lives idle, so that even though the working masses toil from morning till night, the country as a whole is still poor. In Utopia, however, the whole country works, even if it is only for six hours, and this labor power is sufficient for the entire island population to live in abundance.

As for the old and the sick, they are treated with great tenderness and care. There are four hospitals just outside each town. These medical facilities are large enough to be mistaken for a small city from a distance. The food eaten in the hospitals is more delicious than the food eaten by other citizens, as the hospital managers are given the right to choose the food in the market before anyone else. The physicians are very skilled and the care is excellent.

Cities in Utopia are highly organized both in terms of planning and legally. The streets of the rectangular cities are regular and transportation is easy. The city is divided into four equal regions. Each district has a shopping center. Necessary goods and the products of the land are stored in these shopping centers. In order to prevent infectious diseases and to ensure a certain level of hygiene, all the food is thoroughly washed and cleaned in the rivers outside the city before it reaches these markets.

Utopia's economic system is not left to the market and is centrally planned. The food and all other needs of the citizens are determined by very precise calculations. The rulers examine the situation in various regions and determine what is plentiful and where it is scarce. Cities where there was an abundance of a particular item or food would help the city where it was scarce, without asking for anything in return. Since one does not know what the next harvest will be like, production is adjusted to meet all the needs of Utopia for two years. The surplus is either distributed free of charge to the poor of foreign lands or sold to them at fair prices.

Although Utopia occasionally resorts to foreign trade, money is not used inside the country. There is no commercial exchange. Each house leader goes to the market and buys as much food and goods as he wants. Since everything is plentiful and everyone trusts the leaders, no Utopian buys more food or goods from the market than they need, nor would they even think of doing so.

Utopians also do not prefer to eat their food in the privacy of their homes. In Utopia, besides the houses used as dwellings, there is another big house on every street used for gathering and eating together. Although it is not forbidden for a Utopian to buy food from the market and eat it at home, Utopians find it pointless and absurd to deal with kitchen work in their homes. They prefer to eat the food that women cook in shifts in the big house together with the whole street, in unison.

All houses are identical. This sameness is also completely true for the general plans of the cities. Again, like the architecture, there is no diversity in the forms and colors of clothing; everything is completely identical. In More's utopia, people live simply and wear simple clothes. There is an emphasis on cleanliness, health and music.

Utopia tries to prevent a hierarchy based on material things among people. The same language is used everywhere in the country, the same behavioral patterns are seen, customs are identical, the law that applies in one place applies in all other parts of Utopia. Their appearance will also be the same, there will be no variation in urban form. There is no difference in the design or color of clothing. However, this uniformity, which permeates every aspect of life, not only ensures equality, but also leads to monotony. In Utopia, where there is no room for personal tendencies and individual freedoms, the rigid uniformity seen in every aspect of life, the top-downism that determines space with identical city plans, has spread to every aspect of social life.

In Utopia, each city has at least 32 square kilometers of agricultural land. Agriculture is a job that everyone, regardless of their profession, should know how to do; it is done as a duty and taught to the new generations.

Utopians attach great importance to their gardens. Behind each house there are large gardens, with one door leading to the front and the other to the garden behind. All kinds of plants are grown in the gardens and this is done with great pleasure by the citizens of Utopia. Every year there is a competition for the "most beautiful garden" among the neighborhoods of Utopia's cities. This is a motivation for everyone to make their gardens even more beautiful.

Houses in Utopia have flat ceilings. They are covered with a material that is cheap, fireproof and more resistant to rain than lead. Glass is a common material used in these houses, as well as cloths made transparent with amber or oil. This allows the houses to be well protected from the wind and to receive more light.

Since there is no private property in Utopia, no one owns the houses. People exchange residences all the time. Everyone lives in their own house and at the same time in someone else's house. Even on trips, people feel at home. Therefore, there are no locks and keys in Utopia (Kurt 2007:163). Since no one has any private property and everything is everyone's property, anyone who wants to can enter someone else's garden and house. In order to prevent a sense of private ownership and to prevent people from being tied to a house, houses are changed every 10 years by lottery. The way of life in these houses, where several families, at least 40 people, live together, can be likened to the way of life in communes, that is, in houses. In each house, for example, there is a large room where children under the age of five are cared for together. But unlike in Plato's state, mothers take care of their own children in this home. Only babies whose mothers have died or are ill are provided with a wet nurse.

The denial of private property is so important that gold and precious stones are given to young children as ornaments and toys, so that when they grow up they will not value such precious metals. In Utopia, gold is used to make chamber pots and chains for slaves. Thus, Utopians attempt to devalue gold by using it in the most worthless areas. They deny wealth and the ambitions it can bring and the social conflicts that these ambitions can cause, both as a reality and as a concept.

On the island of Utopia, when individuals form families, 30 families come together to form administrative units called philarchs. Under these administrative units live 6,000 families supervised by philarchs. The 10 philarchs, who are the district administrators of each city, together with 300 families, are subordinate to the top administrator (chief-philarch). Two hundred district administrators elect the mayor of the city by secret ballot from four candidates nominated by the people. More did not favor democracy, in which the administration is carried out by the whole people, but meritocracy, in which the administration is carried out by those who are gifted (Cunningham 2007:1). He argues that cities should be governed by the wisest and most skilled people.

The residence of the Philarchs (regional administrators) is located in the center of each street and represents both regional and political power. A total of 30 families live in 15 houses, one on each side of the Philarch's residence. This ensures that each street and its inhabitants are under the control of the philarch. In order to ensure that they do not waste their time, the working life as well as the private life of the monitored individuals is controlled by urban design tools.

In addition to being a political and administrative unit, the philarch is also a work unit. Members of this unit work collectively in the fields. The non-working hours are devoted to education. There is art education for the people. Children are raised communally, meals are eaten in public houses. More proposes an ascetic abundance, in other words, an abundance of basic goods without luxuries or superfluities. Although he was a Catholic, More's proposed good society has some features of the Protestant ethic. This ideology emphasizes work, frugality, self-restraint and the willing fulfillment of one's duties. In More's *Utopia*, the theme of material abundance is linked to the themes of work and participation. Each individual in Utopia has to actively participate in the affairs of society and fulfill his or her part of the work to accomplish things that will benefit society. This threefold achievement of abundance, participation and work is achieved through a series of elaborate means of strict social control, social rewards and punishments.

It is essential that people acquire knowledge and work skills in both areas by experiencing urban and rural life respectively. Syphogrants or Magistrates, each elected to oversee 30 families, are responsible for seeing that everyone fulfills his or her duties. Deviations from work or other duties required by the community are punished with sanctions such as slavery.

Even in their leisure time, "everyone lives under the watchful eye, so that all men spend their leisure hours for good purposes." More's society facilitates the fulfillment of this obligation by banning all ale houses, taverns, gambling houses and other vices, and condemning activities such as hunting. Intellectual pleasures are encouraged by a total educational system that teaches, through the example of Utopia's select group of scholars, how to spend the spare hours reading or attending lectures. Thus, society reaches a level of abundance that everyone works to create and share. This level of abundance is realized and sustained partly because the population remains unchanged. More, like Malthus after him, believes only to a limited extent in the latent powers of increasing labor productivity and fears overpopulation (Meyerson, 1996:116-17). If a surplus of people should arise in Utopia, the space needed for expansion would have to be found on one of the neighboring continents.

All problems concerning the state and governance are discussed in popular assemblies. There are no class distinctions. Only people who have committed crimes can be enslaved in the country. Ownership of everything is common.

This rational design of utopia is defined and criticized by some researchers as the new manifesto of collective life and control (Mumford 1965: 408). It is accused of being a legitimizer of strict and sharp rules, standardization, and being kept in line by the administration; it is accused of creating a monotonous and gloomy living environment brought about by uniformization (Mumford 1965: 408). More was criticized for encouraging totalitarian tendencies both in his own time and in later periods (Alver 2009: 146). More's orderly and uniform cities were designed as an important means of controlling individuals' private lives as well as their working lives.

FIRST UTOPIAS

In 1602, about 80 years after the English Thomas More, the Italian philosopher Tommaso Campanella published a utopia called *Città del Sole* (*City of the Sun*). *The City of the Sun* was included as an appendix in Campanella's *Philosophia realis epilogistica*, published in 1613, and published separately in 1623. Campanella's *Città del Sole*, like all his other ideal city designs, is conceived as a coherent and self-sufficient entity in terms of its spiritual and creative purposes.

There are great similarities in form and content between Campanella's work and More's. The Land of the Sun is also a metafiction and, similar to Utopia, is based on the narrative of a Genoese captain, a traveling sailor. In the architectural structure of the city, as in More's *Utopia*, the houses are not allowed to be architecturally and structurally different, as it might lead to the development of different tastes, affiliations, feelings and even identities among the citizens and disrupt the principle of equality. Everything architectural in the city is uniform and symmetrical. The city is purely rational, geometric and homogeneous, as befits a design on paper. This time, however, the space of the dreamland is imagined not as an island, as in More's Utopia, but as a vast plain just south of the equator. Moreover, unlike More's *Utopia*, the *City of the Sun* is not the size of a country, but of a city. Campanella's *City of the Sun* is an example of utopia designed in the city and intended to be put into practice in the ideal city. Although the structure of the city, which is designed as an ideal living space, reflects centralized planning and strengthens the authoritarian structure of the administration, the urban structure preserves its quality of being an ideal living space.

The City of the Sun is built on a hill rising in the middle of a wide plain. Its diameter is around 3,500-5,000 meters. At the summit of the hill, and therefore the city, is a round temple. This temple is the seat of both religious and political power. The religious and political leader of the City of the Sun is the high priest, called Hoh. From this central temple, the military and war affairs are directed by *Pan* (power), the high priest's deputy; professional, craft and scientific affairs by *Sin* (reason), another deputy; reproduction, education, nutrition and clothing by *Mor* (love), another deputy. The High Priest and his three assistants and three subordinates to each of the assistants make up the 13-member assembly. Apart from this administrative cadre, a small number of the citizens are soldiers charged with protecting the city, while the rest are farmers engaged in agriculture. Although the farmers are responsible for providing the city with provisions, they are passivized in matters such as the regulation and advancement of the good life, the life of mind and spirit, or how the city should be governed (Yüksel 2012:15). They have no voting rights or freedom of opinion.

The city, which spreads around the temple built on the peak in the center of the City of the Sun, is made up of seven intertwined circles. All the necessary facilities and services for urban life are located within these seven circles. Each of these circles is named after the seven planets in the solar system and is separated from each other by walls. These wide and high walls on the outside of the circles are supported by towers, bastions and wide trenches, forming a protective shield against external attacks. The walls are covered with armed guards.

The outermost circle between the city walls is connected by four streets that provide access to the sea through four gates in four main directions. The seven wide walls surrounding the circular form of the City of the Sun contain written and official records of all the sciences and arts; thanks to this feature, the walls are used as the main educational tool for children. Thus, the functions of defense and education merge in the same spatial use. In Campanella's utopia, dwellings consist of multi-story apartment blocks. These buildings are in symmetrical harmony with all other buildings in the city and there is an architectural order in the city (Ertan 2003:151-52). Houses in the City of the Sun are communal. Citizens of the City of the Sun have to change their apartments or the circle they live in and move out of the house they live in every six months. Under this ideal city design, possessiveness and ownership in every sense, down to and including the home, are tried to be curbed and prevented. In this respect, the City of the Sun is quite similar to Thomas More's island of Utopia.

In the City of the Sun, it is thought that poverty degrades people; it leads to cheating, cunning and theft, while wealth makes people selfish, ignorant and proud. Therefore, in this ideal city design, both poverty and wealth are seen as harmful for society. Campanella believes that in a society where there is no personal property and all property is common, both poverty and wealth disappear. Thus, the citizens of the City of the Sun are not slaves to property and only benefit from it. This ensures that there is no selfish person left in the city, because everything is open for sharing.

The absence of property manifests itself even in spouses, for there is no such thing as a spouse in the City of the Sun. In the City of the Sun, it is absolutely undesirable for citizens to have wives or children and to raise them according to their own interests. In Campanella's design, the purpose of mating is the preservation of the common human race, not the individual. Campanella envisions that in a society without a spouse, there would be no family, so that citizens who do not have a family would not be caught up in the struggle for livelihood or the ambition to acquire property, and thus all the people of the City of the Sun would be like one big, single family. In Campanella's design, in such a social environment, selfishness is replaced by the love of coexistence. Personal interests are pushed to the background and love of country is brought to the forefront (Güleryüz 2013:53-54). In the *City of the Sun*, as in all utopias, society is more important than the individual.

In an order where the society is more important than the individual, hard work is praised for the benefit of the society, while rest is disparaged. For this reason, work is very important in the City of the Sun; all citizens work, almost without exception. A person with a physical disability can work as a watchman, unless his eyesight is also impaired. Those who are blind comb wool and separate the thick from the thin. Those who are both blind and physically handicapped, since they can hear in Campanella's design, act as informers on behalf of the state and report what they hear to the rulers. This approach not only shows that all citizens are forced to work with an impulse from the top, but also proves that within the framework of an authoritarian power structure, the state constantly monitors its citizens and establishes a hegemony over them.

Campanella abolished private property and reduced working hours to four hours a day. There is no private property. Everything is managed by the state, including the upbringing of children. The distribution of common goods among the members of society is the work of state offices.

In the City of the Sun, people wear different colored berets according to their professions. There is no habit of using servants or maids in this city, but it is allowed to sell or use prisoners of war as slaves. Women who are painted to look beautiful, who wear high heels to increase their height or long dresses to cover up the imperfection of their feet are punished with death. Their skin should be vibrant and colorful only because they work; their beauty should be in their bodies, in their stature, which develops as a result of their work (Kurt 2007:164-65). He envisioned complete equality between the sexes, an attitude that was quite avant-garde at the time.

Campanella, the author of *City of the Sun*, planned an uprising in Calabria to realize the social justice he envisioned in his design, but when his plans were revealed, he was captured and imprisoned for 27 years.

Another important work that was published after Thomas More's utopia's main characteristics was *Christianopolis* (1619) by Johannes Valentinus Andreae, a clergyman. This work brings a new perspective to the secular structures of previous utopias and urban designs. For, as the title suggests, Christianopolis describes the idea of an ideal Christian society. In other words, it is not a secular but a religious enterprise.

It is known that Andreae was familiar with Campanella's *Città del Sole*, which was created with an atheistic-communist ideal society in mind, as a draft before it was published in 1623, and that he designed his own design with a mystical-Christian ideal society in mind. The interesting aspect of the design is that it was motivated neither by the needs of feudal lords nor by military defense concerns, but rather by an ideal collectivist-Christian society. Christianopolis, in describing Andreae's vision of his ideal Christian society, also reveals the characteristics of the Renaissance city.

Andreae gives a plan and a perspective view of Christianopolis. The city has a square plan, surrounded by a city wall and measuring approximately 215 meters on a side. The squares are placed concentrically towards the center of the city, forming building blocks and roads respectively, with a square area of about 58 meters on a side, with a temple in the center. This arrangement is made by stepping up from the outermost square, the city walls, towards the center. Each side of the concentric squares, the corners of which are emphasized by towers, is designed so that the buildings on each side have a separate function. Four highways connecting the middle of the sides of the squares lead to the central area, which is crossed by vaults under the building blocks.

Christianopolis was designed for a population of 400 people. The city has a total of 264 dwellings, all identically produced. All of them consist of a living room, a bedroom and a kitchen (Morrison 2013:266). Except for the temple in the center, all buildings in the city are two-story. The city was divided into zones, industrial areas were separated according to their qualities, and similar types of industry were gathered together (Yüksel 2012:15-6). Agricultural zones were designed adjacent to the city. With this design, Christianopolis is considered as the discovery of the idea of agricultural zones adjacent to the city in the garden-city designs put forward by Ebenezer Howard in the early twentieth century (Mumford 1922:85).

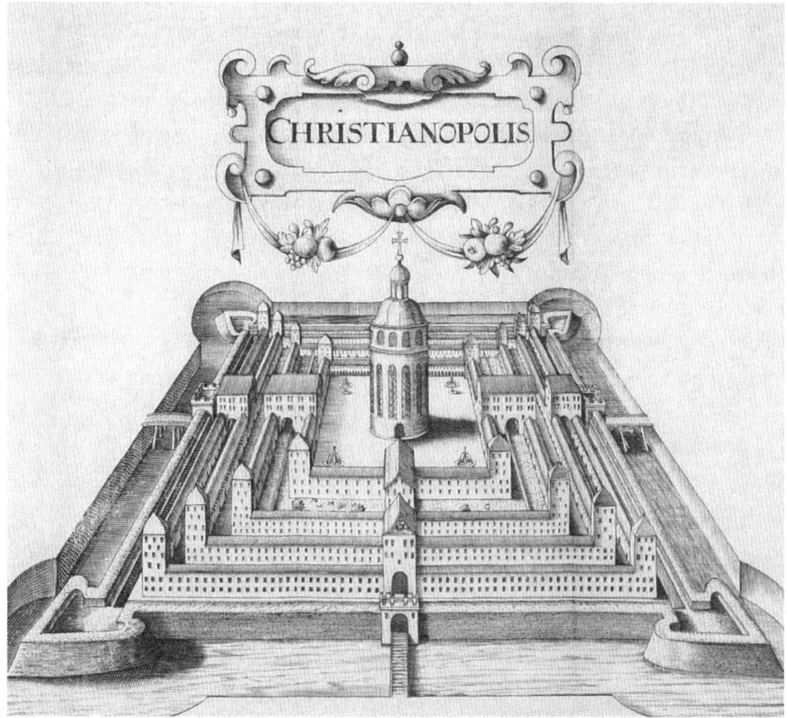

ARCHITECTURAL UTOPIAS IN SEARCH OF THE IDEAL CITY

Another important utopia among the first utopias is *The New Atlantis*, written by Francis Bacon and published in 1627. In *Timaeus* and *Critias*, Plato refers to the island of Atlantis, which is believed to have existed in the Atlantic Ocean in the past, and the happy life on this fairy tale island, and Bacon uses the name Atlantis in his utopia and calls his dreamland New Atlantis.

Bacon's utopian society, called *The New Atlantis*, has many characteristics of More's *Utopia*. However, Bacon paid greater attention to the structure and roles of families and assigned a greater function to technology and science (Cunningham 2007:1). Bacon was unable to complete this work. Therefore, only 50 pages of the book were published. According to this fiction, sailors sailing from Peru to China and Japan arrive at Ben Salem Island, which is called New Atlantis, as a result of a coincidence. Thus, in New Atlantis, true to the utopian tradition, there is a sailor and his narrative of a country that no one else in his community has yet seen. The inhabitants of this island named it Ben Salem. What we learn about the people of Ben Salem remains very limited. Because, unlike More, Bacon's aim is not only to give his

New Atlantis, Francis Bacon

readers an example of a perfect social and political order, but also to point out the importance of science. In Bacon's eyes, civilization is nothing but the sovereignty of science over human life. Like most Renaissance thinkers, Bacon is not aware that science can also develop in the wrong direction and that technical progress and civilization do not always go hand in hand (Urgan 1984:87). This is why he devotes a large part of his book to praising a scientific research institution, which he calls "the noblest institution on earth" and calls the Solomon's House and presents it as a model for every country in the world. At the beginning of the New Atlantis, he writes that he is "telling this story in order to give an example of a scientific institution".

In the New Atlantis, Solomon's House is the most essential spot in the city. For this reason, the entire city is built around Solomon's Palace, famous for its majestic dome. Solomon's House is "devoted to the study of all God's creations" (Bacon 1999:167). This iconography derives from Solomon's Temple. In this respect, Bacon's house/temple is typical, and although it is not referred to as a museum in his text, it evokes the cabinets of curiosities as much as the knowledge systems of his time (universal languages) (McCellan 2008:15).

In Bacon's *The New Atlantis*, a science-oriented utopia, the importance of scientific research is constantly emphasized, where scientific studies guide society. Bacon envisioned an ideal society where science is trusted, scientists are extremely important and scientific results are effectively utilized for social benefit (J.C. Davis 1983:136). At Solomon's House, where scientific studies are carried out, the staff constantly gather information by organizing trips to countries outside the island. The information gathered on other countries, natural phenomena, animals, celestial bodies and everything that comes to mind is gathered and classified in Solomon's House and then stored in the archive.

Due to the importance given to science in the New Atlantis Island, there is a superiority of scientists in society; this class is privileged and prioritized in society. In this context, the principle of equality found in More's and Campanella's utopias is absent in *The New Atlantis*. It differs from More's and Campannella's utopias with these features.

For Bacon, *scientia potentia est* (knowledge is power). According to him, science makes man free against nature and even makes him the master of nature (Ağaoğulları 1986:30). For this reason, Bacon's utopia envisions a city inhabited by people who, through science, make themselves masters of nature and thus can open up a whole new living space for themselves.

UTOPIAS OF ENLIGHTENMENT

All modern utopian visions of the perfect city have common features and principles of urban planning and architecture: First of all, the urban space is pre-planned in a precise, detailed and comprehensive manner, and the city is built from scratch on an empty or vacated site, according to a blueprint that is completed before the foundation work begins. Then, the regularity, uniformity, homogeneity and reproducibility of the spatial components surrounding the administrative buildings, which are placed in the center of the city or on a hilltop from which the entire urban space can be seen, are ensured. All architectural and demographic solutions are aimed at meeting the needs of the city as a whole. Attention is also paid to the spatial separation of parts of the city that differ in terms of the quality of their inhabitants or are dedicated to different functions. The houses that citizens will live in are designed to be identical, that is, completely the same, no matter in which part of the city (Bauman 2004:47-8). The utopian mentality, which plans the city architecturally, also depends on its permission as to who will live in the city. Here, permission is dependent on a rational and pragmatic understanding such as embracing those who contribute to the development and productivity of the city and excluding those who do not.

In the utopias of the Enlightenment period, a standard called "normal" is established for city dwellers, and those outside this standard are deemed inadequate to live in the city. These people who fall outside the standards of normality are those who cannot contribute to social production, such as the sick, the crippled, the insane and criminals.

The perfect city designs of the Enlightenment utopians on paper are not close to the cities in which the inhabitants live and want to live. As Marx put it, the Enlightenment utopians focused on how to change the world, not how to describe or explain it. They are not interested in what is, in the present, but in what should be, in the ideal. They resist the constraints of the existing urban fabric and structure that prevent the realization of ideal designs and aspire to create a reality made from scratch, a reality that bears no traces of historical evolution.

Any ideal city project that was to be created from nothing meant the destruction of an existing city. Enlightenment utopians sought to exchange chaotic cities for ideal cities endowed with a cosmos. The city of the future was the spatial embodiment, symbol and monument of the freedom won in the relentless life-and-death battle of reason against the elusive irrational contingency of history (Bauman 2003:50). Just as the freedom promised by the revolution would purify historical time, the space in the dreams of urban utopians would be a place never polluted by history.

Étienne-Gabriel Morelly, one of the first utopian writers of the Enlightenment, expressed the modern conception of a perfect and ideal urban space in his 1755 work *Code de la nature, ou Le véritable esprit de ses lois de tout temps négligé ou méconnu* (Code of nature, or the true spirit of its laws, neglected or misunderstood at all times). In this homogeneous and orderly urban plan, Morelly arranges public buildings around a large square made up of regular parts, all of which look uniform and pleasing. Again, the necessary halls that allow the public to gather and come together are located in the center.

Around the city center will be lined avenues, each of the same size, similar in appearance and equally divided. The houses of all citizens living in the city will be identical.

Unlike ancient and Renaissance utopias, in Morelly's ideal city, urban growth is not viewed negatively. All areas in the city will be planned in such a way that they can be expanded if necessary, without disrupting the existing built order (Bauman 2000:48). In other words, Morelly designed a utopia that allows cities to expand.

The ideal country of Denis Vairasse, one of the Enlightenment utopians, is *Sévariade*, the perfect capital of Sévarambes, and it is designed as a city where order and order are strictly enforced. This is a design in which the prescriptivism brought by the Enlightenment is intended to be implemented uniformly. The architecture of the city is tried to conform to a rational, clear and simple plan that would make it the most organized city in the world. The city is divided into 260 identical units. In each of these units there is a square, and in each of these squares there is a building with a 15-meter-long façade, a large courtyard inside, four gates and rooms where 1,000 people can "live comfortably".

The streets in Sévarambes are all straight. Each street leads to large squares, also uniform and of different sizes, with public buildings and fountains in the center. All the houses are uniform; only the houses where important people live have extra ornamentation. There are no architectural features that could create chaos in the city. Everywhere there is a perfect and striking architecture of order.

Socially, in a manner entirely in keeping with the general structure of the Enlightenment, no one sick, mentally handicapped or criminal is allowed to live in the city. All of these are banished outside the city. There is no place for anything that has no function. No component of the city is unique and it is compatible with the uniformity of the total. For this reason, each component of the city can be moved around within the city and nothing is noticed in such a change. At the same time, all the cities in this ideal country are identical. Therefore, whoever has visited one city in the country of Sévarambes has learned about all the other cities.

UTOPIAS OF THE NINETEENTH CENTURY

The utopias of the nineteenth century generally manifest themselves as criticisms of the industrial city. The structure of the industrial city that threatened human life led people to seek welfare, happiness, peace and quality of life outside the city. Thinkers and entrepreneurs such as Robert Owen, Joseph Fourier and J.B. Godin devoted their lives to perfecting people's lives (Aktan 2012:100). The utopias of the industrial period formed the prototype of the housing and settlement forms of the future.

The biggest change in the city takes place with industry. New cities become the center of a new economic system based on industrial production and wealth creation based on capital, unlike the trade-based structure of the previous ones. The nineteenth century saw a new form of urbanization, namely the development of the industrial city.

The rise of industry requires the utilization of new resources and new forms of energy for the use of machinery in an increasing number of factories. This leads to the importance of new geographical areas. Factories need labor, and housing for workers develops near new sources of employment. Industrial cities grow rapidly, giving rise to very different residential areas for new workers and bosses. Unlike in the past, power and wealth shift from port and trade cities to the newly established industrial cities.

In industrial cities, urban housing areas, mostly large apartment buildings, emerge near factories and new workplaces. The new physical structure is characterized by narrow streets and crowded housing. In these conditions, urban dwellers are exposed to diseases caused by the new environmental conditions. Air pollution arises as industry switches to carbon dioxide-emitting fuels as a source of energy and heating for housing. Infectious diseases become widespread due to the lack of clean water networks and sewage systems (McDermott 1973:121). Nutrition is often inadequate due to poverty and ignorance.

One of the most common health problems in industrial cities was rickets, a bone disease. This was the first disease recognized to be caused by pollution. It was understood to be caused by the lack of sunlight exposure of children living in poor urban neighborhoods due to narrow streets and poorly planned apartment buildings. This problem was exacerbated by smog, a side effect of industrial production. Rickets became widespread especially in the poor neighborhoods of big cities (Thorns, 2002: 16). The disease drastically reduces the quality of life. For these reasons, the utopians of the nineteenth century criticized the negative effects of the industrial revolution, such as overpopulation, unhealthy conditions and inequality in cities, and sought a new social and urban design. In this period, the gap between the city and nature widened and cities became both remote from nature and uninhabitable. The factory, the center of the new production system, binds all aspects of urban life to itself. The new mode of production and social relations also change the physical space of cities. At the beginning of the nineteenth century, the center of the industrial city consists of factories, warehouses and the housing areas of the poor classes surrounding them. As one moves away from this center, the residential areas of other groups are located in circles with increasing income levels (Aktan 2012:72). Apart from these, there are farms, fields and small rural settlements that provide the agricultural needs of the city.

Given the existing problems, in the nineteenth century, workers' settlements such as Saltaire, Bournville, Port Sunlight in England and Pullman in the USA, which were the most industrialized countries, were built outside the urban areas that were considered to have harmful effects with the strategy of their paternalistic founders (D. Spencer 2016:160). The utopias of these years reflected the longing for places in the countryside where one could breathe and spend time with nature, as opposed to the centralized locations of existing cities. In addition, the innovations provided by technological developments were also desired to be found in cities. As such, the utopias of this period had two different faces: on the one hand, there was a passion for technical infrastructures such as urban lighting, sewage, subways, and on the other hand, there was a longing for the Middle Ages and its monuments.

UTOPIAN SOCIALISTS

One of the most important components of utopian literature beginning with Thomas More is the great emphasis on the principle of equality in ideal societies. The elimination of classes, where everybody lives under the same economic conditions and private property is abolished, would come to be clearly defined as socialism in the nineteenth century.

Such a sharp definition of socialism was made possible by the crowding of the working class that emerged with the emergence of the industrial revolution, the fact that they had a higher literacy capacity compared to the farmer population, and that they lived in cities rather than in the countryside, unlike farmers, and that they had the chance to reach a certain level of consciousness. Thinkers such as Marx and Engels thought that it was precisely through this working class that a socialist and universal revolution could be made.

The utopias that emerged in these years aimed to create a new city for the working class and to ensure that this city was structured according to socialist principles. For this reason, the utopias of the nineteenth century in particular have a socialist tendency and the utopians of this period have been called "utopian socialists".

Utopian socialists, on the one hand, envisioned a new social structure and, on the other hand, integrated their discourse with elements of design. Thinkers such as Saint-Simon, Fourier and Owen, the leading utopians among them, followed the traditions of More's *Utopia* and Plato's *Republic* to provide detailed descriptions of communities of the industrial revolution untainted by class struggles. Unlike More or Plato, however, utopian socialists strived for the immediate realization of their ideal settlements.

Utopian socialist planning was dominated by two trajectories: First, to eliminate the distinction between city and countryside; second, to overcome the physical isolation of individuals and families by placing the community into a single large "family" structure. Many of their designs depict not ideal cities, but ideal communes, small rural units of less than 2,000 inhabitants.

Saint-Simon's ideas and utopian approaches form the basis for utopian socialists. In Saint-Simon's utopia, the main goal of society and urban planning is to maximize production. Since workers are the cogs that will make production, Saint-Simon thinks that the planning of cities should provide an environment where workers can be utilized in the best way. He aims to increase hygiene in the city to reduce illnesses. Therefore, in the case of Paris, he proposes to clean the city by opening a wide canal extending from the Bastille to the Louvre and bringing drinking water to Paris. His plan is to create a "labor army" of workers to ensure complete production efficiency. This army, which would consist of squads, would be led by high-ranking engineers and polytechnicians (Ragon 2010:44). Saint-Simon embarks on urban design with a pure rationality and this attitude directly influenced Auguste Comte, who would leave his mark on nineteenth-century positivism. Saint-Simon's approach would be spread by Comte.

In Saint-Simon's utopia, as industry replaced the agricultural primacy, the management of material objects should be left in the hands of industrialists, while intellectual and moral management should be taken away from clergymen and given to scientists. He believes that the ideal society should be ruled by three assemblies to be elected separately by artists, industrialists and scientists with scientific methods and dictatorial rule, because the nation is actually a "great industry" and a "science of policy-making". In this sense, he favors a hierarchical social organization.

In the industrial society designed by Saint-Simon in a centralized structure, it is aimed to improve the working life of laborers. Improving the living conditions of the poor class should be the main goal of society. Saint-Simon tries to organize the industrial society by uniting religion, science and industry by handing over the management of society and the church, which he shaped with a new understanding of Christianity, to industrialists. Saint-Simon's work, which attempts to harmonize the interests of the proletariat and the bourgeoisie by reflecting the social trends of the period, can be considered a complex combination of technocracy, free market liberalism and new socialism (Geoghegan 1987:9-13). Saint-Simon's alternative to industrial society, based on science, technology and cooperation, would form the starting point of Owen and Fourier's social designs.

Robert Owen has the most interesting life story among the utopian socialists, the most enterprising, the most productive and the most selfless. He was a utopian who started his life in 1771 in Montgomeryshire, Wales, as the child of a low-income family and went on to become a great industrialist (Gordon 1994:279). Before his utopia, he constructed himself and produced his utopias based on his self-construction. He came to London when he was only 10 years old, worked as an apprentice in various workshops and then as a salesman in some stores, and it was at this age that he became interested in utopian ideas. Francis Bacon's *The New Atlantis*, Rousseau's powerful text on how to build a new society, *The Social Contract*, and the works of the utopian socialist Morelly became his bedside books (Usta 2016:17). Utopianism is like an ideal for which Owen has been preparing himself since the early years of his life.

At the age of eighteen, Owen joined a merchant in Lincolnshire and then a business in Manchester as a laborer, and soon formed a partnership with an artisan to manufacture cotton yarn. The number of workers employed by this partnership soon reaches 440. By the time he is nineteen, he becomes the manager of one of the first spinning mills in Manchester; he is now responsible for 4,500 workers. Owen's rapid rise continued here. Based on the premise that improving working conditions would increase the productivity of workers (Aybay 1970:59), Owen succeeded in generating a leap in production quality in a short time with his unique methods and increases the factory's profit by 50%. By the time he was twenty-three, he became a partner with two wealthy industrialists from London and Manchester and started his own business as a business owner. Owen's rapid rise was supported by his social life: he married the daughter of one of the industrialists (Ragon 2010:60). When his father-in-law transferred his companies in New Lanark to Owen, he became an important industrialist. Owen now had control over a sample universe where he can implement his utopia.

The New Lanark factories –where Owen realized his first utopian experiment– are one of the largest industrial institutions in England, 40 kilometers away from Glasgow, Scotland, employing around 2,000 workers (Aybay 1970:62). Owen was the first person to propose a utopian industrial city (Erdem 2005:79). In 1800, Owen started to work on his utopian experiment in New Lanark, and within a few years he transformed the New Lanark factories, and the workers' houses surrounding the factories, and the schools within the framework of his own design and turned the region into an exemplary and alternative living space that attracted thousands of tourists both nationally and globally. Owen transformed the New Lanark universe, whose inhabitants consisted of workers and their families, through education (Engels 1975:62). Within the framework of an ideal city design, Owen's assumptions in this process were as follows:

1. Man's character is not formed by himself, but by his environment.
2. By applying certain methods and means, every community, and even the whole world, can be given any kind of character, from the worst to the best, from the most ignorant to the most enlightened.

Owen published these assumptions on the cover of his first book, *A New View of Society*, published in 1813 and expressed his thoughts in detail (Aybay 1970:62-63). Here lies precisely the assumption that forms the basis for all utopians to write utopias: An unlimited belief in the realizability of social engineering.

The reforms Owen attempted in New Lanark had three main goals:

1. To improve the living conditions of workers and their families,
2. Increase production and productivity,
3. To transform a "miserable society" into a truly happy industrial society.

These goals aim at a socio-economic transformation and assume that the end result will be a happy utopian society.

To achieve these goals, Owen established his own government in New Lanark which controlled everything. Inescapably, the authoritarian nature of utopias found its way into Owen's mind. Starting out with the motto "for the people, in spite of the people", Owen places himself, whom he considers to

be the one who knows, above society, and since he accepts that the people are too ill-equipped to know where their own good lies. He takes all governing powers upon himself as a logical deduction of these assumptions. In his own words, by doing so, Owen wanted to establish a "government" that would apply the principles he had found to govern the people in general, in order to change the environment that had detrimental effects on the character of the people (Aybay 1970:64).

Owen also attached great importance to the architecture of the settlement he designed, and he designed the space to encourage communal living and work. The New Lanark model, which was realized on an isolated and empty rural land, consists of self-sufficient, small and ideal village associations where production, housing and education units are gathered together. In this settlement, buildings are arranged in a rectangle in the center of the farmed area. Three large social buildings house the kitchen, dining hall, kindergarten, reading and liturgy hall, school, meeting halls and library. The workers' houses, each with four rooms, are placed on three sides of the square, with the children's dormitory on the fourth side. Behind the houses are gardens, behind the gardens, in the area separated by trees, are workshops, stables, slaughterhouses and laundries, and even further away are the facilities for the production of beer and flour (Erdem 2005:79-80). New Lanark contains a perfect wholeness with its systematically placed stone buildings, the landscaping between them and the landscape.

The housing units of the ideal city designed by Owen were designed as self-sufficient experimental units. This experimentation stems from the fact that New Lanark dwellings are conceived as country houses with urban functions. Thus, in terms of space and architecture, the New Lanark model aimed to build a hybrid structure that strives to achieve urban-rural continuity in many respects (Güleryüz 2013:60). In addition, the workers' housing units were enlarged compared to their counterparts and the streets were planned in a highly organized manner. The city streets were swept every day, garbage was moved far away from the settlements, and inspectors were appointed to supervise the cleanliness of all houses. In other words, industrial society spatially moved to the countryside, and the chaos, disorder and low hygiene in the city were overcome. By bringing water from the River Clyde, the opportunities for city dwellers to wash and clean were expanded. Doctors were brought to the village and health services were provided free of charge.

Owen both increased the wages of workers and reduced their daily working hours to 10 hours; he also gave them time for rest and entertainment (Ragon 2010:60-61). He put an end to the employment of children under the age of ten (Gordon 1994:284). Reduced working hours also allow workers and workers' families to socialize with each other, creating a commune mentality and tightening community ties.

In the New Lanark model, to further increase socialization and group consciousness, Owen made sure that meals are cooked and eaten in communal dining halls. The burden of raising the children in the community was taken from the shoulders of their parents, and the large group was considered as a single family and the children were raised as the children of this single family. In this way, in his utopia, he wanted to ensure that group members see each other as family as well as group consciousness, and that resources are used more economically.

Owen opened a school called the "Institute for the Formation of Character" for the children of workers in New Lanark and develops and provides them with educational opportunities that are quite advanced for the period. The school offered reading, writing, zoology, botany, history, geography, arithmetic – plus, sewing classes for girls (Aybay 1970:74). In line with his own views, as he argued that people can be shaped by education and environmental conditions, he strived to raise people in accordance with the New Lanark model. Like all utopians, Owen chose to create people suited to the ideal city instead of creating a city for people. By accepting the education and care of younger children as the duty of the community, Owen became the inventor of the kindergarten concept and opened the first kindergarten in the world in New Lanark (Engels 1975:62). Owen believed that well-raised children will produce excellent workers for New Lanark in the years to come, thanks to these facilities.

In New Lanark, Owen tried to achieve order not through discipline and punishments, but through persuasion of the workers, and he was highly successful in this. Thus, it was aimed for the workers to continue to produce industrial goods and to enjoy the peaceful blessings of rural life. According to Owen, happy workers will work more efficiently and thus the profitability of the factory will increase. According to Owen, thanks to this model, people will live a highly organized life full of goodness, brotherhood and harmony, away from the inconveniences of the city and yet without giving up the benefits it provides (Erdem 2005:80).

Owen's successes in New Lanark as a good businessman, humanist reformer and educator led to his experience gaining worldwide fame and attracting many visitors from all over the world. Between 1815-25, some 20,000 visitors, including the Archduke Nicholas II, later Tsar of Russia, toured New Lanark and were amazed by what they saw. Among the visitors were foreign princes, ambassadors, churchmen, nobility, people from all countries and professions. All this brought Owen international fame and the opportunity to take his utopian model elsewhere. Archduke Nicholas, who admired New Lanark, offered Owen to come to Russia with his two million unemployed citizens and establish factory communities similar to New Lanark (Aybay 1970:75). However, Owen would not accept this.

Despite the fact that New Lanark was wondered and praised all over the world, these ideas, which no industrialist before Owen had ever put into practice or even thought of, were characterized as madness in British industrial circles. However, all the industrialists who came to see this utopia come to life were astonished when they encountered the data, for as the welfare level of the workers in New Lanark increased, so did the profitability of the factories. The main reason for this is that the workers here were better qualified than their peers thanks to the education they received, they were more peaceful in a more comfortable home and urban environment, and they did their jobs better because they lived happier lives as they had time for rest and socializing. Owen seemed to have succeeded in building the "workers' army" that Saint-Simon envisioned. He opposed the materialistic and malicious mechanism of his colleagues and praised the "automatism of goodness" (Ragon 2010:61). He did not separate the workers' homes from the workshops, he saw the whole as a giant clockwork machine, and he likened New Lanark to a chronometer that would work flawlessly, ticking away forever, as was common to all utopians.

Famous not only for his factory in New Lanark but also for his articles (in the newspapers he distributed for free) and lectures (he was also a pioneer in the use of modern propaganda methods), in 1815 Owen called a meeting of the main Scottish manufacturers in Glasgow and asked them to emulate his success and improve the living conditions of the workers: "If you understand the real value of your living machines, you will think more of them, and you will find that you can make much more profit." Nevertheless, the manufacturers were unwilling to make changes for the people Owen called "white slaves". After this failed attempt, Owen attempted to force the government to pass a labor law. He targeted workers not only in England but all over the world, sending leaflets to all officials. After a five-year struggle, he succeeded in getting the first law limiting the working hours of women and children in factories passed in 1819 (Engels 1975:64). He was elected president of the first great congress where all the trade unions in England were united into one big, single trade union.

However, despite all his successes and the prosperity he achieved in New Lanark, Owen was criticized by his partners for the high wage policy implemented in the factories and the constant expenditure on schooling (Ragon 2010:61-62). The view that the utopian Owen was not a Catholic, but rather an atheist, and that this unbelief lay at the heart of all he did, became widespread and his partners were disturbed by this situation (Bernard 1988:22). The process gradually came to a point where Owen's power was shaken. So much so that by the early 1820s, Owen began to lose control over New Lanark. His religious partners took action to put an end to practices such as dance lessons, especially in schools. In early 1824, they reached an agreement to stop the implementation of Owen's principles. Owen's utopia did not turn into a dystopia through its natural process (perhaps because it was not tried long enough), but it was brought to an end by an external intervention by Owen's partners. However, Owen did not give up when his partners stop his implementation and decided to put his utopia into practice outside New Lanark. His new goal was to try to establish his ideal settlement and community in the United States.

Today, New Lanark is a museum visited by 400,000 people a year (Koç, 2012). It was inscribed on the UNESCO World Heritage List in 2001 for its importance and contribution to technology, architecture and human values.

After 24 years of experience in New Lanark, Owen traveled to the USA in 1824, where he was very well received. In the US, he both gave lectures about his utopia and held one-on-one meetings at the level of presidents and ministers and was highly respected. In a speech he made in Washington during these contacts, he expressed for the first time that he aimed to establish a "rational religion". This religion would overcome selfishness, build a brand-new social order and ensure a lasting peace among the people of the world (Aybay 1970:176-77). Owen set out to establish his second utopia.

In 1825, Owen bought the village of Harmony in the US state of Indiana, which belonged to a Protestant sect, to use as the place where he would realize his utopia. Settling there, he devoted himself to realizing the economic and social life he had planned. He invited workers and their families from many different nationalities to "New Harmony" for his initiative. He expects such a wide and diverse spectrum to create harmony, as the name of his new utopia suggests.

  ARCHITECTURAL UTOPIAS IN SEARCH OF THE IDEAL CITY

Owen drafted a constitution for New Harmony. Accordingly, the members of the community would not be involved in the administration for the first three years, but at the end of this period, in addition to the four members to be determined by Owen, the members to be elected among the candidates over the age of 21 living in New Harmony would form a general assembly and take over the administration of the community. Buying and selling was prohibited in New Harmony, which would be based on common property. All citizens would live in identical houses, wear uniform clothing, share the same lifestyle and have the same educational opportunities. The main principles of the community are respect for the law, a balance between production and consumption, equal rights for all citizens, common property, social relations based on sincerity, kindness and benevolence, and the right to health.

Like other utopian designs, New Harmony was laid out on paper, with all the details thought out and strict rules to create a perfect whole. The project was to build a society that would be self-sufficient, working both in the countryside and in factories. A place away from the negative effects of the city, but with its advantages. The settlement model of the project is a village settlement based on communal life, equipped with all the necessary services for the community (Batur 1993:17). The settlement was built on a land of 100-150 hectares (Güleryüz 2013:59).

New Harmony was envisioned to function according to the principles of machine, clock, discipline, order and punctuality, and great importance was attached to its plan and architecture. New Harmony was isolated from its surroundings by means of high platforms. It was designed in squares, each of which was planned to accommodate 1,200 people. The square buildings were placed in the center of the agricultural area. It removed "unnecessary inconveniences, unhealthy and uncomfortable streets, avenues, tree-lined paths and courtyards". Public buildings were arranged in parallelograms within the square. The center building housed the collective kitchen and dining halls. To the right was the cultural building, with a classroom for young children on the ground floor and a reading room and place of worship upstairs. The building on the left had a classroom for older children, meeting rooms and a library. On three sides of the square was the four-room house of married workers. On the fourth side were the dormitories for children over the age of three. There were gardens at the back of the houses. Workshops were located further away. Farther away were farms, bakeries and breweries. Industrial buildings were added to the area (Ragon 2010:63). In contrast to Fourier's communal building, Owen recommended detached houses. In this plan, everything was placed in its place as if Owen alone was a god.

It was hoped that life would be shaped by this physical environment, which was determined in all its details, and the social environment that was thought to be shaped by it (Alver 2009:150). In this project where everything

will be in harmony, it was assumed that when the human being is isolated from the negative environmental factors, a healthy society can be created and the example that this modeling will produce will gradually spread all over the world and the ideal society of the future will be created. Unfortunately, these expectations were not realized.

Following Owen's return to England, after he built a transitional social order in New Harmony for a transitional period of three years, problems arose. Owen, who came to New Harmony for the second time, decided in 1826 to end the provisional order and move to a community based on full equality. In 1827, New Harmony units were arranged on the basis of a kind of guild system consisting of professional groups, but the autocratic attitude of Owen, who was put in charge, could not prevent the community from splitting in the face of growing difficulties. The widespread social, religious and racial differences among the members of the community made life in New Harmony difficult and the members began to spend time arguing instead of working (Ertan 2004:7-9). This time, unlike his experience in New Lanark, Owen's utopia collapsed in on itself and turned into a dystopia.

　　ARCHITECTURAL UTOPIAS IN SEARCH OF THE IDEAL CITY

Despite Owen's best efforts, the harmony and order he envisioned did not materialize in New Harmony, and his utopian attempt ended in failure (Benevolo 1981:49). In New Harmony, there were ample opportunities for community members to work, but there were no effective means of social control that would ensure harmony among the diverse personalities that the community attracted. It was a community of misfits, including irrational adventurers as well as those who wish to pursue a philosophical utopia. When religious, social, ethnic and racial differences joined the other existing differences, an environment of conflict ensued in New Harmony (Güleryüz 2013:61). Moreover, the inhabitants of New Harmony were free to work or not, and when some chose not to work due to this prerogative, a certain group of people had to undertake all the work of the community and these people reacted to the situation (Ragon 2010:62). However, Owen believed that the necessary behavioral reactions would arise spontaneously (Erdem 2005:80). The initiative, which failed, ended in 1828. However, New Harmony inspired the establishment of new utopian communities. Independent of Owen, novel "New Harmony" initiatives, sixteen of them in the USA and seven in Great Britain, emerged (Ertan 2004:8). However, all these utopian attempts would end in dystopias and prove unsustainable.

The main social distortions of Owen's time were the agglomeration of the population in the neglected parts of large cities, the oppression of women and children under heavy workloads, and the frustration of the working class, which was suddenly and collectively dispersed from rural to urban, from agriculture to modern industry. Owen tried to put forward a utopia that could overcome all these social distortions.

His philosophy, contrary to the general undrstanding of his time, presented three fundamental challenges: He rejected the notions that "human rights do not exist" (The Co-operative College 2009:4), that "human character cannot change" and that "people are inherently evil" and accepted that "people have inherent rights, and if the environment is improved, so will man". According to him, a person's character is not constructed by the person, but by the person's environment. Therefore, if an environment supported by architecture is established within the framework of the principles of justice and benevolence, the burden of immorality on the shoulders of society will be removed (Owen 1858:60; Owen 1991:ix). In order to shape the new way of thinking in society, Owen paid special attention to education, inventing kindergartens and establishing schools for later ages.

He saw society as a created product and institutions as a mechanical structure that could be changed at will. He perceived the social system as an invention, a new machine to be used to increase happiness. His advice is a mechanistic society to replace the old enculturated society. He argued that the new settlement unit to be created through architecture would raise the standard of living of people, that everyone would live in peace and harmony, and that there would be no need for institutions such as law enforcement, judicial bodies and prisons. Owen suggested that governments and social organizations follow his example.

François Marie Charles Fourier's comprehensive doctrine is based on a *théorie de l'unité universelle* (a theory of universal unity), a theory based on the founding of society on partnership and mutual aid. The basic unit of Fourier's new society is what Fourier called the "partnership of laborers". In contrast to Cabet's centralist approach, Fourier's society consists of communes (Abensour 2009:94). This is a different understanding from radical socialism. Fourier, who divided the historical development of society into four stages: savagery, barbarism, patriarchy and civilization. Fourier was of the opinion that "barbarism", which he saw as identical with the social order that came with the 16th century, "transformed the stage of civilization into a complex, ambiguous, hypocritical form with every shortcoming it experienced".

Stating that civilization proceeds in a vicious circle of contradictions that it constantly recreates without making any contribution to its solution; and therefore, seeks the opposite of what it wants to achieve or what it seems to want to achieve, Fourier made important determinations in terms of the history of society (Engels 1975:75). In this respect, Fourier was one of the first researchers of the crisis of civilization, which is the subject of utopias and counter-utopias, by foreseeing the effects and possible consequences of the civilization process, which constitutes the starting point of utopian thought. Fourier published his most important works between 1820 and 1836, but the influence of his teaching spread throughout the nineteenth century. Fourierism became a widespread movement with its own publications, bookstore and active militants. Fourier's utopia describes a stage of human history that has not yet been passed. According to Fourier, human history had passed through five stages: paradise, savagery, patriarchy, barbarism and civilization. The higher stage, which Fourier's breakthrough will now usher in, is, in Fourier's words, Guarantism, which will lead to a more robust solidarity among all members of society. In the era of guarantism, "family associations" or communes will be formed. These will become widespread and put guarantism on a solid foundation. After the period of guarantism, humanity will experience two imaginary periods: simple partnership, the new "serizophy", and unified partnership, the "harmony" (Ragon 2010:50). He expresses this argument in a pamphlet published around 1820 as a chapter of his *Théorie de l'unité universelle* and published it as a pamphlet in 1849 under the magazine *La Phalange* with the title *Des Modifications à Introduire dans L'archtitecture des Villes*.

Fourier is the first modern urban planner to consider the social system together with a specific type of housing. He approaches the city in a com-

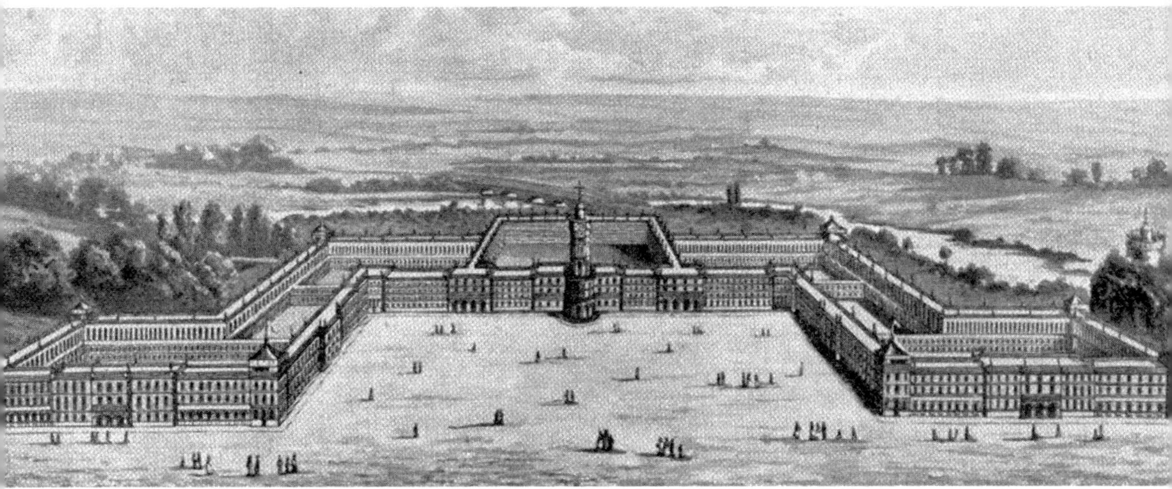

pletely different and avant-garde way compared to the settlements of the past. By blending industrial activities with agrarian works, he anticipated Howard's garden-cities by 70 years and incorporated the countryside into his conception of the city. Like the cities proposed by Howard years later, the cities of the Guarantism era consisted of three interconnected sub-units: The center, where commerce and administration are located, and the surrounding industrial and agricultural units. Fourier proposed that the city should consist of three main belts separated from each other by large green areas: the central city in the first of these belts; suburbs and large factories in the second; and wide avenues and suburbs in the third. Fourier's most important contribution to the design of society was the *phalanstère* (phalanstery) units, which consisted of giant-sized buildings for 1,500-1,600 people called "social palaces".

According to Fourier, throughout the history of mankind, the difficult, even impossible, has always been attempted, and in order to achieve human-environment harmony, it has always been tried to change people, and thus they have failed. However, the solution is not to change people, but to take the differences in people as data and to organize the environment and society accordingly. For this to happen, Fourier thought of creating a settlement he called phalanstery. In Fourier's utopia, people would no longer live in cities but in large buildings called "phalansteries". The population of such a unit is 1,620 people. The members of the unit carry out their work in common, sharing what they produce equally according to their needs. The dwellings in a phalanstery are large, compact, mixed-use blocks where all activities are clustered together. These large blocks, called phalanges, have street galleries that are naturally ventilated all year round, heated in winter and cooled in summer, despite the harshness of nature.

In the phalanstery unit, 7/8 of the population are agricultural and industrial workers, the rest are artists, scientists and capitalist partnerships. In the phalansteries, which are divided into seven or more classes organized in groups of at least 24 people, each individual who is open to change will work in a field that is made attractive according to his capacity. The surplus production of the phalansteries, after the minimum subsistence level is met, will be allocated 5/12 to labor, 4/12 to capital, and 3/12 to talent. The phalanstery units, which Fourier hoped would be established on a voluntary basis, are small-scale and self-sufficient agricultural communities engaged in both agriculture and industry. In phalansteries, the means of production would be the common property of the community, with only small private ownership permitted. Composed of individuals of very different ages, tastes and personalities, the community will be organized on the principle of cooperation rather than competition. The fertility of the soil will be increased, adverse weather conditions will be controlled, nature will be domesticated, and fast and efficient transportation will be implemented (Şenel 1994:100-01). In addition, the activities of individuals will be brought under a certain order and control through daily work schedules.

Believing that it was uneconomical to build houses for everyone individually, Fourier designed community units consisting of buildings for 1,600 people and industrial facilities on approximately 5,000 hectares. In addition, by including common spaces such as theaters, promenades and parks, dining halls, Fourier wanted to make communal life dominant in his phalansteries. The access between the communal units is provided through covered gallery streets and tunnels that are heated in winter and ventilated in summer to protect pedestrians from the adverse effects of weather conditions (Tümer 1997:29). Fourier made the human scale dominant in the spatial and architectural design of phalanstery units.

Fourier pursues a utopian society. He takes his place in the search for utopian cities with the phalanstery he established according to the principles of difference and diversity. He draws both the physical/spatial and social aspects of his utopian city or society in detail. Streets, avenues, houses, workshops, parts of houses are measured and cut out one by one (Alver 2009:150). This is a scene that has now become commonplace: the architect-engineer is in charge and dreams of living spaces for society in spite of human beings.

In Phalanges, the floors are specially organized for different age groups. The elderly live on the ground floor, children on the intermediate floors and adults on the upper floors. All buildings are designed with three floors and an attic, excluding the ground floor. People living in Phalanges use the kitchen and all the halls together, except for the rooms where they sleep (Coates & Stetter 2000:78). In line with the historical utopian tradition, Fourier wages war on individual ownership by advocating "common property". He also structured the utopia he designed in the form of a commune life. Fourier was the first to propose a collective residential building for the workers' community. Fourier proposes the collective building because it is both economical and practical. This building, which he called the *phalanstère*, is a house divided in such a way as to accommodate 30 different families using common material means. Phalanstery has meeting rooms on the ground floor, protected from all bad weather conditions, allowing for communication indoors. The families jointly pay the wages of the kitchen staff and a four or five-course meal list is prepared at different prices. This saves money and time, as well as the pleasure of being part of a whole, and of course improves the quality of the food. Fourier thus proposes public dining halls instead of dining rooms, collective kitchens with butlers and kitchen staff. According to Fourier, private houses are not for the people. It is a pleasure reserved for the rich, like riding in flashy cars (Ragon 2010:53). The phalanstery is a form of community based on actions. Fourier wants to surround poor families living in terrible buildings lacking hygiene and aesthetics with hygiene and aesthetics. However, this collective life will also require certain rules to be followed. There is no place here for the torment of someone setting up a lime kiln or a gravel pit to stink up thousands of families living in a clean environment. Luxury components such as garden walls are also not allowed. Although such structures may look innocent, they actually restrict the field of vision of passers-by who do not want to see a wall. For this reason, gardens in guarantism are not enclosed by walls, but by high supports. In the phalansteries, which he also called "palaces of society", Fourier refused to use the square form, which he found monotonous. In his phalanstery drawings, he depicts a double-winged central building resembling the Palace of Versailles. The central building of the phalanstery is reserved for quiet work. Noisy workshops are located in one of the wings of the building. The other wing accommodates large groups of people visiting the "palace of society". Members live on the upper floors of the phalansteries, which are at least three stories high. By categorizing activities and grouping noisy jobs together, Fourier invented what would later be called "zoning".

Fourier proposed to connect the sectors in phalansteries with passageways. The passageways are covered, i.e., "air conditioned". This is not an entirely new idea, since medieval cities had many streets covered by arches. In Paris, the same system was applied to the Rue Rivoli, the construction of which began in 1811. However, Fourier incorporated this idea into his urban planning designs, giving it an importance it had not had until then. Fourier was talking about climatization of the city in a serious sense: The cold will not be felt inside the phalansteries. All the dwellings would have covered passages with a low level of heating. Thanks to these, everywhere can be reached without being exposed to bad weather. Workshops, dining halls, balls and meetings can be attended without the need to wear boots and furs, without the risk of catching a cold or pneumonia. Access from the phalansteries to the stables can be provided from the inside, thanks to durable underground passages or corridors raised by columns to the first floor. The phalansteries are intended to offer workers a level of comfort they have never experienced before.

In the phalanstery, which is a large building complex that aims to find solutions to the needs that people can meet both collectively and individually, people sleep in separate rooms, but otherwise meet many of their needs together and use many spaces jointly. This complex was conceived as a building in which 1,500-1,600 people of different ages, tastes and personalities would live harmoniously and happily. It is a kind of cooperative where everyone has a share. Wages are abolished and common property and a share in profits are envisaged. According to Fourier, in this complex, where production and consumption take place in the same location, a standard of living would be possible that would provide people with a table richer than the richest tables.

Fourier thinks that a society composed of various classes will develop in stages, the last of which will be the stage of harmony. The phalanstery was conceived as the product of the new era that came after savagery, patriarchy, barbarism and civilization, representing the different stages of history that humanity had gone through up to that point. Fourier advocated that man, having suppressed his savagery under the negative effects of civilization, should unleash his passions, which he classified as sensitive and expressive. These harmonized passions led to new social arrangements such as the phalanstery.

In his utopia, each building should leave a piece of empty land around it at least as large as the area it occupies, and this area should grow larger and larger outwards in rings. Each building should have four sides, the distance between them should not be less than six meters, and the buildings should have gutters to push rainwater into underground channels. The narrowest path should be 17 meters. Alongside this road, there should be sidewalks and pedestrian paths decorated with trees and flowers. In Fourier's city, public spaces make up 1/8 of the city. Fourier rejects the grid system, which Cabet insistently praised, because he believes that it does not allow freedom. However, almost all socialist theorists who followed Fourier and most of the later modern urban planners reintroduced Cabet's mechanical ideal of straight lines instead of Fourier's more "humane" plan.

Fourier's new scheme would provide an income sufficient for subsistence. Fourier advocated the fulfillment of seven conditions to make a life of united labor attractive to all. These are;

1. Every member must share in the profits.
2. Everyone, regardless of sex or age, should be compensated for their work according to the criteria of capital, labor and ability.

3. In every field of work, working hours should be changed eight times a day.

4. Tasks should be carried out by spontaneous groups of friends.

5. Workshops and cultivated land must be well maintained and tidy.

6. The division of labor should allow members of all sexes and ages to work.

7. Everyone should be free to exercise their right to work (Fourier 1971:167).

In order to realize this dream, Fourier, a utopian, spent his life every afternoon in the garden of the Palais-Royal looking for a financier for his project. Only after his death, Victor Considérant implemented his project near Dallas, but this effort did not last long either.

Fourier's utopia was realized by Godin, also one of his ardent followers, in 1859 with the Familistère de Guise. As Ebenezer Howard had tried to do at the beginning of the twentieth century, here, too, agriculture and industry were tried to be united; a structure where workers could meet all their needs without leaving the complex was envisioned. Even though it was considered to be a palace for workers during its construction period (where workers could work in manufacturing or agriculture next to their residences, benefit from the green area, rest and meet their cultural needs), this building was later harshly criticized by socialist circles, especially Engels, and was likened to a barracks due to its strict control mechanism and strict rules (Kurt 2007:166-67). Nevertheless, it has been the longest-lived project that has survived to the present day among its counterparts.

Unlike Cabet, Fourier gives importance to aesthetics as much as absolute functionality. He praises both a generalized aesthetics and the art of urban planning as its direct expression. According to Fourier, the beautiful is not more expensive than the ugly. Architects need to combine utility with beauty in order to advance on the path of naturalness. For Fourier, it is either both or neither.

For example, someone who wants his living room to be beautiful knows that the beauty of the room cannot be separated from the beauty of the roads. If one enters this beautiful parlor through a dirty and untidy courtyard, a ramshackle staircase and a hall with old, rude furniture, it cannot be an aesthetic place. "Why, then," Fourier asks, "do architects not decorate the collective spaces called cities?" His argument is that cities that cannot make their buildings comfortable and beautiful cannot produce social happiness.

Fourier is the most powerful utopian among nineteenth century French thinkers (McWilliam 2011:292). For many researchers, he is considered to have had the greatest influence on urban thinking (Cunningham 2007:1). He claims to base his plans for change on a scientific analysis of human passions. Arguing that physical and psychological impulses are essentially the product of good desires, but because these desires are suppressed and misdirected, they lead to crime and social conflict, Fourier envisions a future where such constraints are eliminated and universal harmony is realized. In Fourier's view, the mastery of the passions could transform work into pleasure, liberate sexual instincts, eradicate poverty, strengthen fraternal relations, and increase individual and collective happiness. The Phalanstery, the setting in which this marvelous change will take place, is depicted in the finest detail by Fourier's imagination.

Unlike Owen and the English utopians, Fourier sees the ideal order not only as a formal working group, but also as a pleasure-based community that appeals to bodily pleasures. In favor of difference and diversity, Fourier, instead of changing the human being to adapt to the social environment in his phalanges, makes the "law of passion" prevail, in which society is changed according to the passions of individuals. Fourier put forward the view that in a good order, individual passions would develop in cooperation to increase social happiness.

The phalansteries are a proposal for an ideal order in which various interests are encouraged and minority tastes and behaviors are allowed. Fourier's failure to foresee the consequences of industrialization based on mechanization led to the short life of the phalanstery society. Unlike Owen's design of society, Fourier favors diversity. To this end, the social wealth of individuals from different walks of life and cultures was reflected in the phalanstery units. As a medium of urban-rural wealth, Fourier designed ideal communities outside the city, combining rural life and technology. As a solution to the urban problems caused by the industrial revolution, Fourier and Owen, in an effort to establish harmony between humanistic values and nature, aimed to create urban-rural continuity. Rural communities —Owen and Fourier's attempt to restructure industrial society in a rural atmosphere— should be seen as efforts to put social and administrative structures into practice through planned spaces (Ertan 2004:10-12).

Between 1842-58, some 40 attempts were made to establish phalanges in North America. Most of these attempts did not last long, but they created experiences and accumulations to establish an ideal living environment (Güçer & Yılmaz 2004:138). Another example of phalange model implementation is the settlement proposal called "Familistère" by Jean-Baptiste André Godin. Godin successfully took Fourier's phalange project and reinterpreted it, adding different perspectives and suggestions to this settlement model. Among these, he suggested that the settlement should combine agricultural and industrial society, that communal life should be abandoned and each family should be given a house, thus developing family autonomy and a sense of belonging (Benevelo 1967:147).

Godin tried to put the Familistère settlement model into practice in 1859 in Northern France, next to a factory he owned. The settlement was built on an 18-hectare forested area with a capacity to accommodate a group of 1,000 workers. Familistère and the nearby factory building are separated by a dense green belt and a river. Two bridges connect the factory and the residential settlements. Familistère consists of three large interconnected residential buildings, a hospital, nursery, kindergarten, theater, gymnasium, laundry, bathroom and various service and storage buildings. The residential buildings have a rectangular plan. In the center of the buildings are courtyards covered with a glass-covered metal structure.

The ground floors of the central building are reserved for consumer stores and offices. The Familistère settlement is defined as a model that combines production, distribution, consumption, education, entertainment and housing with workspaces. In addition to production and consumption areas, the Familistère settlement also included common social areas consisting of entertainment and recreational spaces. In Familistère, which literally means "social palace", a housing model in the form of a social palace was proposed for workers (Güleryüz 2013:61-63). Familistère in Guise, France, one of the first examples of social housing, is now open to visitors as a museum.

Another name who undertook to spread Fourier's ideas was Victor Considérant (1808-1893). Considérant became the head of the magazine *La Phalange*. Although he made a great effort to spread Fourierism, he rationalized this view and removed its metaphysical, poetic and playful aspects (Ragon 2010:54). His approach was dry and formulaic.

Considérant's phalanstery has a form reminiscent of the government palace in Dijon. What Considérant stated to justify Fourier's view of the collective building, Le Corbusier repeated almost verbatim a hundred years later, first in defense of the "vertical garden-city" and then of the "housing unit". The important difference between Le Corbusier and Considérant is that, according to Le Corbusier, the apartments are owned by individuals and the building is composed of different cells. The communal areas were based on the principle that the masters made a profit through the shared use of the workers. In Considérant, on the other hand, there was a commune life.

Considérant mentions a water distribution system to supply water to all parts of the phalanstery and a central heating system to utilize the heat from the kitchens. It suggests issuing subscription cards for services such as laundry supply services. If necessary, people's personal belongings should consist of their clothes and shoes. He emphasizes the idea of a covered passageway street, ventilated and cooled in summer and heated in winter. He describes the passageway-street as the blood vessels carrying blood to the body of the phalanstery, perceiving it as the architectural symbol and reflection of high social participation and the vibrant harmony of the phalanstery. Rising amid cultures, the phalanstery can serve peasants as well as workers.

Considérant does not glorify the traditional rural settlement as an idyllic space against the inferno of the cities.

On the contrary, in his *Description du Phalanstère et Considérations Sociales sur L'architectonique* (1848), he opposes peasant cottages on the grounds that they are not aesthetic enough. He is one of the few critics of the traditional rural dwellings that Romantic writers desperately clung to against the ugliness of industrial cities. Considérant criticizes these dwellings for having a bedroom where everyone, mother, father and children sleep together; that the dwellings still consist of a cellar and attic; and that sometimes a barn and a henhouse are included in the dwelling (Ragon 2010:57-8). He emphasizes that the light-receiving parts of these houses are flattened and narrow and disapproves of the lack of glass in most of them.

On April 14, 1849, Considérant, who had been elected as a deputy during the Second Republic, submitted a bill requesting the state to carry out "an experiment to establish a communal community" near Saint-Germain-en-Laye. But none of the deputies, except himself, were willing to support this bill. At the same time, Louis Blanc proposed the construction of a phalanstery in the poor neighborhoods of Paris with workers' delegates. But the Second Republic did not survive long enough for this project to succeed. Exiled to the United States for his participation in the 1849 Uprising, Considérant founded the Union Colony near Dallas, but this attempt failed.

Another utopia of the period is the Icarian society presented by Étienne Cabet in his 1840 work *Voyage en Icarie* (Journey to Ikaria). In this utopia, there is a deep belief that industry will lead to wealth and peace. As in many utopias, the wealth and peace envisioned in Ikaria will be achieved through an authoritarian order and a minimum of freedom. This modern dictatorship envisioned by Saint-Simon became a myth with Cabet's book. Marx says that Cabet became the inventor of "utopian communism" by developing Saint-Simon's view of statist socialism.

Influenced by Saint-Simon, as well as Owen, Fourier and Considérant, Cabet interestingly combined Napoleonic militarism with the peaceful and united Christian ideal. Saint-Simon's idea of a "workers' army" reappears in a more powerful form.

Here, as in More's utopia, people live in identical houses and use identical furniture. Ikaria is a strictly geometric city, with straight intersecting streets and a river flowing straight down the center. Each of the 60 neighborhoods in the city bears the character of 60 nations (Erdem 2005:80).

Taking pure rationality to extremes creates a very strict regime in Ikaria, where nothing that does not have a function is allowed the right to live. In Cabet's ideal country, Ikaria, all citizens are soldiers and appoint their own superiors. There are no personal workshops in the homes, all workers perform their "workshop tasks" by going to large collective workshops, which they themselves designate.

There are no small shopkeepers in Ikaria. There are only large stores open to the public. The shops are literally open to everyone; there is no monetary exchange, as production is distributed freely. Extremely strict rules have eliminated adultery. Likewise, cafeterias and nightclubs, which were seen as a cause of disorder, were closed.

Cabet does not allow the women of Ikaria to walk the streets in an attractive manner, but constructs a design in which they save their ornaments for their husbands. Celibacy is permitted, but it is considered frowned upon. Because of the principle of utility, all wild animals were exterminated as they were considered to be of no use to humanity.

Cadavers are also burned on the grounds that they are not useful.

In Ikaria, just like in Plato's *Republic*, art is banished. Only art with useful and functional purposes is allowed. We encounter the first ideas of the industrial society's functional understanding of art in Cabet. In Ikaria, all the walls are covered with paper or cloth or decorated with polished and framed or painted paintings, but the paintings are not pictures, but very important educational images that provide essential information for everyday life. The paintings in the kitchen, for example, show the most practical ways of cooking, making it possible to access the necessary information instantly, without wasting time leafing through thick books. The charts hanging on the bathroom wall indicate the temperature settings, time, etc. required for bathing. Charts in children's rooms show them what they need to do during the day. There are very few drawings or paintings inside the frames, which anyone can see by visiting national museums and public buildings.

In Ikaria, the state owns all goods and services on behalf of society. Individuals participate in the production process not to work for themselves but for society as a whole. Ikaria is divided into 100 towns, each consisting of 10 communes, equal in size and population. Money, property and trade disappeared as everyone could freely buy the goods and services they needed. Despite the complete equality in social life in Ikaria, individual freedom was kept to a minimum and each citizen was trained to be each other's supervisor.

In Cabet's utopian cities, there is a strict plan that resembles a military order. All the cities of Ikaria are identical in form. There are the same number of houses on each of the streets that run through the middle of the Tair River, which divides the circular capital Ikaria in two, and which is the center of Ikaria. All the roads are straight, wide, extremely clean and lined with sidewalks, or rather entrances with rows of columns. Ikarians live in identical towns, in houses that are identical down to the furnishings. All the houses are eye-catching, all four-story-high, fenced, with very elegant doors and windows, polished and painted in a variety of colors. Built according to a uniform urban plan, the buildings are characterized by order, harmony and splendor. In Cabet's egalitarian order, uniform cities are home to uniform citizens who submit to unconditional conformity.

The standard uniform house of Ikaria is the house designed as a winner of a public competition. A committee of citizens unanimously accepted the winning plan and decided that henceforth all their houses would be built according to this plan. This makes it possible to mass-produce all the parts that make up a house, farm, town or city, since parts such as doors and windows will be identical. Sample plans were also prepared for farms, various workshops, hospitals, schools, etc.

The same path was followed for the furnishing of houses and furniture. Cabet furnished his houses with uniform furniture. Since the furnishings, like the houses, were uniform, families only made a few special changes, and when they moved, they left the house furnished and moved to another house with the same furnishings. Apartments have built-in wardrobes, wardrobes, sideboards, partitions, etc. and the furniture is built into the walls, fixed or glued. Furniture with internal compartments or drawers has doors on the front and some have shelves on top (Ragon 2010:48). This is a uniformization and standardization in line with modernism. It is the projection of the maxim "one way of thinking" in architecture.

Cabet pays special attention to hygiene. He organizes the city according to medical needs and the needs of traffic. There is neither a cemetery, nor an unsanitary factory, nor a hospital inside the city. All these institutions are outside the city, in breezy areas, near a stream or in the countryside. Not a single piece of garbage is thrown on the street from houses or workshops. In terms of hygiene, Cabet proposes "underground channels" for filth, what we now call sewers. He forbids "riding horses" from entering the city. Keeping to the right is mandatory for both cars and pedestrians. Some streets have underground passages in the form of tunnels. Streets are wide enough for four cars to drive side by side. For postal trains, it proposes "iron roads", a kind of rail system that cannot be used by cars.

Families use small cars pulled by large dogs for their daily outings. In contrast to the herds of animals that clutter and stain the streets of London, causing thousands of accidents, causing anxiety, often horror and death, and accustoming society to the idea of slaughter, here there are never herds of cows or sheep, because the slaughterhouses and butchers of this city are located outside the city.

Cabet also suggests a degree of acclimatization of the city's air. All sidewalks are covered with glass windows that protect the people from the rain without depriving them of sunlight, and retractable roofs that allow the temperature to be controlled. All crossings that allow people to cross the street are covered. The stations of the stagecoaches are covered, taking into account the risk of rain.

In 1847, Cabet made an attempt to establish his utopia of Ikaria in Texas. He buys a large plot of land in Texas and 500 people settle there in the first phase. Later, however, in this area of 3,000 inhabitants, only 250 people remained, living in accordance with Cabet's basic principles. Cholera and arguments scattered this group. Cabet traveled to the United States in 1849 to take matters into his own hands. But he could not save the first Ikarian community. In 1856, he retired with the rest of the community to Saint-Louis, where he died that same year.

However, after Cabet's death, attempts to found a new Ikaria continued. An attempt is made to found a new Ikaria in Cheltenham. But after six years of coexistence, Cabet's followers went their separate ways. Nevertheless, they are eager to create a communist society. Another group left Ikaria and settled on 1,200 hectares in Iowa. A mess hall was built in the center of a large square plaza in the center of the city. On three sides of this plaza, houses were built, separated from each other by gardens. On the fourth side of the square, communal areas such as laundries and bakeries were built. There was a grove very close to the city. The farm that provided the city's food is 1.5 kilometers away from the city. Thanks to this marvelous organization, the city of Ikaria, founded in Iowa, survived for almost a generation until 1880. The reason for the demise of this hugely successful experiment was mostly due to intergenerational problems. Some of the young people born in Ikaria went to California to found a new town called Ikaria-Hope, but this new town only survived for a six-year period between 1881-87. The very famous New Ikaria, built in a park by the elderly, lasted only 15 years (Ragon 2010:48-49). The last remaining town of Ikaria also faded into history in 1895.

In the nineteenth century, the industry located in the very centers of the cities polluted the cities to the maximum extent possible, and health conditions deteriorated significantly. From air pollution to the hygiene of the streets, many problems threatened daily life. Cholera epidemics in Europe lead to the deaths of hundreds of thousands of people. For this reason, establishing a hygienic city is a very important goal among the ideal urban design utopias of the new era. The most famous work on this subject is *Hygeia*, written by Benjamin Ward Richardson in 1876. Hygeia is a city based on strict compliance with public health principles. It was designed for a population of 100,000, living in 20,000 dwellings. The city is 1,600 hectares in size, with an average density of 60 people per hectare. The balanced distribution of population density in the city is ensured by the character of the housing. The buildings are high-rise, but the total building height cannot exceed 18 meters.

A decarbonization system prevents the exhaust gases from fireplaces from polluting the city's air. The houses are made of polished bricks that can be easily washed. There are many hot springs and sports grounds in the city to improve health conditions.

The city has two wide main streets running east-west. A railroad runs under both of them, which is reserved for heavy traffic. Thus, light and heavy traffic flows are separated. Streets and alleys in the north-south direction intersect the main streets in the east-west direction. All streets are wide enough to allow for air flow and sunlight. There are trees and shrubs around the pedestrian paths. The common areas behind the houses consist of gardens. Churches, theaters, banks, educational and other public and commercial buildings stand alone, forming part of the streets. These buildings are surrounded by gardens not only for aesthetic reasons but also for the healthy formation of the city (Yüksel 2012:19-20).

Utopian ideal city designs, which became widespread especially in France in the nineteenth century, made it to the USA in the last decade of the century. The utopian wind that blew in the US in the last decade of the nineteenth century resulted in the successive publication of more utopian books in this short period of time than ever before. The common features of these utopias were that they attributed all the existing problems of society to economic problems, and that they believed that these economic problems could be overcome through specialization and work. This decade-long deluge of utopias asserts that people's economic needs can be realized through technological innovations and economic regulations, and that technicians will be sufficient for these processes. The desired universe was a technocratic world.

The initiator of this great wind was Edward Bellamy with his novel *Looking Backward: From 2000 to 1887*, published in Boston in 1888. The book sold more than one million copies in the US alone (Meyerson 1996:118). In these years, when the US and Europe were going through a serious economic crisis, the working class was plunged into increasing hardship and despair. There was a fundamental unrest in society. Everyone was looking for a way out. This 10-year utopian literary frenzy initiated by Bellamy was the production and circulation of texts that offered a way out for all layers of society.

The ideal society imagined by Bellamy was depicted in Boston, USA in 2000. The well-off protagonist of the utopian novel falls into a hypnotic sleep in Boston in 1887 and opens his eyes in Boston in the year 2000. In the 113 years that have passed, everything has changed in the protagonist's city. The entire economy is in the hands of a government-owned national trust called the "Army of Industry". All capital, manufacturing and sales channels are concentrated in the name of the people of the United States and placed under national control. All production is brought to market from a single giant shopping center and distributed through its branches to every town and village. All citizens between the ages of 21 and 45 are obliged to join the Industrial Army, since there are no jobs outside the Industrial Army, and there is no possibility of capital formation or production. All wages are equal in the Industrial Army (Fishman 1982:36). However, the organizational

     ARCHITECTURAL UTOPIAS IN SEARCH OF THE IDEAL CITY

structure consists of a strict hierarchy and chain of command. Here, citizens are trained to be employed in the trade or manufacturing sectors according to their professional orientation.

Bellamy's utopia was designed with an architecture that could ensure the establishment and continuity of the social order he envisioned. In this utopia, the entire city of Boston is covered with a huge roof to optimize climate conditions. The city is a highly organized space, lined with elegant and beautiful buildings surrounded by small fences, decorated with trees, with kilometers of wide streets (Ertan 2003:153). The buildings do not form continuous blocks, but are closed in on themselves. In every neighborhood, there are large and spacious squares greened with trees, decorated with sculptures and fountains. Public buildings are giant in size with architectural splendor (Yüksel 2012:20). Boston's residential areas are organized in units of 2,000 people on 50 acres.

Looking Backward: From 2000 to 1887 proposes to overcome the crisis of society through a utopian ideal of public cooperation and central planning. It is based on the assumption that economic abundance can only be achieved through strong social sanctions/coercion (Meyerson 1996:119). It proposes a stable and rigid world. It sees this as a condition for the sustainability of economic abundance. Thus, the centralized structure will produce a hierarchical and stratified society in which individuals are kept under constant control. The location of the ideal society is determined as the city.

In the period of US utopias initiated by Bellamy, there were times when utopia designs clashed with each other. *News From Nowhere*, a utopia published in 1890 by William Morris (1834-96) from England as a reaction to Bellamy's ideal society, stands out among these.

In order to better explain the socialist idea, Morris speaks of a communist society that has survived the transitional period, state socialism, and is in a pleasing state of development. The date for this progress would be 1952, a date that seemed distant at the time.

Set in the Thames Valley in England, the book is an example of utopia, which means " an order that does not exist". In the England of the future, designed as a giant garden, residential areas and workshops resembling small farmhouses are scattered throughout the country in a harmonious order and aesthetic. Most of London is covered with fields and gardens; the distinction between city and countryside has disappeared with the transformation of the entire space into village settlements. Market areas in the villages, where products are distributed, are one of the places where citizens come together (W. Morris 1986:242-45). Morris's utopia, which attempts to integrate Marxism and romanticism as a reflection of the aesthetic, moral and economic critique of capitalism, aims to radically reject the Victorian ideology based on industrial and technological growth.

Morris' classless utopia proposes a rural utopia shaped according to the free will of individuals. Adopting a nostalgic approach to overcome the negativities of the industrial city, Morris defended the organic unity of the old cities in the face of a world dominated by indifference and a quantitative approach that emerged with industrialization. Expressing his longing for a rural society based on agriculture and handicrafts, where technology is limited, Morris puts forward a rural utopia that is based on the production of handicrafts and ecological continuity and balance instead of the monotony of industrialization and mechanization.

Morris envisioned an environment where country houses cover the riverbanks instead of factory chimneys by eliminating big cities (Erdem 2005:80). Morris's work is considered to be the first example of the ecological utopias of the twentieth century.

In Morris's utopia, administrative oppression is replaced by a tolerant union of free individuals united on the basis of ethical consciousness. This work, in which the desire is for freedom to triumph over administrative oppression, is an anomaly for the general utopian literature thanks to its framework. Decisions affecting the welfare and future of society are taken by the common will of free individuals. Goods produced with a certain quality and durability are utilized by everyone to the extent they wish. The relationship of buying and selling based on money has disappeared. All work is performed by volunteers in this order, where pleasurable work is done by manual labor and boring work by machines. While social relations were organized on the basis of equality, there was discrimination in favor of men in working life, and women had to take on the duties of motherhood and housework (Ertan 2003:154-55).

In this society there is no parliament, no court, no prison, no army, no police. The only administrative power is the free community. Like factory chimneys and railroads, money has disappeared. The machines that had enslaved human beings are now the slaves of people who have learned to produce what they need with their own strength and without fatigue. Once their needs have been met, people are concerned with their private pleasures, which constitute the most important part of their lives.

The space Morris describes to us is completely far from the city. His attitude is negative towards the concentration of people at one point. The big, black cities, the industrial centers of the old mortar and brick desert, have disappeared, just like old London. On the contrary, small towns have flourished. England's towns soon became more crowded than at any time since the fourteenth century and continued to grow rapidly. The city invaded the countryside, but the invaders, like the warriors of old, were transformed by the environment into peasants. England became a garden where nothing was wasted or destroyed. There are the requisite number of dwellings, warehouses and workshops all over the country. Outside the towns there are many houses in the countryside. As a utopia in which industrialization is negated and freedom is glorified, Morris's utopia clearly differs from other utopias.

CREATIVE DESTRUCTION IN PARIS: HAUSSMANN

One of the most important characteristics of modernity is that it never refrains from making a radical break with the past. This is because it sees the world as a *tabula rasa*, a blank slate on which the new can be written without reference to or ignoring the past. Therefore, whether modernity is gentle and democratic or revolutionary, traumatic or authoritarian, it is always brimming with the potential for creative destruction (Harvey 2005:7). In nineteenth century France, this creative destruction manifested itself in the capital of the country.

During the reign of Napoleon III, through the practices of Georges-Eugéne Haussmann, approximately 70 percent of Paris was transformed by destruction and reconstruction, erasing the memory of the city. Meanwhile, it was renovated by cleansing and organizing, and Paris was granted the characteristics of a dream city (Gökçe 2017:695). The process that led Paris to this great destruction and reconstruction began with the emergence of the risks that the great workers' uprising of 1848 brought for the state and the government.

By the end of the first half of the nineteenth century, the industrial revolution that originated in England had been largely realized in almost all of Europe, and the profits of the new classes that emerged with this great transformation, namely the industrialists and industrial companies, had increased greatly, but the peasants and workers living in villages and cities had to live with extremely low incomes. Not only have the incomes of the poor not increased, but their living conditions have also worsened. Workers could work up to 15 hours a day. The level of hygiene and order in industrial cities was extremely low. However, as the population increased in the villages, the agricultural lands were becoming insufficient for people to make a living, and migration to industrial cities continued. Thus, there were large masses of workers who lived in the cities but suffered great difficulties in making a living and living.

This great social tension was supported by the intellectual theorizing of socialist intellectuals in the same years, and workers were called to resistance all over the world. The most famous text among these calls for resistance, the *Communist Manifesto*, written by Karl Marx and Friedrich Engels, was published in February 1848 (Marx & Engels, 2012). Inviting the working class to make a revolution and abolish private property through this revolution, the *Communist Manifesto* proposed an ideal life, a utopia in which workers would no longer be exploited in a classless and stateless society. These ideas spread rapidly and found many supporters among the working class, which was already overwhelmed by economic and vital difficulties. In the same year that the *Communist Manifesto* was published, workers' uprisings in many parts of Europe shook the continent. One of the most influential of these took place in Paris in 1848.

Napoleon III, who was in exile in England during these developments, was seen as the only leader who could save France from this turmoil. Napoleon responded positively to these calls and won the elections by a landslide and came to power. He then took authoritarian steps, exiled most of the socialist leaders in 1849, gained considerable support within the army, and eventually led to the dissolution of parliament in 1851. In December 1851, he changed the constitution with overwhelming support in a plebiscite and entered Paris amidst chants of *Vive l'empereur!* (Long live the Emperor!)

One of Napoleon III's top priorities was to prevent another uprising in Paris, the imperial capital, with barricaded streets as in 1848, and to build an architectural order that would help the soldiers and police as much as possible in preventing such uprisings. It was also desired to reconstruct the city, which was suffering from hygiene, order and aesthetic problems, as a modern city through a fearless operation. The capital of the new empire had to be positively differentiated from every other city in Europe in every way. Napoleon wanted to give medieval Paris a modern image and transform it into a cosmopolitan city better suited to commerce. His aim was to establish an urban network of wide boulevards running through the old and distorted neighborhoods of Paris (Kılıç & Şenel 2012:146). He imagined a Paris with its wide boulevards, cafes, restaurants, restaurants, arcades and green areas reached by the boulevards: a Paris like a paradise on earth that could become the capital of the nineteenth century.

In 1853, Napoleon III appointed Haussmann to Paris to put his designs into practice. Since ideal urban designs, which always begin with ambitious dreams and rationally organized plans, tend to follow the trajectory of a single mind rather than a multilateral consensus, Haussmann set out to remake Paris from the ground up.

In such an ambitious task, he first chose to eliminate any power centers that might disagree with him. Haussmann's first act was to suspend the city council (Harvey, 2005:133). The municipal council would no longer be formed by popular vote, as in other cities in France, but by the emperor's election. The second step was to neutralize the commission by convincing the emperor that the Public Works Commission should essentially consist of the president (Napoleon III) and the secretary general (the Governor of the Seine). He derived an extraordinary level of personal power directly from Napoleon III's authority and planned to use it to the fullest.

Haussmann was attempting to build a Paris on the intellectual tradition of the utopian socialists. The destruction of the Paris of the Second Empire and its transformation into the most modern city in the world cannot be understood without taking into account the influence of Saint-Simon, especially on Napoleon III. Napoleon III took ideas such as workers' cities, squeezing workers into large buildings, straight roads, sacrificing the city to traffic, defending green spaces, demolishing in the name of order and hygiene, etc. from the writings of Saint-Simon, Considérant and Cabet. As soon as the Emperor came to power, he immediately sought to realize the ideal city described by the utopian socialists. Although it was Haussmann who implemented the urban plans of the Second Empire, the ideas actually belonged to Napoleon III (Ragon 2010:89). The instructions came from the Emperor and it was left to Haussmann to raze Paris to the ground.

Napoleon III wanted to eliminate unemployment in Paris, which had turned into a gigantic construction site for a long period of time, and thus to enlist part of the proletariat. One of the aims of the new plan of Paris was to connect the stations through boulevards. The stations were the new gateways of Paris, and those coming into the city from these stations were meant to enter via huge and very impressive boulevards leading from the stations to the new modern urban machine. These were called "boulevard de la Gare". In Paris, Napoleon III had indecisive engineers agree to an unprecedented width of 35 meters for the Boulevard Strasbourg. The medieval city was coming to an end and a modern city was being created, the likes of which had never existed before.

Haussmann, Napoleon III's enforcer, took refuge behind the vandalistic rhetoric of Voltaire, who hated medieval art, and advocated the wholesale destruction of medieval Paris, razing it to the ground and rebuilding it as a modern city. The wide and straight structures of the station boulevards intersected many medieval buildings in the directions in which they were planned to pass. This resulted in Haussmann's demolition of medieval buildings where the new boulevards were to be built. The tree-lined roads and boulevards that ran on all four sides demolished everything in their path, occasionally ending in front of a historic building and encircling these historic buildings with a square, almost placing them in a jewel box. This building ceased to be an organic component of the city and became a collectible on display.

During this demolition process, for example, the inhabitants of Île-de-la-Cité in the center of Paris almost completely evacuated the area. In Haussmann's plans, the priority was not the settlement, but the avenues and boulevards themselves. One of his most important concerns was the flow of traffic. The length of Rue La Fayette, a five-kilometer straight line, was one of Haussmann's greatest sources of pride. For him, the city is primarily a technical problem. Architecture is nothing more than management. Haussmann drew 165 kilometers of roads: Sébastapol, Temple, Malesherbes, Voltaire Boulevards, the Opera Road, the Bois Road, the completion of the Rivoli Avenue, and many more. Paris was indeed turning into a paradise, but it was a paradise born out of ruins. Every building was demolished and a new urban plan was implemented in its place.

Haussmann aimed to increase the speed of commercial activity by uniting the disparate parts of the city. The wide boulevards running through the center of Paris were also designed to contribute to the prestige of the regime and serve as effective conduits for the security forces to control urban disorder when necessary (Saalman 1971:71). The fear of insurrection arising from previous experience led to the creation of a new urban form that involved demolishing workers' housing in the urban centers. Working classes were pushed away from public buildings and bourgeois neighborhoods. A city, suited for barricades and artillery fire as well as the use of cavalry guns, was built.

With Haussmann, an era of military and police in urban planning began. Haussmann's design aimed to build the city in such a way that internal uprisings could be easily suppressed by artillery. Since the machinists of La Chapelle were the most active members of the June 1849 uprising, Haussmann designed the roads as defensive trenches against Belleville and La Villette. When he cut through the Rue des Écoles, he had in mind isolating the students of the Quartier Latin rather than creating a link. The new Paris was conceived as a well-organized square against internal subversion. On the Place du Château-d'eau (now the Place de la République), the Prince-Eugene Barracks was built, which could accommodate 4,000 soldiers. This barracks was built for the security of the major boulevards. The troops could be deployed at a moment's notice on the two-kilometer straight line that runs along the Boulevard Magenta and also on the Boulevard Magenta. On the other hand, the Boulevard Prince-Eugene (now the Boulevard Voltaire) was a 2,850-meter straight line connecting today's Place de la Republic with the Place de la Trône. The Saint-Martin Canal, located within the Boulevard Reine Hortense (today's Boulevard Richard-Lenoir), was the perfect sighting line to observe the turmoil of the slums of the Temple (Ragon 2010:95). Haussmann's utopia was like a state-oriented dystopia, but the result was very aesthetic, regardless of its purpose.

Haussmann ignored and even exacerbated the adverse conditions of the poor in Paris, which he rebuilt at Napoleon's behest. But his administrative responsibility did not extend to the living conditions of the poor. While Haussmann eliminated poor housing in the capital, he created more of the same in the suburbs. The entire surrounding suburbs fell victim to speculation and parcelization.

  ARCHITECTURAL UTOPIAS IN SEARCH OF THE IDEAL CITY

MODERNISM AND TWENTIETH CENTURY UTOPIAS

As the nineteenth century was coming to an end, the two components shaping the urban structure could be identified as the rise in prosperity generated by the new capitalist industrial economy and the growth of urban reform movements. Real wages increased towards the end of the century, lifting at least some workers out of poverty and poor neighborhoods. Transportation systems improved, allowing transportation to reach longer distances. The railroad expanded in the first decade of the twentieth century, followed by electric trams, buses and finally private automobiles. Suburbs were born thanks to these means of transportation. The advance of industrialization, the development of technology and the accumulation of large-scale capital led to the expansion of industrial cities into rural areas. This expansion was shaped by factors such as proximity to labor and raw material markets or large consumption markets.

The birth of the reform movements was influenced by the public health movement and epidemiology. These new approaches emphasize the link between the frequency of diseases and spatial factors. There is a link between diseases and the lack of clean water and proper sewage systems (Thorns 2002:17-8). This led to reforms to provide better physical and social conditions for urban development.

In the first quarter of the twentieth century, when the modern state structure gradually increased its effectiveness, projects began to seek the perfect city within the boundaries of the industrial city (Aktan 2012:100).

Howard, Wright and Le Corbusier based their ideas on technological innovations such as express trains, automobiles, telephones, radios and multi-story steel and reinforced concrete structures that inspired their era.

In the nineteenth century, overcrowded and smog-choked cities on the one hand, and the romantic allure of nature on the other, pushed wealthy people to live in the suburbs. At the beginning of the nineteenth century, the suburb was a shelter in nature, a refuge from the wretchedness of the city. At the time, in order to live in the suburbs, one had to be affluent enough to have a car or hire one frequently. The architecture of the suburbs was extremely attractive, as it was not subject to the sharp lines of the city. Here nature was preserved to the extreme. There were large buildings, playgrounds, gardens, clusters of trees and groves. But with the introduction of the railroads, the face of the suburbs changed completely. The secluded green areas surrounding the cities, especially those that had been recreational areas, suddenly ceased to be pristine places of refuge. Poor crowds, driven out of the centers by the high cost of living in the cities, flocked to the suburbs. Thus, a displacement took place: The wealthy population returned to the prosperous city, while the poor population transformed the face of the suburbs into a grim town. As transportation facilities expanded, both the periphery of the suburb expanded and the density within it increased. From being a green area surrounding the city, it became a new malady for the city. In the suburbs, which have lost their characteristic of being a countryside and isolation, identical houses took over the natural areas that parcel owners had filled with buildings. It was during such a transformation phase of the suburbs that utopian minds, once again reaching for the old idea of idyllic country life, designed garden-cities in the suburbs.

HOWARD'S SUBURB: GARDEN-CITY

In 1902, Ebenezer Howard published a book called *Garden Cities of To-morrow*. In the book, the garden-city was planned to be built on a circular area of 1.2 kilometers in diameter. The settlement structure consists of spaces that are separated from each other from the center outwards. Layout is established as park (social area), residential and industrial areas outwards from the center.

In the center of the circle, a 2.25-hectare park/square and a center with social and administrative buildings such as the municipality building, concert and conference hall, theater, library, museum, military hospital is proposed. From this central square, six 36 meters wide radial boulevards extending outward from the circular shape are defined. Surrounding the social and administrative buildings is another large park called "central park". This park area is also surrounded by the "crystal palace". Inside the crystal palace, which opens to the park on one side and to the road on the other, there are stores where the products produced in the factory will be sold.

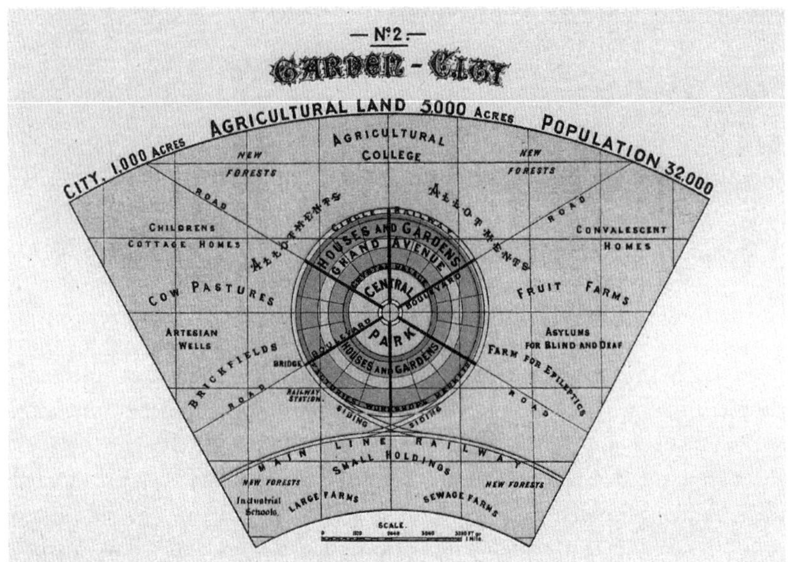

Garden-City
Project plan,
Ebenezer
Howard

The crystal palace also defines the main entrance to the residential area and serves as a promenade in bad weather. In the belt around the crystal palace are residential buildings. The rows of houses with gardens are bisected by a street, the so-called "grand avenue", which is approximately 100 meters wide. The grand avenue is planted with trees and equipped with structures where daily social activities such as schools and playgrounds take place. Therefore, it defines a public space rather than a street. The outermost belt of the circle is the section where the production areas consisting of factories, workshops and farms are located. This section also constitutes the outer boundary of the settlement.

Although the circulation within the settlement is organized with pedestrian circulation in mind as the private automobile is not yet on the agenda, the roads are sized in different widths. The difference in the width of the roads is due to the fact that they play a separating role between spaces and buildings with different functions. The roads are grouped into three categories: ring roads that circulate the circular scheme, roads that cut these roads and open outward from the center, and intermediate roads that connect the rings. The most privileged among this group of roads are boulevards. While the boulevards connect three different functions from the center to the outermost part of the city, they are also very important in terms of establishing a connection with the railway line and the station in a direction tangent to the circle; because the most important issue that makes the garden-city setting possible is the fact that it is located on the railway line that provides transportation to the city.

 ARCHITECTURAL UTOPIAS IN SEARCH OF THE IDEAL CITY

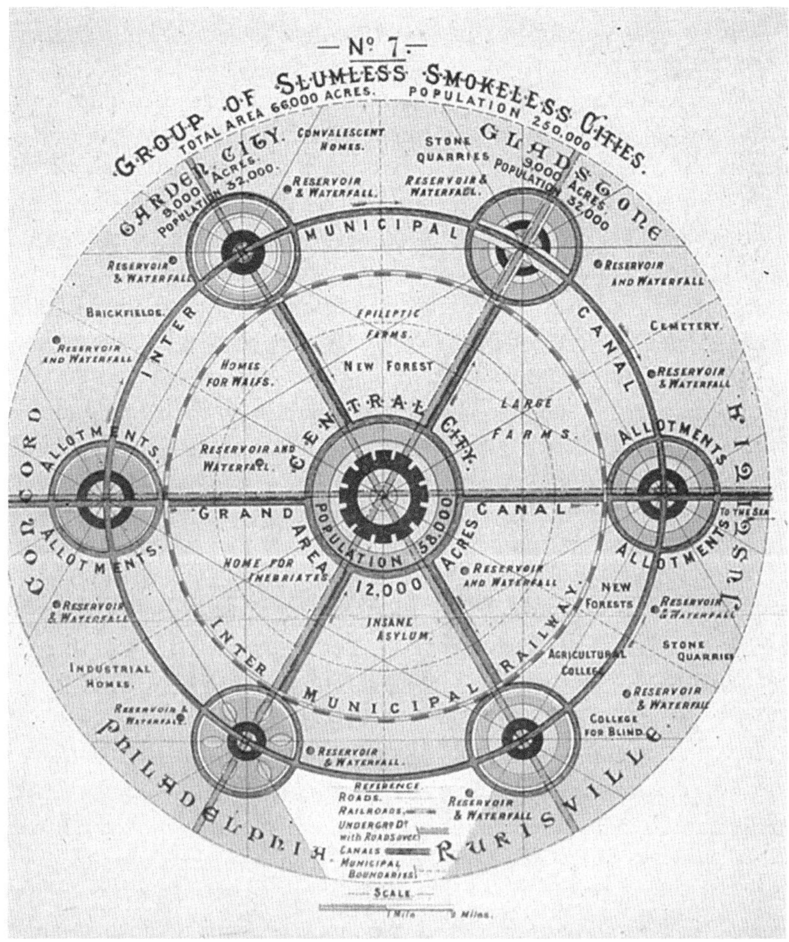

Sub-Cities Project plan, Ebenezer Howard

The garden-city is a settlement outside the city, far away from all the negativities of the city, yet at the same time close to the blessings of the city thanks to the railway, a new product of the age of industrialization. It was envisioned that the quality of life would increase in these settlements, which would be built in the lap of nature and in healthy conditions, and that cultural activities in the city would be moved to the countryside with the establishment of social facilities, and job opportunities would be provided by the establishment of workshops in a different section from the residential areas.

Howard proposed another scheme based on railroad transportation to control urban density. According to this scheme, the city center with a population of 58,000 would be surrounded by six garden-cities with a population of 32,000, connected to each other and to the city center by high-speed trains. Industrial facilities are located outside the garden-cities. Each garden-city is built on 400 hectares of land and surrounded by 2,000 hectares of agricultural land. Howard envisioned that all urban land would be the common property of the community.

From an urban planning perspective, Howard's proposal is not only about creating a garden-city settlement. It also has the ideal of creating "sub-cities" consisting of garden-city settlements separated from the city and each other by green areas but connected to the city and each other by rail-roads, where population density can be controlled in a certain order. In this way, the density in urban centers can be controlled, the population can be distributed in a more planned manner, and the negative conditions resulting from unplanned growth that lead to the collapse of cities can be eliminated.

Howard wanted to build entirely new cities in the middle of the un-spoiled countryside, on land that would remain in the ownership of the community as a whole. Limited in size to 30,000 inhabitants and surrounded by a continuous green belt, the garden-city would be robust, efficient, healthy and beautiful. It would draw people away from bloated cities like London, where wealth and power are dangerously concentrated, while at the same time scattering hundreds of new communities across the countryside where small-scale cooperation and direct democracy could flourish.

LE CORBUSIER PARENTHESIS TO UTOPIA: "CONTEMPORARY CITY" AND "VILLE RADIEUSE" (RADIANT CITY)

One of the most important names in the discipline of modern urbanism is Le Corbusier, the author of the book *Urbanisme*. Le Corbusier played a very important role in determining the design principles of modern architecture and in the rapid spread and globalization of the international architectural style (Merzi 2017:10-1). Moreover, he did not do this in a collective way like the Bauhaus, which was formed with the joint contribution of many people, but rather alone. The popularity of *Urbanism* also brought previous research in the field back to the agenda and put it into circulation (Moos 2009:176). However, Le Corbusier's popularity generated as much anger as enthusiasm. This book ignited the debate on modern urbanism.

Le Corbusier wrote *Urbanism* in an extremely simple, non-technical manner. He built the entire city plan according to the principles of positiv-ism/modernism. He relied on numerical data to identify problems. Func-tionalism, uniformity, homogeneity and standardization dominate the entire work. The book argues that housing and urban planning should be freed from all traditional ties and redesigned with a pure rationality, in a way that is highly compatible with today's technology, and it is argued that such a design is the "Contemporary City" described in the book.

In line with modernism, Le Corbusier believes that a rational de-sign has universal validity. While writing *Urbanism*, he always had Paris in mind; he set out from the shortcomings of Paris and his resentment against it. However, he argued that the city he envisioned in *Urbanism* should be a model for all the cities of the world. This thesis is one of the main arguments of his book: According to Le Corbusier, there is only one common truth for humanity and the human mind is capable of finding it. In *Urbanism*, Le Corbusier claimed that he had found the only common truth in the planning of the modern city. The book draws its foundations from Le Corbusier's diorama of a city of three million inhabitants, which he presented at the Salon d'Automne in 1922. This was followed in 1923 by Le Corbusier's *Vers une architecture* (*Toward an Architecture*), a book of articles serialized in *L'Esprit Nouveau* that laid out the principles of his own architecture. Le Corbusier himself wrote in his preface to the second edition of *Toward an Architecture* that *Urbanism* was the continuation of *Towards an Architecture* (Corbusier 2007:16-7). By 1925, Le Corbusier had textually elaborated this design and brought his proposals to the size of a book, forming a boundary stone, a cult work that influences us to this day. *Urbanism* is Le Corbusier's utopia and one of the most important texts in the history of utopia (Köksal 2014:i).

Le Corbusier divided *Urbanism* into three main sections. The first part is a general discussion, the second part is a theoretical examination of Le Corbusier's utopia of a modern city, and the third part is a discussion of the current situation of the center of Paris.

Chaos Created by the Industrial Revolution

In the general discussion section, Le Corbusier argues that the opportunities provided by technology, particularly in the last 50 years, are in conflict with the low-tech city, which was planned and built with the paradigm of the pre-Industrial Revolution. According to Le Corbusier, the social crisis stemmed from the contradiction between the new way of life created by the Industrial Revolution and the residential architecture that could not respond to the needs of this way of life. The machine turned everything upside down. Development gained an unprecedented speed within a century. A veil was pulled over our habits, our tools, our work, never to be opened again. A vast field unfolds before us (Corbusier 2007:23).

In Le Corbusier's mind, the city is "an instrument of work". The function of the city is to enable work. But cities can no longer fulfill "this function" (Corbusier 1972:ix). With the Industrial Revolution, technology changed rapidly, the mode of production evolved from land-based to industry-oriented, and the population shifted from rural to urban areas. However, the building stock and the streets that provide transportation were designed for the medieval cities before this rapid transformation. Therefore, after the Industrial Revolution, there was a negative contrast between the physical conditions of cities and the requirements of the age. Extant historical cities lacked the capacity to carry the new transformation. Therefore, their functions have been interrupted. Cities have now turned into barriers that prevent development, transportation, work, rest, shelter, entertainment; in short, life in a humane way. For him, in the medieval period, in the absence of motorized vehicles, cities were built along roads on which donkeys which were used for transportation could walk most easily. Many parameters such as the ruggedness of nature, swamps, streams, and the risks of the natural habitat made the donkeys' walking paths winding. As villages, towns and finally cities were also built along these paths, all the cities built before the Industrial Revolution showed an extremely crooked configuration and were abandoned to the irrational trajectories of donkeys. Le Corbusier said, "The donkey has drawn all the cities of the continent, unfortunately also Paris" (Corbusier 1972:6). According to him, these curved roads and planning were no longer necessary in the twentieth century with the transformation of vehicles into automobiles. On the contrary, such curvatures prevent automobile transportation. Le Corbusier, by arguing "The crooked street is the way of donkeys, the straight street is the way of men" (Corbusier 1972:11), prioritizes rational functionalism and suggests that automobile traffic requires straight roads.

According to Le Corbusier, when the city shaped by the Middle Ages encountered technology that developed too fast to be followed, a cacophony, disharmony and chaos ensued. If the ideal form of industrial society could be achieved in urban design, Le Corbusier was of the opinion that the lost order would be regained in a more qualified way, and that a freedom, prosperity and aesthetics unseen in history would be achieved (Fishman 1982:21-2). Le Corbusier, who believed in modernism's optimistic and progressive understanding of history, would try to transform the existing chaos into an atmosphere of order (cosmos).

Bringing Order Under the Leadership of a Single Architect

For Le Corbusier, a design must always be derived from the rationality of the human mind. The world in its natural state is disordered and man must organize the world by overcoming this disorder with the categories of his own mind (Corbusier 1972:15). Rationality, according to him, is order itself: "'The work of man is ordering" (Corbusier 1972:22). For Le Corbusier, a city that is not rationally organized is an obstacle for human beings. The peace of man depends on the perfection of order. What will save us from the chaos of nature is a rational city design designed with rectangles. Geometry is the architectural tool for this. However, today's city is not realized "with the mind of geometry". Therefore, it is a threatening disaster (Corbusier 1972:24). Le Corbusier advocates a transition in urban life from the entropy of romanticism to the rational prescriptivism of modernism that sets standards.

Le Corbusier believes that the architect has duties far beyond constructing buildings; he imposes a much greater duty and responsibility on the architect: To be the leader and pioneer of social development (Corbusier 2007:15-6). By "architect" he actually refers to himself.

According to Le Corbusier, a single mind should build an order by designing an entire city through rational planning. Where there is no plan, there is disorder and arbitrariness. Modern life demands and expects a new plan for housing and the city (Corbusier 2007:34). In *Urbanism*, Le Corbusier constructs this detailed city plan that he has assigned to himself. He designs a "modern city" for "modern life" and creates it with a very "modernist" approach. He described the method of architecture as "the attainment of a theoretical grandeur, a mathematical order, speculation and a perception of harmony in emotional relations". According to Le Corbusier, "geometry is fundamental" (Corbusier 1972:ix). Thus, Le Corbusier identified the tools of architecture that would revitalize the city as mathematics and geometry.

The Instrument of Order: Geometry

According to Le Corbusier, engineers and businessmen using mathematics and geometry had pioneered new forms of production. Now the architect had to design mass-produced houses and radiant cities that would enable everyone to enjoy the "basic joys" of the new age. A whole new environment had to be created in which the techniques of industrialization made the daily lives of citizens easier. In this way, chaos would disappear. For Le Corbusier, the harmony of society became a "problem of construction" (Fishman 1982:180). This was the motivation that drove Le Corbusier to design a utopian city in *Urbanism*. He wanted to produce a machine that would work flawlessly: A city machine.

Since he saw the world in terms of mathematics and geometry, he thought that people's living spaces should also be designed like a machine. For him, " A residence is a machine to live in" (Corbusier 2007:36). The street was a "traffic machine" (Corbusier 1972:126). The river was "a railroad on water". The city was "a machine to live in" (Corbusier 2007:254). Therefore, he designed his utopian city as a machine. A machine without a soul, but one that runs like clockwork.

In the design he made in *Urbanism*, the most defining feature of Le Corbusier's geometry is symmetry. The Modern City design is characterized by absolute symmetry, from the unit element skyscraper to the general plan. This sharp symmetry is placed as a sign of the triumph of reason over chance.

The Romantic Genius Gets Replaced by the Rational Engineer

Suggesting a transition from the particularity of emotions to the universality of reason, that is, from romanticism to modernism, Le Corbusier argues that there is no need for romantic, individual creative geniuses, and that with modernism, the creative genius is replaced by general rational reason, the universal principles of mathematics. He argues that the effect of this in architecture is the transition from the product of passion to the product of reason (Corbusier 1972:42). Le Corbusier equates passion with the creative genius of the architect and reason with the engineer of the modern period. According to him, the work of reason ceaselessly adds to one another, and this is called progress. However, the emotions of passion do not change, even thousands of years cannot change it.

By the nineteenth century, according to Le Corbusier, with the perfection in equipment, reason had overtaken passion. Engineering has triumphed over individual genius. It minimized the importance of genius and then replaced it. In this way, Le Corbusier makes his position clear in favor of standard and universal creations, rather than unique particular creations. Le Corbusier attempted to transform the approach stating that each architectural work and city is a unique work of art towards another approach: in line with the maxim "the way of reason is one", each architectural work and city must be standardized and homogeneous in light of the principles of modernism.

"Everywhere is standard, the uniformity of detail", Le Corbusier called it and aspired to it. According to him, " it is only then that great arrangements can raise their melodies" (Corbusier 1972:67). Showing a thorough modernist reflex, Le Corbusier thus advocates building all urban cells as a uniform, monolithic whole, rather than building the city cell by cell and creating a heterogeneous diversity. Instead of personal structures determined by emotions, he proposes imposing a single and standardized form of structure determined by reason on the entire city. By creating a model that adheres to rules and norms and replicating this model throughout the city, he hopes to achieve a homogeneous and rational city. Advocating a progressive and optimistic understanding of history in line with the principles of modernism, Le Corbusier thinks that the twentieth century will be "like a city from the fairy tales" with the new urbanism.

The Rules of Modernism: Standardization and Homogenization

Throughout the book, Le Corbusier gave no weight to contingency or historicity, and assumed that the logical and rational solutions for similar situations would be one and the same. In other words, the maxim of modernism that "the way of reason is one" is fully embraced. For this reason, the city designed by Le Corbusier is standardized and homogeneous. He focused on mass production. He was influenced by the industrial production models and new material choices of the period (Sevinç 2004:90) and argued that cities and residences should be produced in a serial and standardized manner. Le Corbusier designed a standard and homogeneity between cities as well as a standard and homogeneity within the city itself. He claims to have produced a universal city plan by creating a model that is bound by rules and norms and reproducing this model worldwide. Therefore, the settlement space planned for three million people is not designed for a specific place, but for any place. There is nothing local in its design. It is developed with pure rationality.

Creative Destruction

Modernity, as we have already mentioned, always assumes that there must be a radical break with the past. It always tends to see the world as a "tabula rasa". Therefore, modernity, whether democratic, revolutionary or authoritarian, is always associated with "creative destruction" (Harvey 2005:7). In Urbanism, Le Corbusier assumed the role of the main actor of creative destruction in architectural planning.

Le Corbusier's proposed cure for the salvation of cities was as modernist as his diagnosis of cities. He suggested the complete destruction of the old city, which was not produced by rationality, and the construction of a completely rational city in its place. He advises the demolition of the irrational old city plan, built out of traditions, beliefs and habits, as well as everything that materializes this plan: streets, avenues, buildings, monuments, tombs, everything. Similar to what the modernist French Revolutionaries did in politics, Le Corbusier declared that "every non-rational structure in the city, without exception, must be demolished". Anything without a function is denied a place in his city. Le Corbusier's proposed cure for diseased medieval cities was not a simple Band-Aid, but a radical surgery. Haussmann was his role model, but he would go beyond him in his own project.

Le Corbusier tried to reveal how the ideal city of the twentieth century should be. He believed that his society needed new cities above all. He thought that form would reshape content. For him, physical possibilities would recreate social life in the most positive way. He denied the possibility of gradual rehabilitation. He did not aim to improve old cities, but to completely transform the urban environment. Le Corbusier's design is "a manifesto of urban revolution".

Le Corbusier's ideal city is perhaps the most ambitious and complex expression of the belief that the entire life of society can be radically transformed by reshaping the physical environment. In line with modernism, he dreamed that he could rebuild society along with the city, and he was optimistic regarding this dream. He undertook a social engineering. His action plan is extremely radical. In his view, the classical cities, which concealed themselves within the walls for military reasons, have already overflowed outside the walls in the twentieth century, and since there is no longer any rational design for the walled city to function, it must be completely demolished and rebuilt within the framework of rational principles. Le Corbusier wrote that, "City centers are terminally ill, and their surroundings are as if eaten by moths" (Corbusier 1972:88). He dismisses all history, architectural heritage, monumental structures and cobblestone streets in the name of functionality. Rejecting a conservative evolutionary understanding of urbanism, he puts forward a radical-rational revolutionary urbanism attitude. For the sake of building what is functional, all the past and its cumulative legacy, the traditional lifestyles they signify, and the identities they produce are suddenly and unhesitatingly obliterated.

He also opposes the construction of new and wider urban centers in other areas due to the congestion of the city centers. He firmly argues that the old city center should be demolished and rebuilt – and attempts to prove this claim with various arguments. For him a center is conditional, it exists only with its surroundings. For this reason, leaving that center and rebuilding a new center in another region is not the way to go (Corbusier 1972:91). The center must be replaced where it is. This is Le Corbusier's creative destructiveness. In order to realize the new, he proposes the destruction of the old and insists on this with all his might.

Le Corbusier explains his reasons for the need to demolish the old urban centers. According to him, with the discovery of the automobile, automobiles have started to fill the cities. In 1925, the year he published *Urbanism*, Le Corbusier demonstrated with statistics that the surface covered by automobiles in circulation in Paris was larger than the surface of Paris's roads and asked: "Where do the automobiles go? To the center. In the center there is no room to roam. We need to create it. It is necessary to destroy the center." (Corbusier 1972:108). Le Corbusier points to New York as an example. The traffic density in New York is so high that businessmen have to leave their cars at the periphery and take the subway to their workplaces. Le Corbusier calls this situation a "striking paradox" and shows with statistics that the number of automobiles is steadily increasing and argues that urban centers with fixed road surfaces will become more and more inadequate (Corbusier, ibid.).

Le Corbusier pointed out that, according to statistics, the speed of automobiles in contemporary cities is 16 kilometers per hour, whereas automobile factories produce vehicles that can go up to 200 kilometers per hour. The reason for this technological irony is that cities do not have modern streets. According to him, this situation is a "congestion, suffocation" (Corbusier 1972:110). "In the present situation, the great modern city is an absurdity." (Corbusier 1972:115) Therefore, according to Le Corbusier, urban centers should be demolished and rebuilt according to new requirements.

Le Corbusier's Utopia: "The Contemporary City"

Le Corbusier's utopian urban planning, which advocates the complete demolition of old urban centers and the construction of a new urban center in their place, emerges at this stage. In the second part of Urbanism, "The Contemporary City", Le Corbusier explains the foundations and principles of his utopia. He begins by saying, "With technical analysis and architectural synthesis, I have established the plan of a city of three million inhabitants" (Corbusier 1972:157), and then proceeds to design the way the city should be built in the new century.

Le Corbusier's utopian city is centered on the train station. This station is integrated with subways, buses, other transportation facilities and, via helicopter, with the airport. The station is surrounded by 60-story skyscrapers, each symmetrically arranged at wide intervals. These large complexes will serve to fulfill the commercial needs of the community. In the parks surrounding them, there are upscale restaurants, theaters and shops. The majority of the population lives in spacious, high-rise, elevator-operated apartment buildings with a private hanging garden in every unit, while some live in colonies consisting of detached houses. The streets are three stories high to allow different types of vehicles to flow at different speeds. Raising density to such a high level allows people to be comfortably packed into a small space, freeing up large areas for agriculture, recreation and the enjoyment of nature. Urban development, geometrically arranged in such a widely spaced manner, allows for the provision of cultural and other services required by a dense consumer population and an adequate transportation system. Le Corbusier's idea of the city as a complex machine, a

The Contemporary City, Le Corbusier, 1925

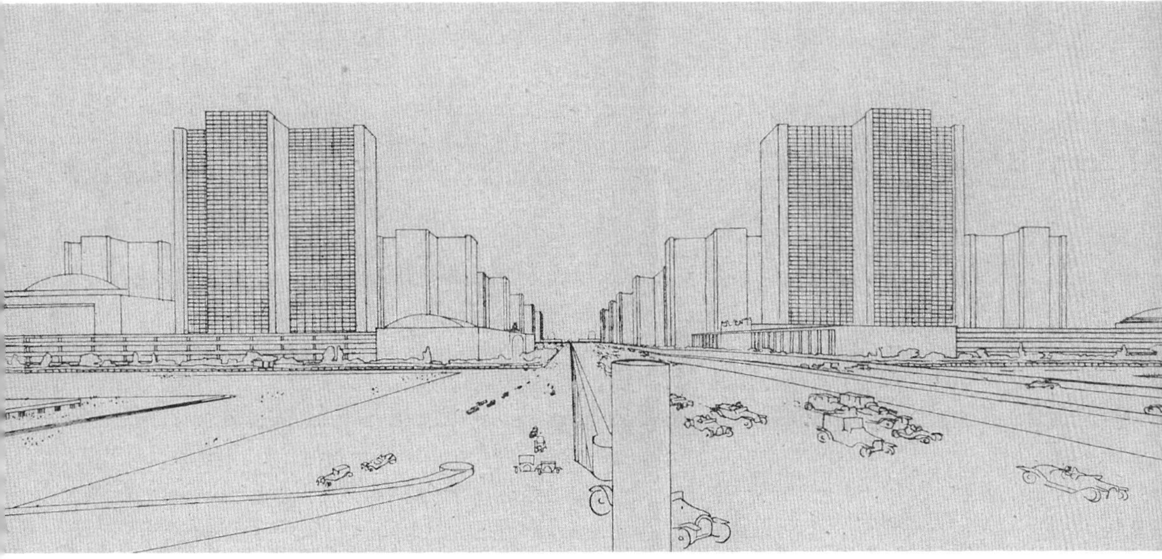

machine necessary for everyday life, also provides everyone with the right to live in privacy and beauty in a light, green, spacious, serene environment (Meyerson 1996:120).

In his urban designs, Le Corbusier excluded everything that was not functional. Traditions, habits, aesthetics, public memory, historicity and everything that seems irrational are the enemies of his urban design. Since he wanted to build a completely rational and profitable city, he made sure that everything was extremely tight and compact. The basic principles of the plan of his utopian city are as follows:

1. De-congestion of the city center,
2. Increasing density,
3. Increasing the number of transportation vehicles,
4. Increasing green areas.

For him, solving the first two items is possible by resolving the traffic and replacing the existing buildings with very tall buildings. For Le Corbusier, the reason for the traffic in the city is not only the inconvenience of the curved roads inherited from the Middle Ages for motor vehicles, but also the distance of the spaces from each other. He tried to solve this problem by increasing the density of the city center and reducing the number of streets and street intersections.

According to Le Corbusier, the number of streets and street intersections in existing cities should be reduced by 2/3. In the current plans, streets intersect every 50, 20 or 10 meters. In his opinion, street intersections are the enemy of traffic. Le Corbusier claimed that the optimum distance for a street intersection is the distance between two metro or bus stops. This corresponds to a distance of 400 meters (Corbusier 1972:162).

With the aim of reducing traffic and facilitating access within the center by increasing the density of the city, Le Corbusier imagines that the increased density of the city can be realized through skyscrapers. Consequently, the grounds on which the existing low-rise buildings sit will be narrowed, and 60-story skyscrapers will be erected on this shrunken ground. Given that the number of floors in the Paris buildings of the period was six, Le Corbusier desired a 10-fold vertical elevation. Hence, he used the skyscraper, in his own words, as a "street in the air".

Distances were shortened as a result of vertical concentration instead of horizontal expansion, and it became possible to reach a large number of places, sometimes on foot and sometimes only by elevator. This provides an important solution to the city's traffic problem.

An additional advantage of retreating from horizontal expansion is that the areas on which buildings are to be erected are considerably narrowed, thus transforming the land on which buildings used to occupy into green areas. According to Le Corbusier, modern work requires serenity and healthy air. However, these are not possible in environments where there are no green areas and buildings are everywhere.

With vertical growth, Le Corbusier not only increases the density of the city and reduces traffic, but also improves the city's quality of air and creates a serene landscape where people will be more comfortable (Corbusier 1972:160). In Le Corbusier's plans for his utopian city, the skyscrapers, which will house 6,000 inhabitants per hectare, will have 95% green space on the ground and there will be squares, restaurants and theaters built around them. Luxury residences on indented plots with 300 inhabitants per hectare will have 85% green space on the ground, including gardens and sports fields. The closed plots, which will accommodate 305 inhabitants per hectare, will have 48% green space on the ground and will include gardens and sports areas (Corbusier 1972:165).

In Le Corbusier's city, boulevards were drawn between skyscrapers over 200 meters high and in the middle of the remaining empty spaces; one-, two- or three-story buildings, cramped, one after the other, with steps leading to luxury stores with their elegant showcases, where shopping, the object of which is to please, is to be done; likewise, restaurants and cafes are located on successive terraces opening to clusters of five trees or similar to the openings of English parks. Above all, the street is reconstructed with elements on a human scale.

Denser than the big cities at the time of Le Corbusier, this city re-establishes its own marketplaces; it claims to create a consoling landscape where trees, flowers and distant lawns are presented to our eyes only with ground floor houses and terraces retreating one after the other (Corbusier 1972:228).

Financing the Utopian City

In order to show that the city plan he designed was feasible, Le Corbusier tried to prove that it was financially profitable to demolish the city completely and rebuild another city in its place. In this way, he wanted to announce to the necessary authorities that he had produced a realizable project rather than a model that could only work on paper. In making the economic modeling in question, he chose Paris as a model city and produced his calculations in the framework of this city. Through this effort, Le Corbusier actually laid the intellectual foundations of today's urban-transformation practice, which has become widespread especially in Istanbul. Indeed, Le Corbusier's design of the time is in practice in today's Istanbul.

If the city is demolished and rebuilt according to Le Corbusier's proposals, it will be worth much more than its former value. He formulates it: "Assume the value of the existing buildings in the city together with the land as (A). Then let's imagine that these neighborhoods, which are suffocating and outdated, whose streets, environment and parks are not habitable, are demolished and replaced with brand new and magnificent neighborhoods, keeping the same number of apartments." In this new situation, according to Le Corbusier, the value of each unit will increase along with the total value increase of the neighborhood. Le Corbusier estimates this increase as (A5). This is not all, because in his plan, neighbourhoods are to be rebuilt collectively in the most optimal way in line with his planning, and all the floors of buildings are to be increased. Even though the total number of units will not increase as much as the increase in floors, the total number of units will increase from 800 inhabitants per hectare to 3,300 inhabitants per hectare; in other words, there will be a four-fold increase in units. Le Corbusier therefore multiplies the land value, which becomes (A5), by four to arrive at 4(A5).

Thus, the public will have spent a considerable budget to demolish and rebuild, but in the end will make a huge profit because of the huge increase in value at the close of the operation. Both locals and foreign investors from all over the world, such as Americans, Germans, British and Japanese, will invest in these new buildings. In this way, Le Corbusier's city will become a world city, and since it will become a city that receives investments from all countries, it will not be at risk of being destroyed in the event of a possible war, since no nation will risk bombing a city where its own investments are located (Corbusier 1972:284-6). Furthermore, there will be a much greater economic return than the budget spent on the construction of the new city.

Criticism of Urbanism

In Le Corbusier's architectural philosophy, the concept of the ideal city represents a search for perfection, clarity, certainty and non-contradiction. His design claims to be purely functional, far from aesthetics, in order to ensure justice and equality and to realize social order. Instead of livable cities, it tends to build regions defined according to their functions. He evaluated the level of creativity of an architect and the aesthetic value of a building according to the benefit it provides to people and society.

According to Le Corbusier, cities should be designed according to an ideal model; this is an urban utopia. His homogeneous city, intended to be circulated all over the world and to be produced with the same standards in every corner of the globe, is a gigantic machine. You can sense this feeling in every corner of the city, even in its plan. Everything that is not functional has been excluded and expelled from this city. For the sake of optimizing productivity, the entire fabric of the past has been eliminated. This radical rupture in the design of the city pertains not only to the design of the city, but also to the entire past. Le Corbusier's proposal is an operation of uprooting. And he hopes that the lines emanating from a single mind will dominate the whole world. Behind the exclusion of what is quintessentially human from all living spaces to the point of mechanizing the house, the street and the city,

 ARCHITECTURAL UTOPIAS IN SEARCH OF THE IDEAL CITY

lies the unconditional sanctification of monopolistic radical rationality and bureaucratic power (Harvey 1991:51). Le Corbusier's design is –ironically– the urbanist projection of the political authoritarianization of modernism, which emerged as an emancipatory paradigm.

Nevertheless, human beings are not merely minds and functions; on the contrary, they are cultural and social beings. In a city design that will be produced by a purely rational planning from a single mind, in which no interventions of its inhabitants are accepted, the public cannot easily be expected to be satisfied, to identify with the city they live in, and to develop a sense of belonging. The city is, in Lévi-Strauss' words, a "social work of art". Its densely interwoven structure is the product of thousands of minds and individual decisions. Its diversity comes from unexpected intersections and unpredictable interactions. As Fishman puts it, "How can a single individual, even a genius, hope to understand this structure? And how can he produce a new framework with equally satisfying complexities? How can a single individual hope to impose his or her idea on history?" (Fishman 1982:25-6) As if the architect, if given the opportunity, could solve all our problems with his or her rational professional insight and planning skills. It is as if society is both one of the instruments of the architect's profession and the object of his actions (Tanyeli 2017:11).

Identifying what is right and necessary for human beings and society only by reducing it to numerical values, focusing on parameters such as square meters, topography and economy within the framework of a simple equation, and producing plans based only on basic human biological functions, can only come from minds that assume that the human being, like the city, is nothing but a machine. Just as the city is not a "working machine", the human being is not a biological machine. An architecture that is conceived with these assumptions is oppressive because it is perceived as a tool to discipline the physical environment and sociality. The design power of the architect, as advocated by Le Corbusier, points to a tyranny that is intended to be established over sociality.

The shapes and sizes of cities are not determined by the personal desires of architects. They are determined by socio-economic forces and interests, institutional patterns and a conception of progress and efficiency shared by the ruling elite. Architects can only propose prescriptions that represent these forces and interests. This is why, as Moos puts it, "in politics and urbanism, simplifying formulas such as *'ville contemporaine pour 3 millions d'habitants'* have not been successful" (Moos 2009:175). What emerges from such practices is nothing but a city without an identity.

As Le suggests, cities cannot be completely demolished and rebuilt continuously with the developing technology. While Le Corbusier advocates the complete demolition of the medieval city and the construction of cities compatible with today's technology, he is actually in a contradiction. Because if the city is not going to develop by articulation, the new city that Le Corbusier will produce will also fall behind in the face of technology after a while. In that case, will this city also be completely demolished and rebuilt? Le Corbusier's contradiction is that he presents the city he will build as if it will last forever. However, existence and the design of existence (the search for truth) are both existences, and therefore, far from being fixed, they are constantly reinterpreted, paraphrased and re-created (Snyder 1991:17). The city is an organism that cannot and will never be completed. It is always in existence.

Another contradiction of Le Corbusier is that although he thought that the buildings created by a single "genius" artist and his divinely inspired buildings were no longer valid and therefore argued that the singular "genius" architect was replaced by " collective" engineers, ironically, he himself assumed the role of the "genius" planner. Although Le Corbusier claimed that he accepted mathematics and geometry as principles, he rejected anything other than his own design and, just like a "genius" artist, he imposed his interpretation of design over everything else. Le Corbusier brackets the sovereignty of the "genius" one-man regimes he criticizes in favor of his own "genius" one-man regime.

The utopian architect attitude of Le Corbusier utilizes reasoning, which he considers to be rational, as a tool of power. Since he has a precise rational understanding, he does not need an environment of consensus and negotiation with "ordinary" people who have not reached this understanding. The omnipotent architect subject argues that all other stakeholders of society should obey his reason (Tanyeli 2017:121). In Le Corbusier's utopian urban design, no one but Le Corbusier knows the most favorable urban design. Like a savior, as the one who knows, Le Corbusier presents the heaven on earth to these masses who are ignorant of what is good for them. Corbusier – the architect-subject who knows– turned the city into his object and assigned himself the task of inventing and building it from the beginning to the end.

Whereas in today's metropolitanized cities, the city is no longer the object of the planner, but the subject of the planner. It is not the planner who will shape the city, but the city that will shape the planner. An architectural production independent of mass culture is not possible.

Since the nineteenth century, the world has been rapidly urbanizing and now urbanization has been escalating towards the metropolitan dimension. Metropolitanization, on the other hand, is dragging cities further towards the subordination of plurality and the destruction of uniformity. While urban planning in the nineteenth and twentieth centuries was concerned with the homogeneity of the physical environment and the integrity of identity, as Le Corbusier did, today the homogeneity of the past can be seen to be a dream in metropolises. Cities are now constituted by different cultural existences, preferences, living habits, ethnic groups, marginalities and subcultural communities. Who can argue that cities should be planned in such a way when the world is not on a path towards homogeneity, the unity of identity or a cultural consensus (Tanyeli 2017:72-3)? It has become impossible for a single architect to plan today's metropolises.

It is also doubtful that geometry, which Le Corbusier instrumentalized for a planning that would establish order, is the right instrument for urban planning. Like the Cartesian philosophy that allowed the algebraic to correspond to the geometric, Le Corbusier assumed a system that would allow architects to match the abstract function or mathematical rationality to the concrete form. The title "Is Descartes American?" in The Radiant City, which he used to point to the rationality of American urban planning, is the result of this assumption (Corbusier 1967: 127). Today, however, the relationship between architecture and mathematics is being strongly criticized as being too linear. It seems impossible to think of what is described under the name of "function" in architecture as a mathematical function, or to believe that it is an object that can be represented as a geometric drawing in a coordinate system. The relationship that is possible with the tautological logic of mathematics does not work in the social world of architecture (Tanyeli 2017:313-4). Le Corbusier's utopia, which seems perfect on paper, fails to find a resonance in the real world, exactly like the entire utopian literature.

Le Corbusier's Second Utopia: The Radiant City

Le Corbusier's design of the *Radiant City* is similar to the Contemporary City in many ways, but reflects a sharper hierarchy. In his proposal for the Radiant City, Le Corbusier, as in the Contemporary City, envisions collective governance in an orderly urban environment, aiming to reflect harmony on the urban structure and the lives of citizens. However, there is now an urban utopia in which the center is much more authoritarian. The Great Depression of 1929, which shook the whole world, changed Le Corbusier.

With the Great Depression, production in the Western world dropped to half of its pre-Great Depression level and unemployment reached 25%. However, in the same period, in the USSR, which designed its economy through central planning, the Soviets doubled their production with the Five-Year Development Plan, full employment was achieved in Germany with the planned economy management put into effect by Hitler, and Italy made great economic breakthroughs. Le Corbusier was influenced by these great economic successes, and in the 1930s he began to believe in dictatorial governments rather than individual freedom. This change in him directly affected the ideal city utopias he designed.

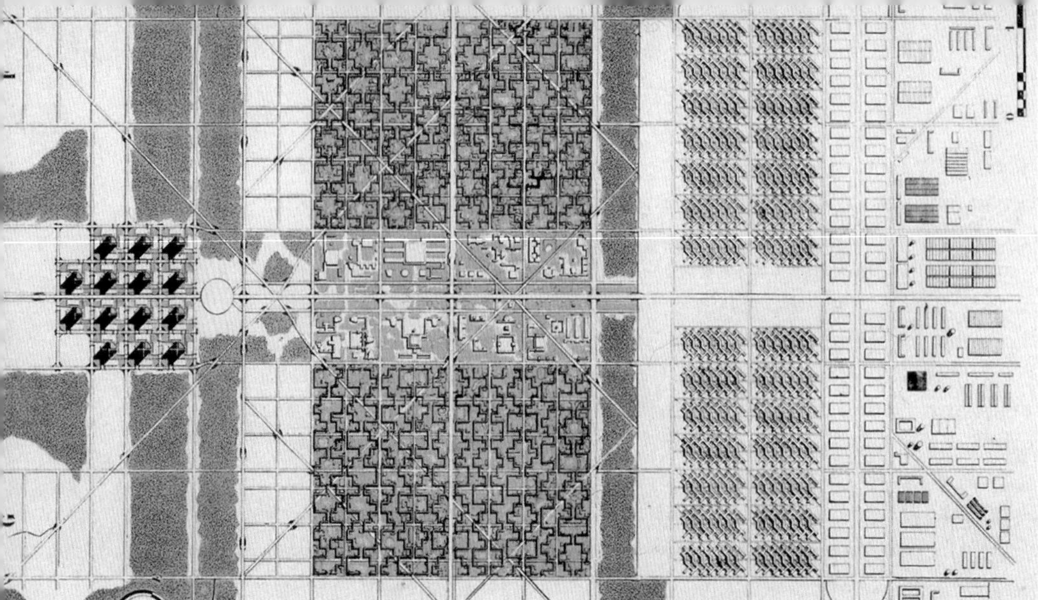

For the Le Corbusier of the 1930s, the freedom of the individual is still absolute, but only in private life. The individual can organize parties and events with his neighbors, but he cannot change the system. It makes no sense for society to vote on important questions concerning the allocation of its resources. Such matters should be determined by experts and applied objectively.

Le Corbusier is of the opinion that the city, created with a humanist understanding, has to be supplemented by a classless society. In the Radiant City, a complex synthesis of the contemporary city devoid of trusts, every element of the production process is managed by higher decision-making bodies according to a single plan. In this plan, holistic management would replace the market and specialists would shape their productive capacities according to the needs of society. The harmony Le Corbusier envisioned for urban restructuring would now be imposed on all production.

Like the Contemporary City, in the Radiant City, the ideal of freedom is reflected in the residential area and the ideal of participation in the collective management structure. The relationship of dependency between the ideal of production and the administrative hierarchy in the Radiant City, which symbolizes the city of organization and freedom, is more hierarchical than in the Contemporary City. The synthesis of freedom and order proposed by Le Corbusier, who aims to create a society based on unity of belief and action, will be made possible by the removal of politics from the private sphere of the ideal city, thereby eradicating crime and poverty.

Le Corbusier did not position the administrative towers in the center of the City of Light. The guest of honor of the Radiant City is the residential area. But the residential area has now undergone a major transformation. The capitalism and market economy that led him to divide the housing

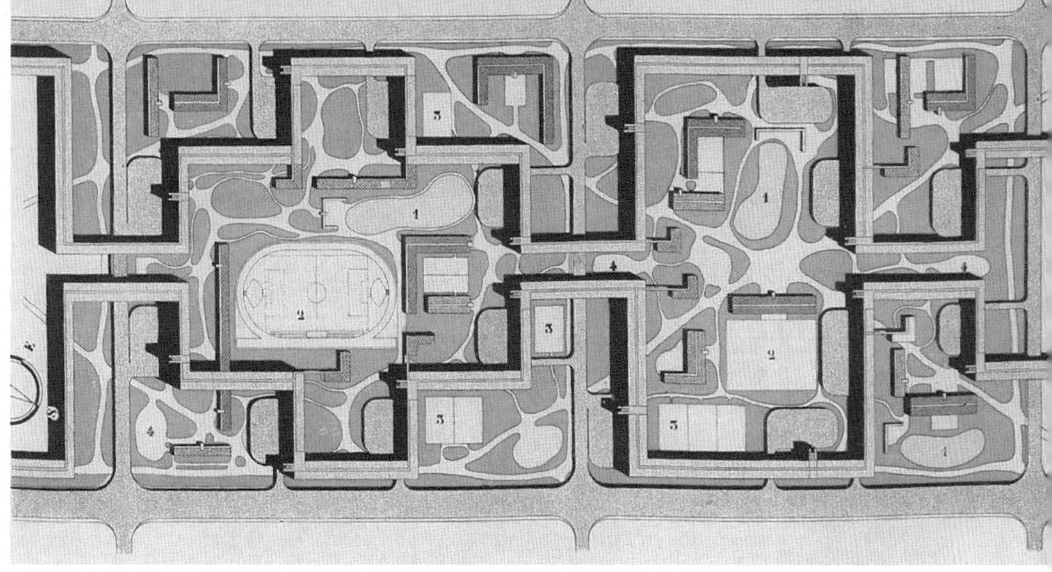

areas in the Modern City into classes, with the elites in the center and the proletariat in the periphery.

Le Corbusier, who had lost his enthusiasm for workers' rights, is now a revolutionary syndicalist who advocates a completely different understanding of workers' rights. The residential area reflects Le Corbusier's belief that the world of freedom must be egalitarian; he designs a classless city.

In the residential units called "Unité", which constitute the space of freedom and abundance that Le Corbusier planned for the elite class, apartment buildings are organized on the basis of industrial hierarchy and the collective provision of urban services is aimed. The most important feature of Le Corbusier's Unité units, which envisioned a new family order in which men and women could work full-time equally, is that they offer a new understanding of the family. Surrounded by large green areas, the skyscrapers tend to preserve the natural landscape. The Unité units, high-rise apartment blocks in which Le Corbusier gave the service provision a collective character, are located at the center of the Radiant City. Unités are 50-meter-high neighborhoods accommodating 2,700 people, each apartment building functioning as a vertical village. These buildings reflect Le Corbusier's principles of contemporary housing. According to him, the city of the future should be the Radiant City, where glass and steel skyscrapers rise, bringing order and harmony to the population density and creating an efficient and ostentatious center for the imposing bureaucracies that govern society.

In Unité, the emphasis is not on individual apartments, but on the communal services offered to all residents. The Unité has a large number of workshops for traditional crafts that are technically inapplicable in mass-production industries. In these workshops, there are meeting places of different sizes for participatory activities that have no place in hierarchical production spaces. There are cafés, restaurants and shops for socializing. Each Unité has a full-scale gym, rooftop tennis courts and swimming pools. High-rise buildings occupy only 15% of the land, and the open space around them is devoted to carefully designed playgrounds, gardens and parks.

The utopia of the Radiant City excludes the traditional family unit, where men are responsible for earning money and women for domestic service. Le Corbusier dreams of a society in which men and women will work equally and full-time. In Unité, cooking, cleaning and child-rearing are services provided by the community. Each building has its own nursery, kindergarten and primary school, communal laundry, cleaning service and food shop.

Le Corbusier's design of strict zoning and geometric plan layout was used in Punjab, India, in 1949, and was applied in Brasilia, the capital of Brazil, designed by two Brazilian architects, when Brasilia was built from scratch on an empty lot. Following Le Corbusier's recommendations of a perfect geometric layout, identical housing units and a sharp functional division, the construction of the city, financed entirely by the Brazilian government, sought to achieve social equality and justice through Le Corbusier's principles. However, the results were not quite as Le Corbusier had expected, and social inequality and crime rates were high in these cities.

PLUG-IN URBAN UTOPIA: ARCHIGRAM

Archigram emerged as a playful and popular representation of a future built on technology in the avant-garde architecture of the 1960s. Archigram originated as a cheap zine; later, it became known as the name of the group and finally as a method of architectural representation consisting of drawings and collages. Taking its name from the telegraph, a technological communication tool of the period, Archigram (ARCHItectural teleGRAM) is a letter-magazine hybrid that aims to influence the architectural environment by questioning the status quo (Özkuş 2005:84). It was born as a reaction to the stereotypical understanding of modern architecture and became the symbol of technology-information based architecture of the future.

The Archigram group was founded in the 1960s in England by a group of architects including Peter Cook, Dennis Crampton, Michael Webb, David Greene, Warren Chalk and Ron Herron. The group explained that their basic idea was to explore a whole new language and way of thinking that paralleled space capsules, calculators and devices of the electro-atomic age. Essentially, it was about bringing high technology to a level where it could respond to all the problems of society, and accepting concepts such as "masses of people" and "silos of individuals" in urban design.

The members of the Archigram group argued that rational urbanization should be a combination of the functions of the city, which were handled piecemeal. For this, they envisioned megastructures that would incorporate urban functions as a whole. Constant's dream of "New Babylon" sought

an answer to the functional distinction between buildings and parts of the city to this end. Following Constant's lead, the British Archigram group also presented Peter Cook's "Plug-in City" at the "Living City" exhibition of 1964. In "Plug-in City", Peter Cook defined the entire city in terms of structures consisting of capsules that can be plugged in and out of the main structure according to the designated function.

Plug-in City is a network of giant-sized space structures that can fit into any terrain topography. In the project, the capsules, which are used as living spaces and discarded when they become obsolete, are attached to the towers, which also contain the plumbing system. Thus, the urban structure can develop in all directions.

Considered close to constructivist architecture due to its passion for technology, Archigram projects have sometimes been criticized as fascist urban fictions because they promote consumption and the commercial attitude it brings with it. Nevertheless, despite these criticisms, Archigram asserts that there is no political side behind its work. The importance of consumption and media culture is inevitable for the members of Archigram, who try to convey their ideas only through drawings and visuals, and extract their materials from popular culture. Particularly influenced by science fiction, Archigram members took the cover of *Archigram No.4 Amazing Archigram* from the cover of the August 1928 issue of *Amazing Stories*, a classic of science fiction comics. They also used the same language not only on the cover but also inside.

The emergence of Archigram is not only a reflection of the popular culture of the 1960s on the art and architecture scene, but also technological developments. In the post-war period, defined by Reyner Banham as the "second machine age", with the introduction of many appliances such as hair dryers, televisions and washing machines into homes, technology was not only incorporated into life, but it was also understood to be something changeable and accessible. Archigram's megastructures, on the other hand, are utopias that emerged with the belief in the inexhaustibility of all these technological developments. Archigrammers, starting from the idea that not only technology but also cities are in an endless change and mobility, argued that the biggest problem in the organization of a city is the coherent combination of parts of different functions and scales. They were more interested in the services a building offers to its users rather than how beautiful or ugly it is, whether it is monumental or not, or whether it is in harmony with the surrounding buildings. Archigram members, speaking of a service network created independently of time and space, have argued that energy and communication are sufficient for architecture, and where these are present, the architectural environment will form spontaneously.

It can be said that various concepts such as mountable-dismountable, mobile, interactive, which we frequently encounter in Archigram's architecture, are concepts that have taken place in the architecture and art community today. Archigram's proposals served towards a new agenda where displacement, metamorphosis and time replaced stasis, where consumption, lifestyle and discontinuity became programs and human civilization became an electronic surface covering the earth (Erdem 2005:83). The ideas put forward by Archigram —a representative of the avant-garde architecture of the 1960s that produced urban utopias— and the attitude it adopted based on consumption and popular culture in the way it put forward these, instead of advocating for the consumer society, paved the way for purging the discourses on architecture and the city from pre-modern remnants with a radical attitude. Archigram is among the first representatives of a future architecture based on technology and information, as opposed to the stereotypical singular solution approach of modern architecture.

In this era, technology enters completely into human life and becomes easily accessible and changeable. Archigram expressed their urban foresights reflecting this endless development and mobility of technology through collages, drawings and the popular means of communication of their time.

Within the Archigram group, the first breaking point lies in their opposition to "traditional" architecture. Archigram produced designs that would not be realized, could not be realized, would remain only on paper, as if to imply that functionality was not a necessity, especially against the Bauhaus' simple and even cold attitude that constructed all architectural elements from a functional point of view. However, within these designs, there are also formal, functional structures that are not far from Bauhaus. We cannot overlook the exaggerated functionality of "plug-in" towers and dismountable cabins that take functionality to the extreme. It is intrinsically contradictory to wage a war against functionalism and an understanding of architectural form that traces its origins to simple geometric shapes through an even

more exaggerated functionalism and a simulation whose building blocks are based on a similar understanding of form. Such a position would only serve to nourish the modern, let alone destroy it.

The second breaking point arises when the concepts of mobility and mobility are linked to freedom. In buildings, everything and everyone is in constant motion. Even cities move in accordance with the mobility required by modern life. This mobility of the structure gives the impression that the individual is also mobile and "therefore" free. But this is just a simulation, similar to modern society. The fact that the city moves does not mean that you move too. As long as your workplace, your residence, and the various spaces where you fulfill your social needs are located within the same city-universe, the movement of the city means nothing to the individuals of utopia. Moreover, given that the dwellings are all constructed as standard rectangular prisms, it does not matter where the dwelling is positioned by crane. The dwelling is always the same. And considering the sophistication of the transportation network, it doesn't matter where the dwelling is located. Even if physically relocated, the dwelling of utopia will be psychologically uniform and fixed.

When we examine the design proposals of the Archigram group in 1964, "Plug-in City", "Living City" and "Walking City", we see that the ideas they advocate are reflected in the cities they envision. They accept the continuous growth and expansion of the city as an irrefutable fact and bring together parts of different functions and scales within this expansion. While constructing this unity, they are also looking for an answer to the question: How can an alternative be offered to the universal city type presented in modern urban planning? They propose kinetic living spaces composed of disconnected modular units. The fact that these units are both disconnected and interrelated replaces the unpredictable, monotonous spaces that we encounter in modern urbanism in the name of creating a whole (Kahya 2007:28-9). Archigram members are particularly interested in the services that a space provides to its users. They argued that the space can fully meet human needs by equipping it with technological tools.

UTOPIAS IN POST-INDUSTRIAL SOCIETY

"What I wanted to do is look at New York as if there had been a plan. Europeans have a lot of manifestos but then don't realize something, but in New York there was a lot of realization but no manifesto." (Koolhaas 1978:7)

In the postmodern or post-industrial period, contemporary architecture comes into close conflict with modernism. Postmodernism is radically skeptical of all the assumptions of modernism, and through the method of deconstruction it attempts to dismantle the entire structure of modernism, stripping it of the meanings it signifies as a whole. As a counter-attempt to macro-narratives, to a holistic understanding of the world, to all modeling from the top, it gives credence to micro-narratives, to the incomprehensibility of the world, and to practices from below.

With postmodern architecture, modernism's perception of producing utopia is also broken. The idea of an ideal city that would function like a machine, planned by a single mind, standing alone at a desk and forcing the masses to comply with this plan, can no longer enforced. Instead, within the framework of the market economy, it evolves into meeting at the point of compromise where consumers and producers converge. This new architectural perspective's relationship with space is thus completely transformed. A new space is envisioned that claims to liberate the subject from the constraints of both modernism and modernity, to reunite the subject with nature, to unleash the subject's nomadic, social and creative tendencies, to restore the old magic to his sensory experience of the world, and to enable him to meet the laws of the material universe with a technology that functions in harmony with formation, spontaneous organization and complexity.

In this contemporary understanding of architecture, sometimes referred to as "new architecture", sometimes as "projectist", "post-critical" or "Deleuzean", figures such as Greg Lynn, Zaha Hadid, Alejandro Zaera-Polo, Farshid Moussavi, Reiser+Umemoto, Lars Spuybroek take a stance that prioritizes freedom, as opposed to a modernist utopian and imposing attitude against freedoms for the sake of realizing an ideal urban planning. They firmly reject hierarchical planning and glorify spontaneous arrangements and spontaneous organizations instead of those produced by a higher mind (D. Spencer 2016:16). The postmodernist approach to architecture makes the ideal city design questionable. In idealized architectural forms, the scale changes, the approach is renewed, and the single decision-maker is replaced by the consensus point where the supply and demand curve intersects within the framework of the market economy.

The reason for this change in architecture is the negative change in the belief in modernist assumptions. Contrary to modernist assumptions, in postmodernist architectural theory, individuals can only acquire a very limited knowledge of the world's extremely complex ontology. Therefore, the planning of society or cities by individuals is a baseless presumption. The market is more adept than the state at calculating, processing and regulating society without interference. Therefore, in urban planning, it is important not to do what is rational on paper, but the expectations of the market, even if they are irrational. In postmodern thought, irrationality is seen as capable of sensing many functional situations that rationality cannot see.

Considering that the market will produce the most efficient combination and arrangement in land use or urban planning, and the forms that can achieve the highest synergy, in the contemporary architectural approach, the architect's clients, i.e., the market, determines the program of land use and the resulting urban and architectural order (Schumacher 2013:120). Instead of the utopian urban planning's attitude towards the domination of the masses, the goal is to highlight subjectivity (Foucault 2007:83). Subjects are not restricted, isolated, and normative standards are not imposed on their attitudes and behaviors and the way they use the city.

In this consensualist approach, models of spontaneous organization, formation and complexity are adopted; cybernetics, systems theory and ecological thinking are defended, the weaknesses of planning are criticized and evolutionary transformations are praised. This architectural approach rejects the enlightened subject of modernity; the subject is a being that can adapt to its environment and is motivated by emotions rather than rationality. As the definition of the subject changes, so does the conception of the ideal city in which the subject will live and the appropriate architecture.

Postmodernism holds that, unlike the modernist abstract mind, which thinks it can know everything, one knows nothing. The world is too complex. In contrast, the perspective of the individual is too narrow to comprehend, let alone direct the course of the world. Whatever he does, he does blindly. We cannot know the rules that govern the social order in which we live. These rules, made up of traditions, institutions, customs and attitudes, are never the conscious designs of the human mind; they have all evolved spontaneously over time. In this view, attributing the origins of cultural institutions, architectural structures, and ideal urban designs to inventions or designs is nothing but a gigantic mistake made by rationalists (Hayck 2013:11). The unpredictable and the unpredictable are the sine qua non conditions for the experience of freedom and the possibility of progress, since progress is maximally dependent on opportunities created by chance and accidents (Hayek 2013:27). What gave rise to all modern planning and the totalitarianism it engenders is the "conscious planning" that rationalism seeks to realize by squeezing society into its own abstract mind. Whereas, according to postmoderns, the outcome of planning is, at best, tyranny. Humans have not imposed on the world a pattern created by their own reason. Rationality is a system that is constantly changing as a result of its effort to adapt to its environment (Hayek 2006:22). Social order cannot be grasped in its totality and any structure that attempts to control, manage or invent this order is on the road to totalitarianism (Foucault 2008:110). The idea that spontaneity and the decision-making process of the society is sanctified instead of top-down planning, and that the market should be the authority that decides everything, manifests itself in architecture and urban planning with Adam Smith's "invisible hand" analogy (Polanyi 1998:196). The postmodern architectural approach emphasizes the liberating effect of the polycentric market against the oppressive imposition of a single mind in urban planning. Cities, precisely because of their complexity, cannot be artificially organized by external interventions or from a single center. They can only be determined spontaneously and immanently, through the interaction and coordination of their elements, that is, through the market. Only by relying on "self-organizing" supra-personal forces that create spontaneous patterns, we can transcend the capacity of individual minds. In an attempt to comprehend the world with such assumptions, the more comprehensive and detailed a plan is, the greater the dystopia it leads to.

This new assumption and philosophy in architecture and urban planning was quick to create various fields of application for itself. By the 1970s, thousands of commune settlements were established in the US alone. These communes, established far away from the cities, attempted to distance themselves from the power structures of modernism instead of directly challenging them. In Drop City in Southern Colorado, as well as in many other communes modeled after it, the "new communards" manifested themselves as small group organizations based on cooperation (Turner 2008:4). These groups are also very attentive to interacting with each other.

Postmodern architecture rejects Platonic perfection and the search for perfection, arguing that no single mind in architecture can find the "true" and "ideal" urban planning. Hadid said this in her 2004 Pritzker Prize acceptance speech: "I believe that the complexities and the dynamism of contemporary life cannot be cast into the simple platonic forms provided by the classical canon, nor does the modern style afford enough means of articulation. We have to deal with social diagrams that are more complex and layered when compared with the social programs of the early modern period." (Hadid, 2004). However, this postmodern approach does not perceive architecture as a completely "free form". It recognizes a specific legitimacy for contemporary architecture. Unlike utopian architectural approaches, this field of legitimacy is not sharply delineated, it is ambiguous and prone to be marked by tendencies. In Hadid's words, "They proliferate infinite variations rather than operating via the repetition of discrete types. They are indeterminate and leave room for active interpretation on the part of the inhabitants." (Lavin 2011:28). Schumacher, on the other hand, expresses his views as: "I am trying to imagine a radical free-market urbanism. ... I am trying to theorize an architectural discourse that does not rely on or create its order through state planning and heavy central, prescriptive regulation but could be possible through open-ended interventions by many participants." (Schumacher & Eisenman, 2013:28). In this sense, architects such as Hadid and Schumacher argue that the formal complexity of their work corresponds precisely to the social complexity of the conditions that architecture serves.

In contrast to the modernist utopian search for a pure order, the new ground on which architectural discourse and practices will be based is complexity. Complexity is seen as the harbinger of a new advanced order in which productivity, creativity and innovation are freed from the interventions of an external mind and left to the market choice of a public base. Only complex mechanisms of choice and taste can capture complex urban structures. Therefore, there is a shift from macro-planning to micro-planning, from the order produced by a single mind to the reconciliation of the complexity produced by multiple minds with complex urban structures. Utopian arrangements are thought to bring dystopian destruction.

"DEGENERATE UTOPIAS": DISNEYLAND AND SHOPPING MALLS

Nowadays, the postmodern city has a structure where entertainment stands out. Areas with a high concentration of places to spend leisure time are

now considered the center of the city. In this framework, spectacular entertainment centers such as restaurants, bars, shopping malls and casinos begin to be perceived as an indicator of the quality of the city. Such places are expressions of the desire to end the fragmentation of everyday life into separate practices, times and spaces (Lefebvre 2000:385). As well as providing entertainment, such service centers also provide employment for city dwellers. However, in addition to this flashy and illuminated face of the postmodern city, there is also a dark side. On this dark side, there are the ghettos, those living in public housing, the poor, the homeless, who are almost completely excluded from the city's glamorous side. Today, the postmodern city is polarized to a degree never seen before in any city (Dear 2000:191). This division is partially masked by the illusion created by print and visual media. Through the computer or television screens in their homes, city dwellers watch the same programs and have the chance to build a common culture. Thus, even if their economic worlds are different, there is a visual commonality. Baudrillard attempts to explain this situation by stating that the difference between reality and dream has disappeared and the entire city has been transformed into a huge amusement park. According to Baudrillard, the birth of amusement parks and the spread of entertainment and leisure activities have changed the city. In this context, he points to Disneyland as the most utopian initiative. Baudrillard defines Disneyland as "a perfect model in which entire orders of simulacra are intertwined" (Baudrillard 2014:29). According to him, all cities now structure themselves by taking Disneyland as an example.

Designed as a theme park, Disneyland is a utopian space decorated with the heroes of the famous animator and filmmaker Walt Disney and reflecting the universe he created, aiming to break all connections with one's daily life and include one in Disney's fairytale alternative universe.

This city is a space of leisure, spontaneity and fun. It offers opportunities for excitement and engaging experiences. Disneyland's status as a phase of Epcot, the utopian city Walt Disney designed in his last years –the ideal city–, is the ultimate expression of this.

There is indeed a great distance between Plato and Walt Disney, which demonstrates the diversity of the ideal city tradition. Nevertheless, the main feature that the *Republic* and Epcot share is that they are both systematically designed environments (Kumar 1991:31). Although the *Republic* was never implemented, the utopian space called Disneyland was realized, the first of which opened in 1955 in Anaheim, California, on 160 acres of land. Since its opening, Disneyland has opened a number of new and expanded attractions, including New Orleans Square in 1966, Bear Country (now Critter Country) in 1972, Mickey's Toontown in 1993, and Star Wars: Galaxy Edge in 2019 (Savvas, 2017). The number of people who have visited Disneyland from its establishment in 1955 to 2019 is 726 million. That's more than all other theme parks in the world combined. In 2018 alone, the park attracted 18.6 million visitors. In 2018, the total number of visitors to Disneylands around the world was 157 million (TEA/AE-COM 2019:9). The number of employees in Disneylands is 30,000. These gigantic figures show us how big an organization Disneyland is and how big a center of attraction it is.

But Disneyland is not designed as a place to live in permanently. It is not a place to move to and then remain in for a lifetime. On the contrary, it alludes to discontinuity and is disguised as a day-to-day floating utopia squeezed in the middle of regular everyday life. Marin describes this condition of Disneyland as "degenerate utopia". According to Marin, Disneyland is a supposedly happy, harmonious and conflict-free space; Disneyland, which aims to calm, soften and entertain, is isolated from the "real" world outside by the fetishism of commodity culture (qt. in Harvey 2000:205). Produced as a world of pure fantasy, through the collaboration of technology and imagination, Disneyland presents a futuristic utopia.

Disneyland is characterized as a "degenerate utopia" because, contrary to the utopian tradition, instead of overthrowing and replacing the existing system in a revolutionary way, Disneyland reinforces the existing system. Disneyland offers its visitors a world that they do not live in on a daily basis, but this world is not a critique or an alternative to the "real" world in which they live, on the contrary, it is an enhanced version of it. It directly embraces and glorifies the fetishism of commodity culture produced by the liberal market economy. In this sense, it also differs from the dystopias that utopias produce in practice. Since there is no intention to be thrown out of the system, and since it provides an experience in which the codes of the system itself are magnified, it does not involve the dangers and risks that might derail the purpose of building an ideal alternative world. It is like an advanced version of the existing world. Moreover, the existing world, within the framework of the capitalist system, actually strives to resemble Disneyland. In this sense, Disneyland represents a design, movement and practice aimed at perfecting the status quo within itself.

The most flawless version of the existing system, which is a safe, climate-controlled, pleasure- and shopping-oriented modeling within an area surrounded by walls with clear boundaries, has spread around the world in the form of shopping malls. Shopping malls are designed as important meeting places where many different activities can take place with their closed and climate-controlled physical environment and safe social environment, rather than just centers where shopping activities are aimed to take place. Those who walk through the shopping centers are relatively free from the unpredictability of adverse weather conditions as well as the unpredictability of criminal acts that can disturb them on the city streets (Ritzer 2014:157). The aesthetic qualities of the space increase the satisfaction of the users of the space, attract potential users to the space and give people morale by distracting them from the urban pressure. With the designer's touch, these buildings appear as important places of "pleasure and enjoyment".

Shopping centers are detached from their surroundings and contexts, they are introverted. There is a contemporary public space, an urban space, designed as an interior within the structure. A shopping center is a building type that creates new urban focal points by integrating a large number of stores with one or a few department stores, a supermarket/hypermarket and social activity areas in a well-climatized and illuminated environment, with its functions and formal features.

In these freely accessible spaces, there is no obligation to buy, and window-shopping is common. Consumers are allowed to look at, grasp and try out the products in a carnival-like atmosphere. Consumers try commodities that do not belong to them in this space (Fiske 2000:314). This space offers a different world to the person and allows them to make direct contact with this world.

People do other things in shopping centers along with the act of buying; for example, they participate in experiences. The consumer combines buying and consuming in a short period of time or in an event in the shopping center. Although such purchases and consumption involve tangible or intangible goods, the act of consumption still remains experiential. This is especially the case when eating in a restaurant, walking around, sitting down to rest, going to the movies, visiting an art gallery. In this sense, the shopping center contains resources for experiences that are not commodified, and the world of objects is of secondary importance here (Falk 1997:5). There is a new universe in the shopping center.

The urban space reconstructed within the shopping center loses its self-renewing quality and becomes a "space created at once" within a "closed box". Behind the rich image created through the decorative arrangements and landscape elements used in the urban/public space that is taken into the interior (constructed), lies a monotonous and user-directed spatial organization. In the building, the features of the real urban space are superficially simulated in order to recreate the complex, chaotic environment of the city in a sterile environment. In Baudrillard's words, in the shopping center, "where everything is taken over and superseded in the ease and translucidity of an abstract `happiness', defined solely by the resolution of tensions." (Baudrillard, 1998:29). These structures turn into an artificial urban space designed with a focus on commercial success, which can be controlled and easily manipulated. Today, shopping malls are surreal spaces where entertainment elements such as carousels and ice skating arenas, technological elements such as panoramic elevators and escalators, and architectural elements such as arches, domes and bridges, which have no semantic or spatial relationship with each other, come together.

FROM DEFEATING NATURE TO MAKING NATURE RENEWABLE IN URBAN DESIGN: ECOTOPIA

Ecological utopias emerged in the 1970s, when ecology became a part of world politics. Until then, in utopias, nature was perceived as a rational being, a phenomenon that would serve the purposes of man with an abstract mind, a resource that he could consume without any conscientious responsibility, a capital whose renewability did not need to be considered. The role of nature in urban planning was not to be respected by the city, but for it to contribute to the aesthetics of the city with small touches. However, since the 1970s, developments in the science of ecology as well as the environmental problems experienced in contemporary cities, the psychological tensions caused by excessive concretization, congestion, the general climate change, and the fact that the individual no longer feels at home in the city, but like a hostage, have led some people away from social, economic or spatial utopias and towards ecological utopias. Thus, in the search for the perfect city, the compatibility of the city with nature manifests itself as a new utopian condition or form.

The assumptions shared by different thinkers of ecological thought suggest that the workings of the human mind, nature, art and computers are patterns emerging from the interaction of materials and energies in specific environments. Since everything comes into existence through the interaction with its outside, the planning of cities cannot be in the hands of a ruling external force (D. Spencer 2016:73). The city can only survive if it is structured in a way that is intrinsic to the functioning of the system.

Ecological utopias first appear in utopian literature through writers such as Ernest Callenbach, Ursula Le Guin, Frank Herbert and Marge Piercy. Ecological utopias do not completely reject technology, but are extremely cautious about it. Unlike other forms of utopia, they do not encourage production. They do not find the meaning of human existence in producing or consuming. Therefore, they also exclude consumption as a method of happiness. In ecological utopias, consumption and production are both low.

In Ernest Callenbach's famous ecological utopia *Ecotopia*, published in 1975, Washington, Oregon and Northern California secede from the US in 1980 for political, economic and ecological reasons and declare their independence. The reason for the region's secession from the US was the reaction to the US policy of "industrialization at all costs" (Bagschik 1996:147). In Ecotopia, people live together with other species without disturbing the natural balance. They equate work with play and entertainment. Families, which form the basis of society, are in units of 5 to 20 people. In urban planning, there is no district-type organization that divides cities into various subdivisions. Instead, quieter and smaller cities are created. The ideal city population is between 40,000 and 50,000. Transportation is provided by electric taxis, minibuses, battery-powered buses and bicycles within the city, using renewable and environmentally friendly energy sources, and by rail between cities (Callenbach 1990:23). The city is not divided into different areas such as commerce, shopping centers and residences; all areas coexist.

Ecotopians have restricted technological development to be in harmony with the ecological system and abandoned excessive consumption patterns. With long-term economic policies, production is localized in each city and region. Although private property is still valid in Ecotopia, nature is considered a public good and is prioritized over both social and economic interests. In the factories where a semi-automated system is established in the production process, weekly working hours are reduced to 20-24 hours. The ecotopian ethic of living in balance with nature is reflected in the production and consumption processes through industrial activities and work programs. The habit of reuse is practiced in every field. Agriculture, fisheries and forestry enterprises, which have reached a permanent balance through the reuse of wastes, have been localized, and health services have been expanded and made cheaper.

Ecotopians are oriented towards renewable energy sources such as solar energy, geothermal heat, water and wind. All citizens are well equipped and knowledgeable about the environment and the protection of environmental values. People who damage environmental resources face heavy prison sentences.

It was recognized that the preservation of plant and animal species diversity depends on reducing population pressure on natural resources, and through various birth control methods, the population of Ecotopia has been reduced over the last 15 years. In the second stage, new small-scale cities were established by spreading the population density in large cities in

The image
of Ernest
Callenbach's
Ecotopia
project
by Mark
Harrison

order to radically localize the economic life of the country. Ecotopians have also allowed the expansion of small regional communities, provided that ecological and cultural resources are preserved. At the end of long political struggles during the independence process, the regions inhabited by black people gained the title of city-state within Ecotopia, and the inhabitants of these regions established their own administrative units and industrial systems. Ecotopia's president is a woman, and she is the leader of the Fight for Life Party, whose majority of members are women. In other words, blacks and women, the most disadvantaged members of society under white, European and male-dominated modernism, have become first-class citizens of Ecotopia.

Ecotopia does not discuss the details of urban planning in detail. The significance of this work is that it is the articulation of a new utopian city in the ecotopia genre. Ecotopia is conceived in a closed geographical area, surrounded by the Sierra Nevada Mountains. In a society based on small urban communities, new cities are built while empty lands are transformed into woodlands, fruit plantations and gardens. Streams that were closed during the US era are reopened to nature within the city, and efforts are made to integrate the city with natural elements. The chaos created by the crowded masses is replaced by silence and peace. The majestic Market Street Boulevard, which cuts through the city, has been replaced by a shopping center adorned with thousands of trees and flowers. The street where bicycles, electric taxis and minibuses used to flow by has narrowed to a two-lane road with bike lanes, fountains, sculptures, kiosks, benches and small gardens. Pergolas scattered throughout the pedestrian zone serve as shelters against adverse weather conditions. Large stores and factories in small towns are integrated with an underground conveyor belt system to facilitate distribution services. In Ecotopia, small-scale urban development is supported, while urban-rural continuity is aimed by introducing elements of rural life into existing large cities.

Callenbach's Ecotopia proposes a social organization open to technological development and in harmony with nature. As an example of ecological utopia, an industrial structure, economic system and social order compatible with ecological values are desired in Ecotopia.

The ideal city design in the form of ecotopia is not limited to literature. Just as there are various practices that precede Ecotopia, some practical experiments are also attempted within the framework of Ecotopia. In these experiments, existing cities are left alone with their problems and ecological utopias that design brand new cities are produced.

In practice, the principles of the pioneers of ecotopia have gradually developed over time. Howard's Garden-City movement can be shown as the pioneer of these principles. In Garden-City, Howard focused on limiting

the size of the city and protecting nature. Following Howard, in the 1940s Frank Lloyd Wright suggested the use of local building materials, Ralph Erskine suggested orientation to the south, façade planting and greening. In the 1960s, practices in the USA and Europe included the use of renewable energy, the use of local materials, recycling, energy saving; in the 1970s, Bengt Warne incorporated principles such as not harming and even improving nature with housing, the use of rainwater and gray water, the use of organic waste, the use of heated air in housing, the use of soil heat into the ecological design process.

One of the greatest ecological utopias of our time in terms of ecological design, and perhaps the main one, is Auroville, which was designed in India and put into practice in 1968. Auroville is both an ecological utopia and the realization of a spiritual space. At the inauguration of this ideal urban design, representatives from all states of India were present, as well as participants from 124 different countries. Five thousand people attended this inauguration ceremony and all the representatives brought symbolic amounts of soil from their respective countries to mix with the soil of Auroville (UNESCO, 1972). The formation of Auroville was also approved by UNESCO within the framework of the supervision of intercultural cooperation and development and UNESCO declared Auroville "the universal city of the future" with its multicultural structure (https://www.auroville.org/contents/538).

Auroville, designed as a galaxy, is divided into various zones such as Peace Zone, Industrial Zone, Residential Zone, International Zone, Cultural Zone and Green Circle. The Peace Zone is located in the center of the city. The Industrial Zone is located in the north of the city, but it is green industry, not heavy industry. The primary task of this zone is to ensure the economic independence of Auroville. It hosts small-scale industry, handicrafts, training centers and municipal administration. The Residential Zone is organized for residential purposes and is the largest zone. Only 45% of the area is dedicated to buildings. The rest is protected as green space. In the International Zone, many different nations have cultural clubs with their own cultural values. The aim is to build a humanist unity through national diversity. In the cultural zone there are institutions for education, arts, culture and sports activities, where practice and research are carried out simultaneously. The so-called Green Circle consists of a 1.25 kilometer radius of green space that wraps around a 1.25 kilometer radius of the urban area. This area includes organic farms, gardens and forests.

Auroville was designed with the motto "the city the world needs" and the settlement of 50,000 people is surrounded by a green belt. According to the city's website, its purpose is to "realize human unification" (www.auroville.org). The city is in the middle of four large local villages. Matrimandir, the spiritual space of Auroville, is the center of the city. Apart from the peace zone in which Matrimandir is located, there are different zones in the city such as the green industrial zone, the international zone, the commercial zone and the residential zone. Thirty-five hectares in size, the city is home to some 1,500 inhabitants from 35 different countries according to 2001 statistics.

The utopia of Auroville is a unique and valuable initiative as one of the rare examples of utopia that has not yet turned into dystopia.

Another ecological utopia initiative is Arcosanti, designed by Paolo Soleri. This initiative, which began in 1970 in Phoenix, Arizona in the USA, is a prototype of a mother city for a population of 5,000 people. Built in the middle of the Arizona Desert, Arcosanti was built by volunteer university students from around the world.

The name of the city, Arcosanti, refers to the concept of archiology, a play on words derived from combining the concepts of architecture and ecology. The basic principles of *archiology* are proximity, high density, diversity and efficient use of resources. The aim of Soleri, the city's designer, was to

build a model showing that a city, even in the middle of the desert, can be self-sufficient without any external needs. This idea resulted in dense, small, efficient, car-free and low-energy settlements.

The building that architect Paolo Soleri designed here was expected to be a self-sufficient, three-dimensional city capable of accommodating 100,000 inhabitants. Sitting on a base of one square kilometer, the building would be one kilometer high. The Hyper Building, a new kind of city, was to be built to last 1,000 years.

By Hyper Building, we mean a city made up of a building that structurally combines architecture and the city. It was intended to be a unity of buildings consisting of many buildings integrated into each other. The project would include all the institutions, structures and organizations that should be in a city within the scope of these buildings. It was to be a highly concentrated and complicated city within a narrow area. However, the construction was left unfinished for many reasons and Arcosanti became the city of this incomplete construction.

Arcosanti continues to live as a residential unit that utilizes environmental technologies in heating, cooling, energy, waste recycling systems, information and communication technologies in its residences and working spaces, and uses high technology in the architectural details and construction of the city with contemporary and recycled materials. Arcosanti, a compact city, stands out as an example of a city that places ecology and new technology at its core with its open and closed spaces, special and unique design.

Arcosanti Project by Paolo Soleri, Arizona

Arcosanti was built as a 25-story prototype building on 1.648 hectares. Only a small part of the project was realized (Yüksel 2012:32). Environmentalist food production, recreation and natural living activities are carried out in the city. However, the city has become a culture and art center with touristic features rather than a center of life. The death of Soleri, the designer of the utopia, in 2013 also played a role in this, as the project underwent several changes after Soleri's death. The city is not a self-sufficient living space; it is sustained by funding from individual and corporate donations and the income left by tourists.

Today, Arcosanti hosts monthly events such as classical music, chamber orchestra, theater, ballet, modern dance, art exhibitions, recitals, festivals, etc., and the city survives thanks to the producers and consumers who are willing to participate in them. Those who come and go are mostly non-residents of the city.

It seems that the ecological utopias that have emerged since the late 1960s seem to have lasted longer than other utopias. However, this is largely due to their extremely small scale and the fact that they are more of a tourist destination than a city. Since nature-friendly utopian practices are not as sharp, interventionist and top-down as modernist utopias, their risk of turning into dystopias seems to be low.

THE DISTORTION OF THE MENTAL DESIGN WHEN CONFRONTED WITH REALITY: DYSTOPIA

Bauman describes today's world as "modern in its intentions, postmodern in its consequences" (Bauman 2000:140). While modernity established itself as a utopia, postmodernity owes its existence to the collapse of the utopia of modernism into the dystopia of postmodernism. Our era is utopian in terms of its intentions and dystopian in terms of its consequences (Hazır & Dereci 2017:95). Looking at the historical process of utopias, all utopias have turned into dystopias since their implementation. Starting with humanist modernity, the process of producing utopias ended with authoritarian and totalitarian modernity, and all utopian attempts resulted in dystopias.

Just as utopias can be traced back to Plato's design of the ideal state, dystopias can be traced back at least to Aristophanes' *The Birds*. The main theme of texts such as *The Birds* is the lack of freedom in a supposedly good society (Meyerson 1996:119). Dystopia emerged as a critique of the suppression and sacrifice of the individual for the sake of society in utopias. However, just as the emergence of real utopias is much later, the production or realization of real dystopias is also much later.

Dystopia is, in Kumar's words, "the deformed image of utopia in a cracked mirror" (Kumar 1987:172). In venturing into the future, utopia aimed to be the pinnacle of historical evolution. In the nineteenth century, when modernism was at its peak, the forces of utopia were major forces such as democracy, science and socialism. In the course of history, however, it became clear that these major forces produced authoritarian climax parodies rather than the pinnacle of human history. Democracy was producing Napoleonic dictatorships or slipping into populism. Science and technology, on the other hand, instead of giving meaning to life, were making it even more meaningless (Kumar 1987:187). They believed that the societies in which utopias, with a pure mind, dismantled all the irrational remnants of the past in a single blow, would make the cities they planned from scratch more perfect than ever before in history, but the results showed that contrary to the utopian designs of perfect periods, they remained in the past, not in the future.

The fact that utopias, instead of creating an ideal and perfect society or city, created a society or city that was inferior to the status quo soon attracted the attention of thinkers and writers. Thus, a new literature was gradually annexed to utopian literature: Dystopian literature. In dystopian literature, writers describe in detail the design of a society and a city in worse conditions than the ones they are currently living in, indicating a specific time period (Sargent 1994:74). Here, like utopia, there is a fiction, but the ontology that the fiction points to is exactly the opposite of utopia. Dystopian literature has set itself the task of "debunking utopia" and defines dystopia as "a nightmare in which our worst fears come true" (Sargisson 2009:26). Utopia, with its violence, seems to refer to nothing but a series of dystopian practices (Zizek 2008:66). In general, dystopian literature tries to shed light on the troubles in the society in which it is written, criticize the failing aspects of society, show what existing problems can lead to if not corrected, provide insight, evoke emotions such as empathy, pathos and catharsis, and bring a critical view of its own society. In the imaginary social order presented in dystopia's fictional form, the conflict between the individual and the system is the subject and it is emphasized that the system oppresses the individual. Social, political and economic inequalities are depicted (Claeys 2010:156). In dystopian literature, the structure that governs society works with social engineering or social engineering methods in order to preserve its existence, to shape individuals according to the system, and to provide the ideal utopian order. Dystopian writers want to expose underbelly of those who rule the society and the system. The destruction of the individual in the name of the happy society envisioned in the utopian approach protects the existence of the system, but the result is now far away and opposite to the utopia that was initially produced and turns into a dystopia. Individuals are uniformized, mechanized and abstracted from their individual characteristics.

Although it seems possible to start the dystopian literature from the second quarter of the eighteenth century, it can be said that the period when

it was effective as a movement coincided with the end of the nineteenth century and the beginning of the twentieth century (Atasoy 2017:60). This century full of exploitation, oppression, state violence, war, genocide, disease, famine, ecological destruction, depression and debt has led to the emergence of this fictional narrative, which is the dark side of utopian imagination.

Etymologically speaking, dystopia is a term derived from the Greek words δυσ (*dus* – difficult) and τόπος (*topos* – place). Just as utopia is derived from the word topos with the prefix eu, which gives the meaning of negativity, and refers to the "non-place", the term dystopia refers to the "difficult/challenging-place" (Sarcey 2003:149). The first use of the word in the modern world belongs to John Stuart Mill in 1868. In his speech before the British Parliament, Mill pointed out that utopias produce very bad results in practice and said, "It is, perhaps, too complimentary to call them Utopians, they ought rather to be called dys-topians, or cacotopians. What is commonly called Utopian is something too good to be practicable; but what they appear to favour is too bad to be practicable." (Hansard's Parliamentary Debates, 1867–68: 1517).

The pioneering text of the dystopian genre is Swift's entertaining *Gulliver's Travels* (1726). Samuel Butler's *Erewhon* (1872) followed it. As modern scientific and industrial utopia became more and more familiar and applicable for many people, antiutopia became less about farce and ridicule, and more about scaring and shocking. In works such as Wells' early anti-utopian novels (*The Time Machine* in 1895 and *Dr. Moreau's Island* in 1896), Zamyatin's *We* (1920), Huxley's *Brave New World* (1932) and Orwell's *1984* (1949), anti-utopia employs all the techniques of the modern novel to present a chilling landscape of an alienated and enslaved world (Kumar 1991:47).

Although dystopia is seen as the name of the not-ideal world that emerges instead of the ideal world intended at the end of utopian attempts, it also has a structure that can be designed in advance, just like utopia. In other words, dystopia is not always just a practical outcome, but can also be designed on paper, just like utopia. These dystopian designs on paper are criticisms directed against the critique of utopia, which claims to find the perfect society and the ideal city through critical thinking. While utopias are based on hope, optimism and happiness, dystopias are based on fear, threat and pessimism. The utopian, optimistic approach, which was especially evident in the Renaissance and towards the end of the nineteenth century, gives way to pessimistic expectations in the late twentieth century. The modern city of the twentieth century marks a period in which the utopian visions of designers are reflected in the city, and cities become boring, monotonous, and devoid of difference and diversity. The mechanical understanding brought by technology, which provides order and perfection in utopias, is transferred to human beings and society; while the social organization is mechanized, the human being is objectified. Written and visual works depicting the frightening and suffocating scenarios of technology and urban combinations are created (Kahya 2007:22).

Orwell's *1984* dramatically describes how oppression and control drag life into a disastrous situation. The work is about how the government changes and manipulates the concept of reality in its favor to establish pressure and control over society. History, changing according to the current circumstances and whose reality is supported by objective records, is utilized by the power as desired. Under these conditions, the knowledge that is only stored in our own memory is doomed to be lost. A revolution has taken place and people are kept under absolute oppression. The revolution was made to estab-

lish a dictatorship. Thought and freedom are the greatest crimes. Therefore, the limits of thought and freedom are being narrowed until they are almost completely destroyed. The utopian technological and bureaucratic revolution, intended to increase people's happiness, closes in on itself, restricting all kinds of people's rights, especially freedom, and thus creating collective unhappiness. Utopia turns into dystopia within its own functioning.

Although dystopian criticism emerged in fiction and science fiction as a reaction to uniformism and the alienation of the individual from society, this reaction also manifested itself as a social movement in the form of resistance to the crises in economic, social and physical life. Dystopias in all their incarnations manifest themselves in a dark period of distrust regarding the basic promises of modernity, i.e., a period in which the dominating power of science and technology, disasters such as the two great world wars, and totalitarian regimes such as Nazism and Stalinism are experienced (Çörekçioğlu 2015:26-7). In *The Open Society and Its Enemies*, Karl Popper claims that utopianism leads directly to totalitarianism and tries to prove this claim with his analyses ranging from Plato to Marx. According to Popper, utopianism is essentially a political attitude and is based on rationalist and idealist thought. Since rationalist and idealist thought is based on the "ideal", that is, an ultimate "goal" that is rationally given, whenever this ideal is applied to the political sphere, it inevitably results in the idea of a project. This political project or political theory is by definition rational and involves a rational method for organizing society. This method, by its own logical structure, requires the reconstruction of society or the political

sphere in accordance with the aims of the project in question. The process of reconstruction is what Popper calls social engineering and inevitably results in totalitarianism. Utopianism begins by searching for ways to organize the disordered, uncertain society of chaos that exists within the framework of modernist assumptions. Utopianism, which describes the plural and heterogeneous field of existence as chaos, constantly produces waste in the process of constructing its utopia through the domination it establishes for the sake of realizing its utopia and the violence it involves in order to establish this dominance, and excludes those who do not conform to its norms (Bauman 2003:11). The monist monist logic of utopias excludes those who are not homogeneous by resorting to violence every time, but the plurality of life manages to turn utopia into dystopia by finding another way each time.

Utopias, born of monist dreams of happiness, thus turn into totalitarian structures and become dystopias. Utopia is the dream, and dystopia is the wreckage of the dream itself, which disintegrates and scatters when it collides with reality. No utopia celebrates democracy or pluralism. As a result of monist domination, all utopias turn into regimes of oppression and produce suffering.

Contrary to the utopians, the 1960s were shaken by the revolts of the unions formed by the consensus of the masses against the designs emerging from the abstract intellect of a single mind. These rebellions, demonstrations and uprisings open gaps in the centralized and patronizing attitude of utopian modernism and generate disintegration in the city. Mass and standardized production patterns are unable to meet different and changing demands. By the 1970s, a strong anti-modernist movement emerged all over the world. The functional and uniform industrial city, which aims for high efficiency, began to evolve into the post-industrial city with its contradictions, irrationalities, unplannedness and dilemmas. The cultural infrastructure of the post-industrial society is postmodernism. In this sense, we observe the emergence of unprecedented designs and pluralistic urban proposals with differentiated discourses on the city. The discipline of architecture loses faith in the ability of planned new forms to solve urban problems. Utopian hope gives way to disillusionment and cynicism. Architectural discourses emerging at this time display a dystopian attitude (Kahya 2007:25). Dystopian architectural works, whether they propose a new urban structure or not, have transformed the view of the city. By directing individuals and society to think and act more freely, they have contributed to people adopting a questioning and critical attitude towards what is happening around them.

All environments, whether natural, technological, architectural, pharmacological or communal, begin to be perceived as a new space of individual liberation. Emancipation is brought to the fore in a cosmic order that offers escape routes from bureaucracy, central planning, and the master mind in urban organization, and consists of infinite connections between individuals and institutions within the city in crisscrossing forms. The imposition of a plan from above is replaced by a state of "becoming".

As the utopian universe design of modernism collide with implementation in the field, its structure disintegrates, in postmodernist language, it undergoes deconstruction. The deconstruction of this utopian structure leads to postmodernism, the dystopia of modernism. In this respect, postmodernism is not the opposite or the other of modernity, but what remains from the self-destruction of the modernist utopia (Hazır & Dereci 2017:107). Dystopian society oscillates in a universe of "post"s such as post-industrial (Bell, 1999), post-capitalist (Drucker, 1993), postmodern, post-structural and post-truth (Alpay, 2017). None of these definitions contain any opposition. They describe the beyond, the after, disintegration, unfinishedness, trivialization. The idea of order, which forms the basis of modernism, actually means coercion, regulation, pressure or forced renunciation, and the absence of freedom has given birth to postmodernity (Bauman 2000:21). The main characteristic of postmodernity is a state of uncertainty. It is a heterogeneity that resists homogenization efforts and disorder that resists the idea of order. Postmodern dystopia is the continuity of uncertainty. This constant state of uncertainty creates endless anxieties and these anxieties turn into fears. A society living in fears and a social order operated by mechanisms based on these fears emerge.

While utopia is a desire for certainty, dystopia is precisely the ground of ambiguity, the enemy of utopia. It is the exact opposite of utopian rigidity with its focus-shattering structure of uncertainty, its blurriness and fluidity. The utopian dream of order becomes more rigid with the fear created by all the uncertainties it cannot dominate. As it solidifies, it draws boundaries. Utopianism, despite its internal consistency on paper and its seeming control of everything, in practice relies on order, regulation and discipline, that is, on limitations imposed against the natural and instinctive impulses of man (Beauchamp 1975:161). Utopias are met with resistance in practice due to the ontology of the individual and society, and when they use force to overcome this resistance, they end up in totalitarianism, integrated with oppression and violence. This natural resistance in the individual is in fact the urge for freedom, which always remains a breach in the social order and the oppressive unity of society (Beauchamp 1973). Wherever utopia is born, it must be remembered that it is only a pure abstract thought, and it must be realized that abstraction from a single mind alone cannot transform a chaos such as life, which is extremely complex, intricate and involves the intervention of multiple minds, into a cosmos. Otherwise, the attempts of singular abstract thought to squeeze pluralistic concreteness into its own structure, as we have analyzed throughout the historical process, without exception end up in dystopias, in other words, at the very opposite end of utopia. Life, politics and architecture are much more than being shaped by the abstract thoughts of a single mind. Attempting to narrow them in an oppressive way has produced nothing but a totalitarian dystopia, and it seems that it never will.

Dystopia depends on utopia to be born; if there is no utopia, there is no dystopia (Hazır & Dereci 2017: 97). Dystopia is nothing but a "waste society" (Bauman 2004:155) that is left over from the utopian arrangement, from the socialized nature, but not a raw society that resembles a pre-order nature. Dystopia is the return, like a boomerang (Beck 2011: 37), of all kinds of harmful substances that are thrown away from a refined society: it sweeps away everything that is intended to be protected. What remains of a project of transcendence without metaphysics is a waste society.

THE EROSION OF HOMOGENEITY IN URBAN DESIGN: HETEROTOPIA

Heterotopia is an anatomical term that means that an organ or tissue is not located where it should be located or is located in a different place (Nakıboğlu 2015:384). In medicine, it is the formation and growth of a tissue in another place as an anomaly instead of where it belongs. Foucault used the word "heterotopia" as a definition against "utopia" and associated it with space, giving it a completely different meaning in social sciences (Foucault 1989). In Foucault, the concept of heterotopia refers to a spatial situation where different, opposing and incompatible entities can live together in the same context.

For Foucault, heterotopia is a contradictory place where everyday life is suspended and the semantics of spaces are transformed. It accommodates many categories in one place at the same time. The prefix "hetero" here also serves to refer to this situation. A heterotopia is a "topos" (place) that draws the person outside of his or her own life, time and history. The sameness of a "homotopia" does not exist in a heterotopia.

According to Foucault, our life, time and history are being eroded in the interior spaces we live in today. This space, which directly affects people and "erodes" them in Foucault's terms, is a heterogeneous space (Foucault 1982:779). In this heterogeneous space, people live in a set of relations that define positions that cannot be reduced or superimposed on each other in any way. In other words, there is a relationship between positions.

Foucault categorizes these spaces, which on the one hand are somehow related to all positions and on the other hand deny all positions other than their own, into two main types. He calls one of them "utopia" and the other "heterotopia". Foucault's conceptualization of "heterotopia" develops an alternative approach to space in parallel with counter-utopian criticisms. According to Foucault, utopias, by their ideal essence, are locations without real places, unreal spaces. Heterotopia, on the other hand, refers to the kinds of places that are outside of all places, even though they can actually be situated in a real place (Foucault 1982:781). While Foucault characterizes heterotopias, which he calls "counter-spaces", as "utopia effectively realized", he points out that these spaces actually turn into spaces that reverse the rules of society when the utopia designed as perfect is realized. In this framework, Foucault's conceptualization of heterotopia, which provides an intellectual space that is quite open to reinterpretation, opens up the possibility of a pluralist social space that allows for multiple (micro) utopias as an alternative to the singularist and holistic classical utopian thought. These places are different from all the positions they reflect. Foucault defines heterotopia as unplanned, spontaneous physical or mental spaces. In this sense, it is opposed to utopia, which is completely planned and designed in such a rational way that there is no room for spontaneity.

Heterotopia is a concept that emerged at the end of the twentieth century and means "a place that offers different functions and units as a whole". The so-called unity formed by divided units such as shopping, working, housing and entertainment that today's cities have is one of the characteristics of heterotopia (Sevinç 2004:146). This fragmentation and intertwining of parts also creates a certain lack of definition.

Foucault's heterotopia is based on six principles:
1. It is universal and has many forms.
a. Heterotopias of crisis (sacred and forbidden places for those in crisis, such as the elderly, pregnant women, etc.)
b. Heterotopias of deviation (spaces for people who deviate from the norm: prison, mental hospital, nursing home)
2. Places that were part of the social order in the past but whose functioning has changed over time (cemeteries and their removal from settlements).
3. They present multiple spaces together in one place (theaters and cinemas).
4. Heterotopias relate to different times. They bring together content from different times (museums and libraries).
5. Spaces conducive to isolation and inclusion (the phenomenon of opening and closing).
6. It is in relation to all other spaces but manifests itself as an independent entity (Foucault 1982:780).

Today, many places from museums to passages, from train stations to movie theaters exhibit the characteristics of a heterotopia. These spaces with their multiple purposes, just like utopias, can only be designed with a pure rationality because they do not impose themselves as a direct necessity in everyday life. They can only emerge as a result of a spiritual development, through a refined aesthetic and refined sensibility of a developed mind.

These utopias can manifest themselves as a component of ideal city designs, and stand out. However, they do not carry all the characteristics of an ideal city, they do not go beyond being a part of a city in terms of scale, and remain functional within the framework of specific purposes. They participate in urban life as transitional spaces, not as living spaces. They are public and do not claim to produce a perfect revolution. But in perfect harmony with the postmodern era, they reinforce the assumption that the parts are important, not the whole. They are spaces where the temporary, not the permanent; the part, not the whole; the volatile, not the profound, are emphasized. In the face of utopia's desire for radical and radical change in the framework of modernism, they have been constructed and implemented as structures that can only make sense within the context of postmodernism.

ATTEMPTS TO FIT THE CITY INTO THE SCALE OF A SINGLE BUILDING: HYPER BUILDING

Utopias, the inclusive ideal city designs of modernism, recede from the city scale to the scale of gigantic buildings with the singularist approach of postmodernism. This is due to the transformation of modernism's macro perspective into micro in favor of postmodernism.

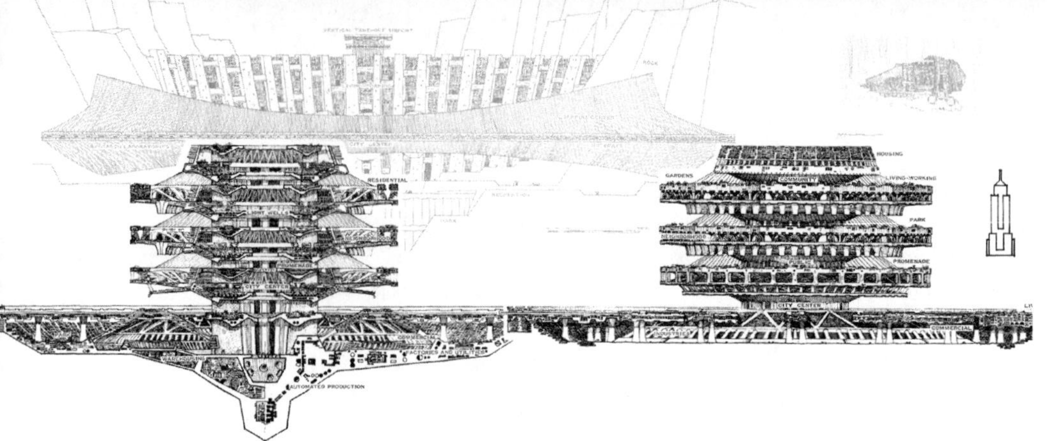

The most famous representative of this approach is architect Paolo Soleri. Soleri sees existing cities as sprawling forms and thinks that they take up too much space on the land. Soleri's solution to this overcrowding is that cities should be conceived and designed outside of their traditional forms. Within the framework of Soleri's views on the structure of new cities in the world, four points stand out:

1. "Arcology" (architecture + ecology),
2. Put an end to urban sprawl,
3. Abandonment of low-rise buildings in urban planning,
4. Utopian urban planning (Özdeş 1985:121-2).

Soleri's solution based on thewse assumptions is the new cities that will be created by the construction of megastructures.

These gigantic complexes, which Soleri calls "hyper buildings", will be cities in their own right. These buildings will have the capacity to accommodate hundreds of thousands or even millions of inhabitants. Thus, while people live in these buildings, the rest of the planet will remain untouched wilderness.

With Arcology, described as the city of the twenty-first century, Soleri envisions a city that is healthy, reflective, accessible at all points by walking, that relies on information technology, efficient use of resources through appropriate technology, that is predominantly mixed-use, interactive and socially offers an extensive cultural life: a city with a long-lasting structure.

With Arcology's compact structure, up to 90 percent more space than today can be allocated for agricultural areas. In such a system, the automobile has no place (Aktan 2012:94). Everything is measured in terms of pedestrian walking distances within the structures.

In "Babel", one of the utopian hyper building designs designed by Soleri in 1970, a biostructure in accordance with Arcology principles was deemed appropriate and a population density of 8,200 people per hectare was estimated. Structurally resembling a tree, this hyper building has four residential levels suspended around a central core containing social spaces and an internal park (Dahinden 1972:39). Light and air penetrate the building through climatic control and through the building's hanging gardens.

Paolo Soleri's designs were put into practice for the first time with Arcosanti, previously discussed in the chapter "Ecotopia" in this book. Arcosanti, a hyper building exemplary of the Arcology concept, was designed as an "urban building" that could accommodate 5,000 people. However, as I mentioned before, Arcosanti is still in existence, but it is an unfinished construction. A large part of the building was not built.

In 1996, after Paolo Soleri's unfinished hyper building Arcosanti, the design of a self-sufficient city consisting only of buildings came back to the agenda. The hyper building, which emerged as a research and goal of OMA/Koolhaas, was decided upon for the Universal Studios Headquarters project in Los Angeles.

Rem Koolhaas, the main executive of the project, is known for his work on the philosophy of architecture as well as architectural practice. He emphasizes the effects of globalization on architecture and contemporary cities and welcomes the chaos it brings. As a theorist, he has expressed his thoughts in various books and articles. Koolhaas still teaches seminars at Harvard University and is the recipient of many awards, including the Pritzker Prize. Rem Koolhaas constantly strives to place beauty in what others see as urban debris, and in doing so, he encourages us to remain more open to the other.

The architecture of the Universal Studios Headquarters consists of four vertical towers connected by a horizontal layer of office floors, rather than the stark volumetric agglomerations characteristic of size. Each tower is designed to serve a specific component of the company. Between these towers hangs the "Corporate Beam". In its organizational capacity, the unified structure of the hyper building approximates architecture to urban planning (Spencer 2016:171-2). Universal Studios is a city plan, a map, rather than an office plan. It is a building that organizes different components. The organization scheme is more reminiscent of a subway plan than a building plan.

The packed towers and intersecting beams of hyper buildings such as the Universal Studios Headquarters, the hyper building in Bangkok and the Togok Towers in Seoul contain a compositional logic regarding the integration of infrastructure. The task of hyper buildings is not to counter or critically reshape circulation and communication systems within their territory, but to facilitate their functioning (Spencer 2014:155). Combining architecture with the organizational forms of urbanism, OMA's hyper building architecture is based on the same foundations as the managerial practices that first emerged in the second half of the nineteenth century.

Like the 200 meter buildings designed by Le Corbusier in his "Contemporary City", which transformed most of the horizontal traffic in the city into vertical traffic via buildings and made many places accessible only by elevator rather than by car, the hyper building is a type of urban planning that emerged with the intention of enclosing a large part of the components

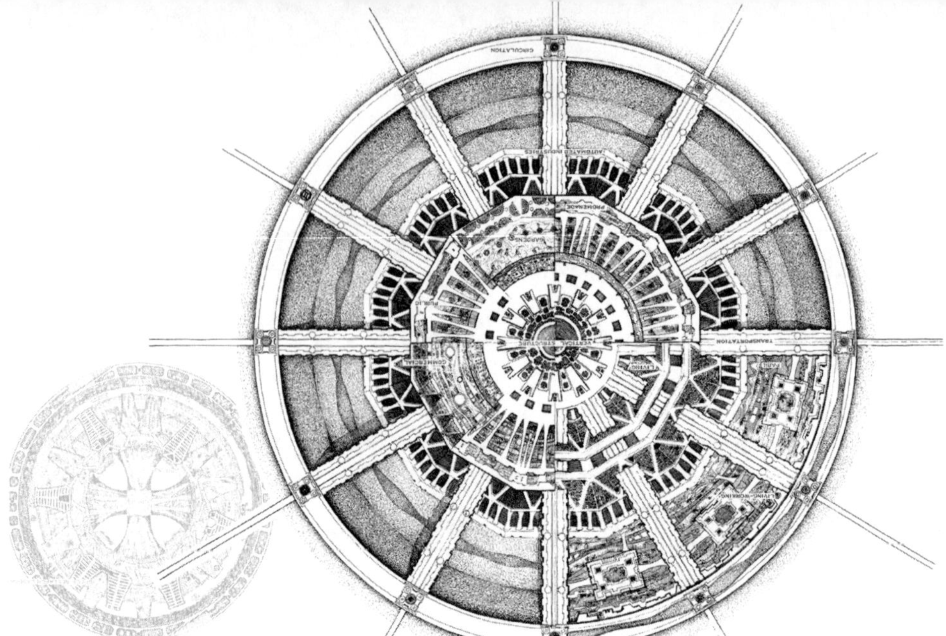

that should be present in a city in a single building. The hyper building, claiming to offer many features, from air conditioning to traffic problems, from functionality to luxury, in a single, closed form, is like a cruise ship to be lived in not only for a certain vacation, but for eternity. It is a single enclosed space where all urban elements are brought together and concentrated in a narrow but luxurious way. It is like a gigantic shopping center with housing and public buildings.

The hyper building, being the most distanced form of urban design from nature, is completely derived from the human mind and detached from the natural state as much as possible. For the sake of functionality, everything historical and cultural has been expelled from urban design, and the city has been produced to be nothing more than a concrete machine. The hyper building has no aim of harmonizing with its environment, culture, the past or nature. As a pure utopian design, it is born out of total abstraction. In sociological and psychological terms, it will result in the alienation of the individual from society and from himself, and thus entails a very strong possibility: dystopia.

A hyper-
building
design by
OMA - Rem
Koolhaas

Conclusion

"To conceive a *true* utopia, to sketch, with conviction, the structure of an ideal society, requires a certain dose of ingenuousness, even of stupidity, which, being too evident, ultimately exasperates the reader. The only readable utopias are the false ones, the ones that, written in a spirit of entertainment or misanthropy..."
Cioran (2015:83)

Utopia is above all a work of oneiric fiction. This dream is a social dream (Sargent 1994:3-4). Its purpose is to create a certain way of life and to achieve a perfect social structure by creating a social construction that will protect it (Kumar 1991:47). The underlying desire is to achieve a better existence and way of life (Levitas 1990:119). Although it is an abstract project, it is dependent on a place, a space, without exception, since it can only come to life in a concrete space. The author of utopia designs a different space from the one in which he or she lives. Thus, the utopian space is born. This space usually corresponds to a city (Alver 2009:142). Within the framework of urban planning, utopia is an engineering of life and society.

Every utopia is the product of an intellectual revolt against the injustices, oppressions, injustices and irregularities of its time. Utopia is people's dream of a better world (Eurich 1967:vii). However, this dream is not a dream shared by all the people of that period or a whole society, but rather it is related to the creation of the world that the utopian or the person who wrote the utopia wants to live in (Çörekçioğlu 2015:20). The utopian is first and foremost a social critic. Utopia is an alternative paradigm arising from the criticism of the current situation (Goodwin 1980:384-5). However, it is not content with criticizing, it wants to radically change the existing (dis)order. It produces a model of society in which the practiced will disappear and attempts to implement this model. Such utopian attempts are an attempt to overcome the concrete situation with an abstract reason. Abstract reason seeks perfection in utopian creations. It desires to design society on paper and rebuild it like an engineer. In utopianism —an idealist attitude— utopians undertake the mission of changing society with their designs and believe that they can succeed (Kurt 2007:160). In this perfect universe where everything is designed with pure rationality, they think that human beings will live in a heaven on earth. In this sense, utopia is a call for radical social change.

Utopias deal with possible worlds, not real ones. Their fictions are closer to the genre of science fiction than traditional realism or naturalistic fiction. They consist of a future design constituting an antithesis to the present. And this future design is a fiction that has not been experienced or practiced before, that has not yet found its place in history. It does not seek what exists, but what is ideal with the thought of " what could have been done to make it perfect". Therefore, utopia is a pure untested idea. And interestingly, there has never been a utopia that has successfully passed the test. Utopia is a proposal that has not succeeded so far.

Utopias almost without exception claim to have an atmosphere of freedom compared to their predecessors. This approach is based on the thesis that irrational social structures or urban plans limit human possibilities. The utopian approach aims to relocate the individual, who is crumbling under the weight of traditions, customs, tendencies, conflicts, social conflicts, and social mechanisms due to abusive rulers, to the most perfect of all possible worlds in a frictionless society, thereby liberating the individual who has been squeezed under the pressure of society and irrationality.

Utopianism desires a society in which all conflicts of conscience and interest are eliminated; a society that removes all obstacles to a dignified life on behalf of all people (Kateb 1975:17). Accordingly, the primary goal of utopia is not freedom, but the maximization of the happiness of individual people and society as a whole. When utopia is first enacted in order to achieve the utopia, that is, the social form in which people and society can be the happiest, the relationship with freedom has often been eroded over time in order to sustain utopia. For utopians have no problem with some sacrifice of freedom in order to maximize happiness. But in the efforts to put utopias into practice, often the libertarian components do not last long and the number of freedoms sacrificed quickly rises. The rate of suppression of freedoms becomes more and more excessive and often, after a certain period of time, leads to an almost total suppression. For its own survival, utopia becomes a total suppression of the freedoms of people and society. Utopia, which was created with the aim of freeing the individual from the pressure of society and elevating them to the happiest they can be, swings in the opposite direction and turns into a much more oppressive system. It closes in on the individual and puts countless tasks on his shoulders, making him completely indebted to utopia. In Izzetbegovic's words, people in utopia are more like a function of utopia rather than living in it. They do not live because there is no freedom. There is no personality (Izzetbegovic 1984:244-6). In utopia, while trying to create a world in which a person can be the happiest, there is the possibility of imprisoning him in a world in which he can be the most miserable. It seems that every utopia, unfortunately, carries the risk of turning into a dystopia, something that is most likely the opposite of what it wants to be. When we look at the practices in history, we see that almost every attempt has ended in a dystopia.

A fundamental component that turns utopia into a dystopia is that it destroys the entire past and builds something brand new in its place, and then does not allow any change or alteration (Meyerson 1996:119). Since utopia claims to be able to achieve the most perfect, any change that can take place in terms of its own logical sequence can only be in the direction of deterioration. In order not to fall back from the perfect order, utopia is very strict about not changing its system under any circumstances and conditions (Riesman 1947:111). In the monotony of this perfection (Reader 2007:163), the individual is hardened by the system, robbed of his humanity and automatized. In this sense, utopias are literally status quo.

Utopia determines the social model down to the smallest and finest details, especially through architectural structures and urban planning, in order to capture and preserve the perfect. In utopia, reason has become the sole criterion for everything (J.C. Davis 1983:14). A single mind, with a pure reason —which is nothing but an abstract approach— embarks on the audacious task of tearing apart and dividing a life, a living organism, a society and a city (which contains many components that are both rational and irrational) as it pleases, discarding many parts, replacing them with many things that have never been tried before, or leaving some of them blank. In this sense, in utopia, not only the innovations that are dreamed of, that have not existed until that day and that have only been produced by it are important, but also the things that were found in the old society but are no longer included in utopia, that have been abolished. In utopia, the existing world has been abolished and transcended (Havemann 2005:19-20). As everything is tied to pure rationality, individuals are represented not as flesh and blood but as robots on paper, as if they were fictional products or symbols. Neither individuals nor society can transcend the status of a dream,

     ARCHITECTURAL UTOPIAS IN SEARCH OF THE IDEAL CITY

a ghost (Cioran 2015:84-5). In this environment where authenticity seems to have been lost completely, utopia seems to have lost its way in the middle of a universe without a point of reference.

This top-down approach, which excludes any kind of social consensus, is based on individual reason, not collective reason. In this sense, it is a product of the great man paradigm. Powered by its internal consistency and flawless appearance on paper, it is built in a way that excludes any kind of social change and development. In order to lead people to maximum happiness, individuals are left in a state of rigid stasis and immobility. Moreover, this is not just an abandonment, but an imposition. The individual is conceived as someone who fails to construct his or her own happiness, society is conceived as a mass of these failures, and in place of this mass of people who fail to think, an intellectual utopian thinks about their happiness for them. Therefore, for the utopian, the masses' opposition to this situation is irrelevant. Because they are the masses who are unaware of how to ensure their own happiness. They need to be guided by a representative of abstract reason. If the masses are reluctant to do so, then it is necessary to force them. Thus, once again, the doors open to the opposite direction of utopia: Dystopia.

The utopian man, to whom the system "imposes" how he should behave, what, how, when and how he should do by society, loses his freedom to take initiative even in the smallest of matters. Paradoxically, utopias, which react to the absolute power systems of their time, take people into a totalitarian order and put them under the yoke of a much more despotic power (Ağaoğulları 1986:35). The triumph of utopian dreams can lead to the nightmare of totalitarianism and the complete collapse of civilization (Kołakowski 1982:247). The "I" is replaced by the "we". The personality is dissolved in society, the human being is reduced to the likeness of thousands and millions of his or her fellow human beings.

The homogenizing approach of utopia requires a certain standard that determines what this homogeneity will be. It tends to call this standard "normal" (Alexander 2001:580). Since it wants to homogenize the standard for everyone, it desires to "normalize" everyone. It describes and excludes those who are outside this normal as "abnormal". It perceives abnormality as formlessness, irregularity, irregularity and imperfection. However, the flow of life itself is a deviation, a rupture, an irregularity (Cioran 2015:85-6). While utopias create a dreamy abstract ideal, as they clash with these realities of life, the purely rational design, which is intended to be fitted to an irrational life, becomes narrow to the masses it is applied to, constricts and crushes them. It restricts and limits their movements, eventually rendering them immobile. Each individual eventually turns into a servant of the great utopian design. At the end of the road to happiness and freedom, unhappiness and slavery await. When the abstract utopia that emerges from the mind collides with the concrete reality outside the mind, the resulting alloy is none other than dystopia.

Utopia produces a rigid organization and planning in order to ensure the unconditional compliance or obedience of the utopian community to the utopian mind. In this organization and planning, bureaucracy and technology are the two main components that take on the task of ensuring that the masses obey the perfect order of utopia. While bureaucracy keeps people under constant control and pressure to establish and then maintain the order, technology is used to produce the methods and instruments necessary for the utopian order.

Apparently, the dominant characteristics of utopias are: An order in which personal and social freedom is suspended, isolationism, authoritarian and totalitarian attitudes, absolutism and oppression (Mumford 1961:362-3). It is the blow of the set of rules emanating from the pure mind to daily life. It is the challenge of a single pure mind to an entire evolution of experiences and traditions.

In a world that has now entered a postmodern phase, the possibility of a city being designed from start to finish by a single mind in pure abstraction seems to have disappeared. After 1960, the possibility of functional urban planning became highly questionable in Western Europe and the USA. The "natural forces" that enabled the organic development of old cities where utopian planning was not practiced regained popularity, and utopian urban models produced by mechanized society were condemned. According to this argument, rational and utopian attempts at urban planning often turn the city into a concentration camp, a dystopia that requires absolute obedience instead of absolute freedom (Ragon 2010:669). Utopian functionality, once a symbol of progressivism, is increasingly perceived as a reactionary attitude that serves nothing but the centralization of power. If it is not known what society can become or what it should be, how can it be known what the city can become or what it should be?

Cities today are more cosmopolitan and heterogeneous than ever before in history, comprising different classes, social strata, beliefs and ethnic origins. Especially in the postmodern era, when identity politics are at an all-time high, designing a city in a purely modernist manner, with the design of a single abstract mind that seems functional on paper, seems to produce nothing but a dystopia that alienates all urbanites. Like the "invisible hand" in economics, cities are now an organism in a constant state of becoming, evolving in line with the market –i.e., the collective habits, economic competencies, expectations from life and the city, and political views of all actors living in the city– aided by the municipality and the central government. The modernist cities, designed in a single stroke and capable of resisting time forever, which have been and are finished, finalized, completed and, in addition to that, displaying an imperious attitude towards their inhabitants, have been transformed into fluid cities in a state of constant becoming, expanding, evolving and transforming.

The needs of today's cities have gone beyond an abstract universal mind, and have evolved into a structure that both transforms and reshapes society as it is impacted by many micro identities, ideologies, changing modes of production of goods and services, and differentiated modes of communication and transportation. There has been a step back from the design of a city by a single mind behind a desk to the design of micro areas, buildings and formations that are micro parts of the city. The indexing of cities to the collective mind and changing common needs of urbanites is now leaving utopias that seek absolute order in favor of an amphibiousness that can manage chaos. As for the utopias that persist, history shows us that the result is always the same: Dystopia!

/ Hall, P. (2014). *Cities of tomorrow: An intellectual history of urban planning and design since 1880*. London: John Wiley & Sons, Fourth edition.

/ Abensour, Miguel; *Utopia from Thomas More to Walter Benjamin*, trans. R.N. MacKenzie, Univocal Publishing, 2017

/ Ağaoğulları, M.A.; "Klasik Ütopyalar: Özgürlükten Despotizme", *AÜ Basın-Yayın Yüksekokulu Yıllık 1983-1985*, S. VIII'den ayrı baskı, 1986.

/ --------- ; *Eski Yunan'da Siyaset Felsefesi*, Verso, Ankara, 1989.

/ Aktan, E.Ö.; "İdeal ve Ütopik Kent Modellerine Ulaşım Bağlamında Biçimsel Yaklaşımlar", *İdeal Kent Dergisi*, S. 5, 2012.

/ Alexander, J.; "Robust Utopias and Civil Repairs", *International Sociology*, C. 16, S. 4, 2001.

/ Alpay, Y.; *Yalanın Siyaseti*, İstanbul, 2017.

/ Alsaç, Ü.; "Düşünsel Mimarlık: Rönesans Ütopyaları Aracılığıyla Bir Örnekleme", *ODTÜ Mimarlık Fakültesi Dergisi*, C. 4, S. 1, 1978.

/ --------- ; "Ütopyalar ve Kent Düzenlemesi Konusunda Bir Söyleşi" der. A. Mengi, *Kent ve Politika*, İmge, Ankara, 2007.

/ Alver, K.; "Ütopya: Mekân ve Kentin İdeal Formu", *Sosyoloji Dergisi*, C. 3, S. 18, 2009.

/ Aristoteles; *Poetika*, Mitos Boyut, İstanbul, 2009.

/ Aslanoğlu, R.A.; *Kent, Kimlik ve Küreselleşme*, Asa, Bursa, 1998.

/ Atasoy, E.; "Ütopyacılık, Ütopya ve Distopya Üzerine Genel ve Eleştirel Bir Bakış", *Doğu Batı Dergisi*, S. 80, 2017.

/ Aybay, R.; *Sosyalizmin Öncülerinden Robert Owen*, Remzi, İstanbul, 1970.

/ Bacon, F.; *New Atlantis: Three Early Modern Utopias*, Oxford University Press, New York, 1999.

/ --------- ; *The New Atlantis*, Watchmaker Publishing, Orgeon, 2010.

/ Baczko, B.; *Utopian Lights: The Evolution of the Idea of Social Progress*, Paragon House, New York, 1989.

/ Bagschik, T.; *Utopias in the English-speaking World and the Perception of Economic Reality*, Peter Lang, Frankfurt, 1996.

/ Batur, A.; "Ütopyalar ve Mimarlık", *İstanbul Dergisi*, S. 5, 1993.

/ Baudrillard, J.; *The Consumer Society, Myths and Structures*, London: Sage Publications, 2008.

/ --------- ; *Simulacra and Simulation*. Ann Arbor: University of Michigan Press; 1994.

/ Bauman, Z.; *Intimations of Postmodernity*, Routledge, London, 2003.

/ --------- ; *Liquid Modernity*, Polity Press, Oxford, 2000.

/ --------- ; *Wasted Lives*, Polity Press, Oxford, 2004.

/ --------- ; *Globalization*, Polity Press, Oxford, 2005.

/ Beauchamp, G.; "Of Man's Last Disobedience: Zamiatin's We and Orwell's 1984", *Comperative Literature Studies*, C. 10, S. 4, 1973.

/ --------- ; "Utopia and Its Discontents", *The Midwest Quarterly*, C. 16, S. 2, 1975.

/ Beck, U.; *Risk Toplumu, Başka Bir Modernliğe Doğru*, İthaki, İstanbul, 2011.

/ Bell, D.; *The end of ideology: on the exhaustion of political ideas in the fifties*. Harvard University Press; 1999.

/ Benevelo, L.; *The Origins of Modern Town Planning*, Routledge, London, 1967.

/ --------- ; *Modern Mimarlığın Tarihi I*, Çevre, İstanbul, 1981.

/ Bernard, P.R.; "Irreconcilable Opinions: The Social and Educational Theories of Robert Owen and William Maclure", *Journal of the Early Republic*, 8/1, 1988.

/ Binboğa, S.; "Uyan", *İdeal Kent Dergisi*, S. 5, 2012.

/ Bumin, K.; *Demokrasi Arayışında Kent*, Batıkent Konut Üretim Yapı Kooperatifleri Birliği, Ankara, 1986.

/ Callenbach, E.; *Ecotopia*, Bantam Books, New York, 1990.

/ Campenella, T.; *The City of Sun*, Dodo Press, 2007.

/ Cioran, E.M.; *History and Utopia*, trans. Richard Howard, The Arcade, 2015.

/ Hansard's Parliamentary Debates, Third Series, Vol. 190, 1867–68, London: Cornelius Buck, 1868.

/ Claeys, G.; "The origins of dystopia: Wells, Huxley and Orwell", Utopian Literature, Part-I. Cambridge: Cambridge University Press; 2010. p. 107–35.

/ Coates, S.; Stetter, A.; *Impossible Worlds: The Architecture of Prefection*, Birhauser, Basel, 2000.

/ Corbusier, L.; *The Radiant City*, Faber & Faber, London, 1967.

/ --------- ; *Urbanisme*, MIT Press, Cambridge, 1972.

/ --------- ; *Toward an Architecture*, Getty Publications, Los Angeles, 2007.

/ --------- ; "İkinci Baskıya Önsöz", *Bir Mimarlığa Doğru*, çev. S. Merzi, Yapı Kredi Yayınları, İstanbul, 2017.

/ Coşkun, İ.; "Şimdinin Eleştirisi: Thomas More ve Bir İmkân/Öneri Olarak Ütopyalar", *Hece Dergisi*, S. 90, 91, 92, 2004.

/ --------- ; "Ütopya ve Kent", *İstanbul Üniversitesi Sosyoloji Dergisi*, C. 3, S. 9, 2004.

/ Cunningham, F.; *Cities: A Philosophical Inquiry. Centre for Urban and Community Studies*, University of Toronto, Toronto, 2007.

/ Çörekçioğlu, H.; *Modernite ve Ütopya*, Sentez, Bursa, 2015.

/ Dahinden, J.; *Urban Structures for the Future*, Pall Mall Press, London, 1972.

/ Danışman, G.; "Ütopya, Mimarlar, Anti-Ütopya", *Mimar-İst Dergisi*, S. 18, 2005.

/ Davis, J.C.; *Utopia & The Ideal Society*, Cambridge University Press, Cambridge, 1983.

/ Davis, K.; *Cities: Their Origin, Growth and Human Impact*, W.H. Freeman and Company, San Francisco, 1973.

/ Dear, M.; *The Postmodern Urban Condition*, Blackwell, Oxford, 2000.

/ Drucker, P.F.; *Post-Capitalist Society*, Butterworth-Heinemann, Oxford, 1993.

/ Eaton, R.; *Ideal Cities, Utopianism and the (Un)built Environment*, Thames & Hudson, New York, 2002.

/ Eck, C.V.; "The Structure of 'De re aedificatoria' Reconsidered", *Journal of the Society of Architectural Historians*, C. 57, S. 3, 1998.

/ Elliot, B.; Macrone, D.; *The City Patterns of Domination and Conflict*, Palgrave Macmillan, London, 1982.

/ Engels, F.; Socialism: *Utopian and Scientific*, Foreign Languages Press, Peking, 1975.

/ Erdem, E.; "Tarihte Ütopya ve Mimarlık İlişkisi", *Mimar-İst Dergisi*, S. 18, 2005.

/ Ertan, K.A.; "Kentin Tükenişi ve Ütopyalar", *Amme İdaresi Dergisi*, C. 36, S. 2, 2003.

/ --------- ; "20. Yüzyıl Kent Ütopyaları", *Çağdaş Yerel Yönetimler Dergisi*, C. 13, S. 3, 2004.

/ --------- ; "Ütopya Tasarımlarında Kent", *İdeal Kent Dergisi*, S. 5, 2012.

/ Eurich, N.; *Science in Utopia: A Mighty Design*, Cambridge, Mass., 1967.

/ Falk, P.; Campbell, C.; "Introduction", *The Shopping Experience*, Sage Publications, New Delhi, 1997.

/ *Urban Utopias in the Twentieth Century*, MIT Press, Cambridge, 1982.

/ Fiske, J.; "Shopping for Pleasure Malls, Power and Resistance", *The Consumer Society Reader*, The New Press, New York, 2000.

/ Foucault, M.; "The Subject and Power", *JSTOR*, Vol.8, No:4, pp.777-795, 1982.

/ --------- ; *The Order of Things*, Routledge, London, 1989.

/ --------- ; *Security, Territory, Population: Lectures at the Collegé de France, 1977-78*, Palgrave Macmillan, New York, 2007.

/ --------- ; *The Birth of Biopolitics*, Palgrave Macmillan, New York, 2008.

/ Fourier, C.; *The Utopian Vision of Charles Fourier*, Beacon Press, Boston, 1971.

/ Geoghegan, V.; *Utopianism and Marxism*, Methuen, London, 1987.

/ Goodwin, B.; "Utopia Defended Against the Liberal", *Political Studies*, C. 28, S. 3, 1980.

/ Gordon, P.; "Robert Owen", *Prospects*, C. 24, S. 1/2, 1994.

/ Gökçe, H.; "Haussmann'ın Paris'i İhya mı? İmha mı?", *Bilecik Şeyh Edebali Üniversitesi Sosyal Bilimler Enstitüsü Dergisi*, S. 2, 2017.

/ Grafton, A.; *Leon Battista Alberti: Master Builder of the Italian Renaissance*, Harvard University Press, Cambridge, 2002.

/ Güçer, Z.; Yılmaz, G.; "Kent Ütopyaları Kapsamında Konut Tipolojileri", *Gazi Üniversitesi Fen Bilimleri Dergisi*, C. 17, S. 4, 2004.

/ Güleryüz, M.; "Bir Ütopya Hareketi Olarak Eko-Köyler: Türkiye'deki Örnekler Üzerine Bir İnceleme", yüksek lisans tezi, İstanbul Kültür Üniversitesi Fen Bilimleri Enstitüsü, İstanbul, 2013.

/ Gürsel, Y.; "Düş ve Düşülke Üzerine Çeşitlemeler", *Mimar-İst Dergisi*, S. 18, 2005.

/ Habermas, J.; *The Philosophical Discourse of Modernity*, MIT Press, Cambridge, 1987.

/ Hadid, Z.; "2004 Laureate Acceptance Speech", https://www.pritzkerprize.com/sites/default/files/inline-files/2004_Acceptance_Speech.pdf, 2004.

/ Harvey, D.; *The Condition of Post Modernity*, Wiley-Blackwell Publications, London, 1991.

/ --------- ; *Spaces of Hope*, Edinburgh University Press, Edinburgh, 2000.

/ --------- ; *Paris, Capital of Modernity*, Routledge, Oxford, 2005.

/ Havemann, R.; *Yarın: Yol Ayrımındaki Sanayi Toplumu Eleştiri ve Gerçek Ütopya*, çev. E. Özbek, Ayrıntı, İstanbul, 1990.

/ --------- ; "Ütopya ve Umut", *Yarın: Yol Ayrımındaki Sanayi Toplumu Eleştiri ve Gerçek Ütopya*, çev. F. Özçelik, Kaynak, İstanbul, 2005.

/ Hayek, F.A.; *The Constitution of Liberty*, Routledge, Oxford, 2006.

/ --------- ; *Legislation and Liberty: A New Statement of the Liberal Principles of Justice and Political Economy*, Routledge, Oxford, 2013.

/ Hazır, M.; Dereci, T.; "Hayat Bir Distopyadır, Modernlikten Postmodernliğe Bir Ütopya - Distopya Dikotomisi İçinde Toplum", *Doğu Batı Dergisi*, S. 80, 2017.

/ Izzetbegoviç, A.; *Islam Between East and West*, American Trust Publications, Oak Brook, 1984.

/ Kahya, G.Y.; "Kentsel Gelişme Olgusu Bağlamında Gelecek Öngörüleri: Siberşehirler", yüksek lisans tezi, İTÜ Fen Bilimleri Enstitüsü, İstanbul, 2007.

/ Kateb, G.; "Utopia and Good Life", *Utopias and Utopian Thoughts*, der. F.E. Manuel, Houghton Mifflin, Boston, 1966.

/ --------- ; *Utopia and Its Enemies*, Collier-MacMillan, London, 1975.

/ Kılıç, P.; Şenel, A.N.; "Tüm Kentlerin Masalı", *İdeal Kent Dergisi*, S. 5, 2012.

/ Koç, A.; "Ütopik Sosyalistlerin Deney Köyü New Lanark", *Hürriyet*, 24.9. 2012.

/ Kołakowski, L.; "The Death of Utopia Reconsidered", *The Tanner Lectures on Human Values*, University of Utah Press, Utah, 1982.

/ Koolhaas, R.; *Delirious New York: A Retroactive Manifesto for Manhattan*, Monacelli Press, New York, 1978.

/ Köksal, A.; "Açık Bir Metin Olarak 'Şehircilik'", L. Corbusier, *Şehircilik*, Daimon, İstanbul, 2014.

/ Kumar, K.; *Utopianism*, University of Minnesota Press, Minnesota, 1991.

/ --------- ; *Utopia and Anti-Utopia in Modern Times*, Blackwell, London, 1987.

/ --------- ; "Aspects of the Western Utopian Tradition", *Thinking Utopia: Steps into Other Worlds*, Berghahn Books, New York, 2007.

/ Kurt, H.; "Kentsel ve Çevresel Sorunların Çözümünde Ütopyacıların Mirası", *Komisyon, Kent ve Politika*, İmge, Ankara, 2007.

/ Lampard, E.; "Historical Aspects of Urbanization", *The Study of Urbanization*, John Wiley and Sons, 1968.

/ Lang, S.; "Sforzinda, Filarete and Filelfo", *Journal of the Warburg and Courtauld Institutes*, C. 35, 1972.

/ Lavin, S.; *Kissing Architecture*, Princeton University Press, Princeton, 2011.

/ Lefebvre, H.; *The Production of Space*, Blackwell, Oxford, 2000.

/ Levitas, R.; *The Concept of Utopia*, Syracuse University Press, New York, 1990.

/ Mannheim, K.; *Ideology and Utopias*, çev. L. Wirth ve E. Shils, Routledge & Kegan Paul, London, 1979.

/ Marx, K.; Engels, F.; *The Communist Manifesto*, Verso, 2012.

/ McCellan, A.; *The Art Museum from Boullée to Bilbao*, The University of California Press, Berkeley, 2008.

/ McDermott, W.; "Air Pollution and Public Health", *Cities: Their Origin, Growth and Human Impact*, W.H. Freeman and Company, San Francisco, 1973.

/ McWilliam, N.; *Sanat/Ütopya Mutluluk Hayalleri: Sosyal Sanat ve Fransız Solu (1830-1850)*, çev. E. Soğancılar, İletişim, İstanbul, 2011.

/ Merrill, E.M.; "The Trattato as Textbook: Francesco di Giorgio's Vision for the Renaissance Architect", *Architectural Histories*, C. 1, S. 1, 2013.

/ Merzi, S.; "Çevirmenin Önsözü", L. Corbusier, *Bir Mimarlığa Doğru*, Yapı Kredi Yayınları, İstanbul, 2017.

/ Meyerson, M.; "Ütopya Gelenekleri ve Kentlerin Planlanması", *Cogito*, S. 8, 1996.

/ Moffett, M.; Fazio, M.W.; Wodehouse, L.; *A World History of Architecture*, Laurence King Publishing, London, 2004.

/ Moos, S.V.; *Le Corbusier Elements of a Synthesis*, 010 Publishers, Rotterdam, 2009.

/ More, T.; *Utopia*, Penguin Classics, London, 2003.

/ Morris, A.; *History of Urban Form Before the Industrial Revolution*, Longman, London, 1994.

/ Morris, W.; *The News From Nowhere*, Penguin, Harmondsworth, 1986.

/ Morrison, T.; "The Architecture of Andreae's Christianopolis and Campanella's City of the Sun, Proceedings of the Society of Architectural Historians", *SAHANZ, 30 Open*, Australia and New Zealand, 2013.

/ Moylan, T.; *Demand the Impossible*, Menthuen, London, 1986.

/ Mumford, L.; *The Story of Utopias*, Boni & Liveright, New York, 1922.

/ --------- ; "The Garden City Idea and Modern Planning", E. Howard, *Garden Cities of To-morrow*, Cambridge, Mass., 1965.

/ --------- ; *The Myth of the Machine*, Harcourt, Brace & World, New York, 1962.

/ --------- ; *The City in History*, Harcourt, Brace & World, New York, 1961.

/ Nakıboğlu, G.; "Ütopyadan Doğmak, Ütopya Doğurmak: Heterotopya Kavramı ve Heterotopya Bağlamında Balık İzlerinin Sesi", *FSM İlmî Araştırmalar İnsan ve Toplum Bilimleri Dergisi*, S. 5, 2015.

/ Noble, R.; "The Utopian Impulse in Contemporary Art", *Utopias*, Whitechapel Gallery, Cambridge, 2009.

/ Owen, R.; *The Life of Robert Owen*, C. 1, 1858.

/ --------- ; *A New View of Society and Other Writings*, Penguin Classics, London, 1991.

/ Özdeş, G.; "Şehirlerin Fonksiyon Bölgeleri", *Şehircilik*, İTÜ Basımevi, İstanbul, 1985.

/ Özkuş, B.; "Renkli Rüyalar Görmek: Archigram", *Mimar-İst Dergisi*, S. 18, 2005.

/ Pearson, C.; *Humanism and the Urban World: Leon Battista Alberti and the Renaissance City*, Pennsylvania State University Press, 2011.

/ Plato; *Timaeus and Critias*, çev. D. Lee, Penguin Books, Harmondsworth, 1977.

/ Platon; *Yasalar I*, Kabalcı, İstanbul, 1998.

/ --------- ; *Kritias*, Sosyal, İstanbul, 2001.

/ --------- ; *Timaeus*, Say, İstanbul, 2015.

/ Polanyi, M.; *The Logic of Liberty: Reflections and Rejoinders*, Routledge, Oxford, 1998.

/ Ragon, M.; *Modern Mimarlık ve Şehircilik Tarihi*, çev. M.A. Erginöz, Kabalcı, İstanbul, 2010.

/ Reader, J.; *Şehirler*, çev. F.B. Karlıdağ, Yapı Kredi Yayınları, İstanbul, 2007.

/ Riesman, D.; "Some Observations on Community Plans and Utopia", *Yale Law Journal*, C. 57, S. 2, 1947.

/ Ritzer, G.; *Toplumun McDonaldlaştırılması*, Ayrıntı, İstanbul, 2014.

/ Roccasecca, P.; *De re aedificatoria...*, 2009, Architectura: http://architectura.cesr.univ-tours.fr/traite/Notice/ENSBA_20A4.asp?param=en (erişim tarihi: 29.6.2017).

/ Rosenau, H.; *The Ideal City: Its Architectural Evolution in Europe*, Routledge, London, 2007.

/ Russano, M.; "Ideal City" Paintings Express Renaissance Concepts, The Epoch Times, 20-26 Haziran 2012.

/ Saalman, H.; *Haussmann: Paris Transformed*, New York, 1971.

/ Sarcey, M.R.; Bouchet, T.; Picon, A.; *Ütopyalar Sözlüğü*, çev. Turhan Ilgaz, Sel, İstanbul, 2003.

/ Sargent, L.T.; "Three Faces of Utopianism", *Utopian Studies*, C. 5, S. 1, 1994.

/ Sargisson, L.; "The Curious Relationship Between Politics and Utopia", *The Use Value of Social Dreaming*, Peter Lang, Oxford, 2009.

/ Saunders, P.; *Social Theory and Urban Question*, Hutchinson, London, 1986.

/ Savvas, G.; Disney Parks Blog, 2017, Disneyland Resort: https://disneyparks.disney.go.com/blog/2017/02/star-wars-themed-lands-at-disney-parks-set-to-open-in-2019 (erişim tarihi: 09.12.2019).

/ Schumacher, P.; "Free Market Urbanism - Urbanism Beyond Planning", *Masterplanning the Adaptive City - Computational Urbanism in the Twenty First Century*, Routledge, Oxford, 2013.

/ Schumacher, P.; Eisenman, P.; "I am Trying to Imagine a Radical Free-market Urbanism", *Log*, S. 28, 2013.

/ Sennet, R.; *Uses of Disorder: Personal Identity and City Life*, Faber & Faber, London, 1996.

/ Sevinç, A.; *Ütopya: Hayali Ahali Projesi*, Okuyanus, İstanbul, 2004.

/ Snyder, J.N.; "Introduction", G. Vattimo, *The End of Modernity*, Polity Press, Cambridge, 1991.

/ Spencer, D.; "The Architecture of Managerialism - OMA, CCTV, and the Post-Political", *Architecture Against the Post-Political: Essays in Reclaiming the Critical Project*, Routledge, London, 2014.

/ --------- ; *The Architecture of Neoliberalism: How Contemporary Architecture Became an Instrument of Control and Compliance*, Bloomsbury Academic, India, 2016.

/ Spencer, J.R.; "Filarete and Central-Plan Architecture", *Journal of the Society of Architectural Historians*, C. 17, S. 3, 1958.

/ Şenel, A.; *Çağdaş Siyasal Akımlar*, İmaj, Ankara, 1994.

/ Tanyeli, U.; *Yıkarak Yapmak, Anarşist Bir Mimarlık Kuramı İçin Altlık*, Metis, İstanbul, 2017.

/ TEA/AECOM, 2018 Theme Index and Museum Index: The Global Attractions Attendance Report, 2019.

/ The Co-operative College; *Robert Owen Day Exploring Social Enterprise From The Past To The Future*, The Co-operative College, Manchester, 2009.

/ Thomson, D.; *Renaissance Architecture: Critics, Patrons, Luxury*, Manchester University Press, Manchester, 1993.

/ Thorns, D.C.; *Transformation of Cities: Urban Theory and Urban Life*, Palgrave Macmillan, New York, 2002.

/ Turner, F.; *From Counterculture to Cyberculture: Stewart Brand, the Whole Earth Network, and the Rise of Digital Utopianism*, University of Chicago Press, Chicago, 2008.

/ Tuztaşı, U.; Civelek, Y.; "Rönesans'tan Modernizme Mimarlık Kuram ve Pratiğinde İdealleştirme Olgusu (1)", *Mimarlık Dergisi*, S. 364, 2012.

/ Tümer, G.; "Kent Ütopyaları", *Bilim ve Ütopya Dergisi*, S. 37, 1997.

/ UNESCO; *Auroville City Open to the World*, The UNESCO Courier, Ekim 1972.

/ Urgan, M.; *Edebiyatta Ütopya Kavramı ve Thomas More*, Adam, İstanbul, 1984.

/ Usta, S.; *Platon'dan Jambulos'a Antikçağ Ütopyaları*, Kaynak, İstanbul, 2005.

/ --------- ; *Türk Ütopyaları*, Kaynak, İstanbul, 2014.

/ --------- ; *İlkçağ Ütopyaları*, Kaynak, İstanbul, 2015.

/ --------- ; "Sosyalizmin Öncülerinden Robert Owen'in Bilinmeyenleri", 2016, www.odatv.com: http://odatv.com/sosyalizmin-onculerinden-robert-owenin-bilinmeyenleri-0805161200.html (access date: 2.7.2017).

/ Vitruvius, P.; *Ten Books on Architecture*, Cambridge University Press, New York, 1999.

/ Weebers, R.C.; Ahmad, Y.; Zuraini, M.A.; "Simon Stevin's Ideas on Settlements", *IPCSIT*, 2011.

/ Yüksel, Ü.D.; "Antikçağdan Günümüze Kent Ütopyaları", *İdeal Kent Dergisi*, S. 5, 2012.

/ Zizek, S.; "The Violence of the Liberal Utopia", *Distinktion: Scandinavian Journal of Social Theory*, C. 9, S. 2, 2008

BIBLIOGRAPHY FOR IMAGES

/ p. 44 - Ideal city plan, Vitruvius. Reproduced image based on "Vitruvian Town Plan" from NCSU Libraries, Design Library Image Collection. *https://images. lib.ncsu.edu/ll/detailView.html?&manifestUrl=https%3A%2F%2Fimages.lib.ncsu. edu%2Fluna%2Fservlet%2Fiiif%2Fm%2FNCSULIB~1~1~18876~105780%2Fmanifest&os =0&q=vitruvian%20town%20plan&baseUrl=%2Fluna%2Fservlet%2Fas%2Fsearch&mediaType= Image#?c=0&m=0&s=0&cv=0&r=0&xywh=-88%2C22%2C366%2C186*

/ p. 50 - Sforzinda city plan, Filarete. *https://www.alamy.com/stock-photo-sforzinda 143337733.html*

/ p. 51 - Sketch of one of Leonardo Da Vinci's ideal city designs. *https://www.alamy.com/plan-for-an-ideal-city-1488-1490-1954artist-leonardo-da-vinci-image262759183.html*

/ p. 52 - Plan drawing of one of Leonardo Da Vinci's ideal city designs. *https://www.alamy.com/drawing-of-the-plan-for-a-model-city-leonardo-da-vinci-image224093476.html*

/ p. 53 - A plan of Albrecht Dürer's ideal city design. *https://www.digitale-sammlungen.de/view/bsb11254921?page=157*

/ p. 54 - An ideal city design of Daniel Speckle. *https://www.alamy.com/franais-vue-gnrale-de-la-ville-de-strasbourg-1587-daniel-specklin-15361589-alternative-names-daniel-speckle-daniel-speckel-daniel-specchelius-daniel-speeckle-daniel-spekel-daniel-speckin-description-german-cartographer-engineer-architect-and-author-date-of-birthdeath-1536-18-october-1589-location-of-birthdeath-strasbourg-strasbourg-authority-control-q327761-viaf12610013-isni0000-0001-1038-9564-ulan500021112-lccnn94020367-gnd118751808-worldcat-argentina-bei-specklin-image184897141.html*

/ p.64 - City image, Thomas More's Utopia. *https://www.alamy.com/stock-photo-the-island-of-utopia-from-woodcut-in-thomas-mores-utopia-1st-edition-83360855.html*

/ p. 65 - Ideal state image, Thomas More's Utopia. *https://www.alamy.com/stock-photo-headpiece-from-thomas-moores-work-depicting-an-ideal-state-where-reason-57286898.html*

/ p. 72 - The City of the Sun, Tommaso Campanella. Spiral Transit (Tránsito en espiral) by Remedios Varo, 1962. *https://educacion.ufm.edu/remedios-varo-transito-en-espiral-oleo-sobre-tela-1962/*

/ p. 74 - Description of the Republic of Christianopolis, Johannes Valentinus Andreae. *https://www.alamy.com/stock-photo-view-of-christianopolis-from-reipublicae-christianopolitanae-descriptio-77036967.html*

/ p. 75 - New Atlantis, Francis Bacon. *https://tr.pinterest.com/pin/380061656035078535/*

/ p. 87 - New Lanark, Robert Owen. *https://johnroeluna.tumblr.com/post/183298831958*

/ p. 92 - New Harmony, Robert Owen. *https://johnroeluna.tumblr.com/post/183298831958*

/ p. 95 - Phalanstère, François Marie Charles Fourier. *https://www.alamy.com/stock-photo-fourier-charles-741772-10101837-french-philosopher-view-of-a-phalanstere-106898234.html*

/ p. 116 - Garden-City Project plan, Ebenezer Howard. *https://www.showhouse.co.uk/news/garden-cities-peaceful-path-social-reform/*

/ p. 117 - Sub-Cities Project plan, Ebenezer Howard. *http://www.mediaarchitecture.at/architekturtheorie/garden_cities/2011_garden_cities_links_en.shtml*

/ p. 125 - The Contemporary City, Le Corbusier, 1925. *https://i.pinimg.com/originals/f7/78/ae/f778ae44c6bc60702d9445f428c9e989.jpg*

/ p. 132 - The Radiant City, Le Corbusier, 1922. *La Ville radieuse, Éditions de l'Architecture d'Aujourd'hui, Collection de l'équipement de la civilisation machiniste, Boulogne-sur-Seine, 1935.*

/ p. 133 - The Radiant City, Le Corbusier, 1922. *La Ville radieuse, Éditions de l'Architecture d'Aujourd'hui, Collection de l'équipement de la civilisation machiniste, Boulogne-sur-Seine, 1935.*

/ p. 135 - Archigram, Peter Cook, 1964, Plug-in City. *https://architizer.com/blog/inspiration/collections/drawings-that-changed-architecture/*

/ p. 137 - Archigram, Ron Herron, 1964, Walking City. *https://www.moma.org/collection/works/814*

/ p. 142 - Paris Disneyland, night view. *https://www.shutterstock.com/tr/image-photo/paris-france-10302017-disneyland-magic-light-1052533727*

/ p. 143 - "The small world" in Hong Kong, Disneyland. *https://www.shutterstock.com/tr/image-photo/hong-kong-china-10-february-2018-1416093038*

/ p. 147 - The image of Ernest Callenbach's Ecotopia project by Mark Harrison. *https://www.steevithak.com/2018/07/22/ecotopia-by-ernest-callenbach/*

/ p. 149 - An ecological utopia in India, Auroville Project. *https://ourgoodbrands.com/auroville-india-utopia-eco-town-prototype/*

/ p. 150 - A detail of Arcosanti Project by Paulo Soleri, Arizona. *https://www.alamy.com/view-of-arcosanti-paolo-soleris-utopian-community-70-miles-outside-image69632819.html*

/ p. 151 – Arcosanti Project by Paulo Soleri, Arizona. *Photo by Rob Jameson. ARCOSANTI - EAST CRESCENT COMPLEX. Birdseye view from south – drone shot. The Cosanti Foundation Archives.*

/ p. 154, 155, 156, 157 - A dystopia modeling. *Shutterstock.*

/ p. 162 - "Babel", hyperbuilding design by Paolo Soleri. *Photo by The Cosanti Foundation. BABEL IBB Arcology, Population 520,000. A hyperstructure over 1 kilometer high and 2 kilometers in diameter at the bowl base. From the book "Arcology: City in the Image of Man" by Paolo Soleri, original publication by M.I.T. in 1970, image 1 and image 2. The Cosanti Foundation Archives.*

/ p. 164 - A hyperbuilding design by Paolo Soleri. *Photo by The Cosanti Foundation. BABEL IBB Arcology, Population 530,000. From "Arcology - City in the Image of Man", by Paolo Soleri. Original drawing black ink on velum. 1969. The Cosanti Foundation Archives.*

/ p. 165 - A hyperbuilding design by OMA - Rem Koolhaas. *https://www.oma.com/projects/hyperbuilding*

UTOPIAS
ARCHITECTURAL UTOPIAS IN SEARCH OF THE IDEAL CITY

Author
Ece Ceylan Baba

Published by
ListLab
info@listlab.eu
listlab.eu

ListLab Editor-in-Chief
Alessandro Martinelli
asma.meetarch (IG)

Translation
Selim Karlıtekin

ListLab Art Director & Production
Blacklist Creative
blacklist-creative.com

Sales, Marketing & Distribution
distribution@listlab.eu
listlab.eu/en/distribuzione

 This book is part of the
BABEL Theory series

ISBN 9788832080926

Printed and bound
in the European Union,
December 2024

Born as an academic publisher, ListLab controls
the quality and originality of the publications
issued to disseminate adequate and up-to-date
knowledge. For this purpose, ListLab has an Editorial Board and an editor-in-chief that supervise the
choice and development of the publications. Also,
ListLab has an international Scientific Commission,
the members of which operate or manage the
peer-review assessment of the publications. In
particular, ListLab adopts a two-round-minimum
single-anonymized peer review process with the
contribution of at least two different reviewers.
This book passed the peer review process and was
consequently edited.

For more information about the Editorial Board
and Scientific Commission, please visit:
listlab.eu/en/board

ListLab was established in 2007 and has elaborated on the idea of an international editorial laboratory with a multidisciplinary approach to architecture, planning, arts, photography, and design. List
Group, found in 2021, aims at creating networks
and promoting debates and cultural exchange, but
also organize events from which new knowledge
about architecture, cities, and landscape can
develop. Today, List Group is composed of ListLab,
the publishing house, Blacklist, the graphic design
studio, Instaura, the informational weblog, and
Us/Them/Yours, a creative agency that aims at a
multimedia approach to information.